Introduction
to Accounting

PEARSON
Education

We work with leading authors to develop the strongest educational materials in accounting, bringing cutting-edge thinking and best learning practice to a global market.

Under a range of well-known imprints, including Financial Times Prentice Hall, we craft high quality print and electronic publications which help readers to understand and apply their content, whether studying or at work.

To find out more about the complete range of our publishing please visit us on the World Wide Web at www.pearsoned.co.uk

Introduction
to Accounting

Geoff Black

FINANCIAL TIMES
Prentice Hall

An imprint of **Pearson Education**

Harlow, England · London · New York · Reading, Massachusetts · San Francisco · Toronto · Don Mills, Ontario · Sydney
Tokyo · Singapore · Hong Kong · Seoul · Taipei · Cape Town · Madrid · Mexico City · Amsterdam · Munich · Paris · Milan

Pearson Education Limited
Edinburgh Gate
Harlow
Essex CM20 2JE
England

and Associated Companies throughout the world

Visit us on the World Wide Web at
www.pearsoned.co.uk

First published 2000

© Pearson Education Limited 2000

ISBN 0582-38168-1

British Library Cataloguing in Publication Data
A catalogue record for this book can be obtained from the British Library.

10 9 8 7 6 5 4
07 06 05 04 03

Typeset by 30 in Stone Serif 9/12pt
Printed and bound in Great Britain by Ashford Colour Press, Gosport, Hampshire.

Contents

A Companion Web Site accompanies *Introduction to Accounting*, by Geoff Black

Visit the ***Introduction to Accounting*** Companion Web Site at
www.booksites.net/black to find valuable teaching and learning material including:

For Students:
➤ Study material designed to help you improve your results
➤ Short answer and multiple choice questions to help you consolidate learning
➤ Practice exam papers to prepare you for the real thing
➤ Electronic glossary

For Lecturers:
➤ A secure, password protected site with teaching material
➤ Secure practice exam papers for use in teaching
➤ PowerPoint presentations for use in lecturing; one for each chapter (except chapters 6 and 12)

Also: This regularly maintained site will also have a syllabus manager, search functions, and email results functions.

Preface

The typical ... accountant is a man past middle age, spare, wrinkled, intelligent, cold, passive, noncommittal, with eyes like a codfish, polite in contact, but at the same time unresponsive, cool, calm, and as damnably composed as a concrete post or plaster of Paris cast; a human petrification with a heart of feldspar, and without charm or the friendly germ, minus passions and a sense of humour. Happily, though, they seldom reproduce – and all of them finally go to Hell.

H. L. Mencken, as quoted in *Accounting for Life* by Henry Benson[1]

My aim in writing this book is to make your initial study of accounting interesting and enjoyable and to help you complete your studies with a much more positive image of accountants than that quoted above. Who knows, you might even become an accountant one day! This is said in the knowledge that most students think that accountancy requires:

➤ advanced mathematical skills
➤ an IQ of 200+
➤ a high boredom threshold.

In the 12 chapters of this book, I have borne in mind that most students reading it will be coming to the subject for the first time, with or without these preconceptions. Many will be on modular courses lasting one semester, with limited access to tutorial help and higher demand than supply in terms of library and other support. To make the learning process as smooth as possible, there is a logical progression in the subject matter from chapter to chapter. I have chosen the pattern of topics to reflect most closely the majority of introductory courses within universities and colleges.

Each chapter commences with a statement of objectives, indicating what you should be able to do after completing that chapter. There are two revision chapters – Chapters 6 and 12 – which will help you to consolidate your knowledge. Within each chapter you will find a number of further features in addition to the textual explanation of the subject matter:

➤ ***Pause for thought***   Either a thought-provoking or a humorous diversion to get you looking at the topic in a different way, or an added explanation of a difficult topic

---

[1] Benson, Lord (1989) *Accounting for Life*, 1st edition, London: Kogan Page

➤	*Did you know?*	A factual item of information to back up the subject text
➤	*Activities*	Practical exercises for you to tackle to ensure that you have understood the subject matter. Answers to these follow directly, so to get the maximum benefit you should conceal the answers whilst attempting each activity
➤	*Glossary*	A glossary of terms found within the chapter
➤	*Self-check questions*	Multiple-choice questions with answers in Appendix 1 at the back of the book
➤	*Self-study questions*	Longer questions with answers in Appendix 2
➤	*Case study*	To provide a synoptic link between chapters, each chapter has a case study based on a business which starts in Chapter 1 and then develops and expands throughout subsequent chapters, to form a 'book within a book'. Each case study is self-standing but builds on the knowledge gained in the previous chapters
➤	*References*	Most of the references given are to pages on the World Wide Web. These are to enhance research into particular areas, or else to provide further practical activities. Web site references have a habit of changing over time, but with perseverance and the use of search engines such as NorthernLight.com, most sites can be accessed.

The chart following shows how the book is structured.

I am always interested in getting feedback from students and lecturers using this book, whether they like it, dislike it, find errors in it or simply want to give suggestions for improving it. Feedback can be sent directly to me at IntroAcctg@hotmail.com, or by contacting the publishers. I sincerely hope that you do enjoy studying accounting and that by the time you get to the final page you will take a kinder view of accountants than the one which I quoted previously.

Geoff Black

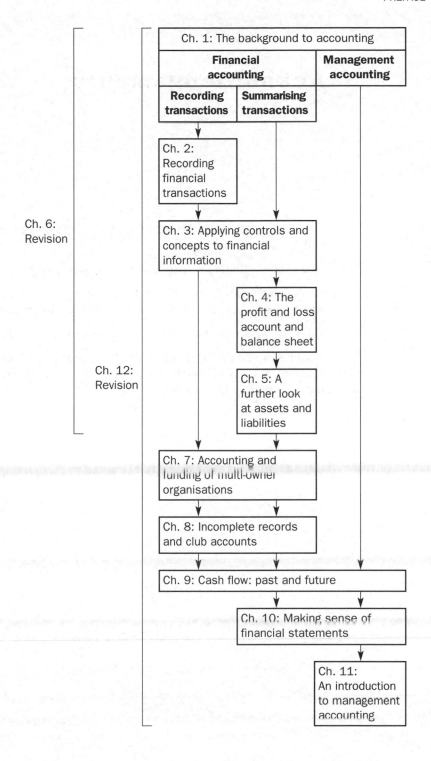

Acknowledgements

I would like to thank the following for permission to reproduce illustrations and textual extracts:

Hyde Mahon Bridges, solicitors, for permission to reproduce Figure 10.2

Peattie and Taylor for permission to reproduce the *Alex* cartoon on pages 180–1, which was first published in the *Daily Telegraph* on October 28th 1997.

The *Guardian* for permission to reproduce an article by Dan Atkinson (page 138)

Finally, I would like to thank Paula Harris of Pearson Education for her encouragement, and my wife Linda for her love and support. This book is dedicated to my son Michael: *Nil satis nisi optimum*.

CHAPTER 1

The background to accounting

Objectives

When you have read this chapter you will be able to:

➤ Explain what is meant by 'accounting'
➤ Distinguish between financial accounting and management accounting
➤ Identify the main users of accounting information
➤ Understand the fundamental concepts on which accounting is based
➤ Distinguish between assets, liabilities, capital, income and expenses
➤ Understand the 'accounting equation'

1.1 Introduction

This chapter introduces you to the whole area of accounting – what it is, who it is for, and who makes the rules and regulations which govern it. Accounting has a number of divisions, the main two being financial accounting and management accounting. The two areas are explained in this chapter, as well as the fundamental concepts that underpin accounting. The chapter also introduces some key terms: assets; liabilities; capital; income and expenses and how they are linked within an 'accounting equation'. This equation helps us to understand the logical basis of accounting and see how the financial affairs of even the most complex organisation can be summarised and analysed.

1.2 What is accounting?

You may think that you know nothing at all about accounting, but consider this snippet of conversation:

'Rita wrote her car off yesterday. She'd gone into the red to pay for it, but – would you credit it – the car wasn't insured. There's no accounting for some people. The bottom line is – you need to protect your assets!'

You may be surprised that this contains six separate accounting references! Most of the terms are so familiar that they are used without thinking where they came from. The origins of accounting can in fact be traced back to ancient times, with the need for accurate records of trading transactions. A logical system of recording financial information, known as double-entry bookkeeping, was in use in medieval Italy, and the first published accounting work, *Summa de Arithmetica, Geometria, Proportioni et Proportionalità*, was

1

written in 1494 by a Venetian monk, Luca Pacioli. The principles of double-entry bookkeeping are still in use today, even where all financial data is processed by computers.

Accounting can be defined simply as the recording, summarising and interpretation of financial information. A more detailed definition is that offered by the American Accounting Association (1966), as follows:

> The process of identifying, measuring and communicating economic information about an organisation or other entity, in order to permit informed judgements by users of the information

The key aspects of accounting are therefore *identifying, measuring* and *communicating*:

> ➤ **Identifying** the key financial components of an organisation, such as assets, liabilities, capital, income, expenses and cash flow;
> ➤ **Measuring** the monetary values of the key financial components in a way which represents a true and fair view of the organisation;
> ➤ **Communicating** the financial information in a way which is useful to the users of that information.

1.3 Who needs accounting?

In the United Kingdom, an Accounting Standards Board (ASB) was set up in 1990 with the aim of improving standards of financial accounting and reporting. In 1999 the ASB produced a *Statement of Principles*[1] which set out certain fundamental principles for the preparation and presentation of financial statements. The Statement of Principles identifies the following seven groups of users of financial information, together with the information which they need from the financial statements:

User group	Information needs
Investors	Investors need to assess the financial performance of the organisation they have invested in to consider the risk inherent in, and return provided by, their investments
Lenders	Lenders need to be aware of the ability of the organisation to repay loans and interest. Potential lenders need to decide whether to lend, and on what terms
Suppliers and other trade creditors	Should suppliers sell to the organisation? Will they be paid?
Employees	People will be interested in their employer's stability and profitability, in particular that part of the organisation (such as a branch) in which they work. They will also be interested in the ability of their employer to pay their wages and pensions
Customers	Customers who are dependent on a particular supplier or are considering placing a long-term contract will need to know if the organisation will continue to exist

[1] Accounting Standards Board (1999) *Statement of Principles for Financial Reporting*, London

User group	Information needs
Governments and their agencies	Reliable financial data helps governments to assemble national economic statistics which are used for a variety of purposes in controlling the economy. Specific financial information from an organisation also enables tax to be assessed
The public	Financial statements often include information relevant to local communities and pressure groups such as attitudes to environmental matters, plans to expand or shut down factories, policies on employment of disabled persons, etc.

We could also add an eighth group – *the management of the organisation* – as they are the 'stewards' of the organisation and need to have reliable financial information on which to base their decisions.

DID YOU KNOW?
In medieval times, a steward was a trusted person who managed the affairs of a household or an estate for the owner.

1.4 Financial accounting and management accounting

Accounting information can be classified broadly between *Financial Accounting* and *Management Accounting*.

Financial Accounting is the day-to-day recording of an organisation's financial transactions and the summarising of those transactions to satisfy the information needs of the user groups listed above. It is sometimes referred to as meeting the *external* accounting needs of the organisation, and as such is subject to many rules and regulations (a 'regulatory framework') imposed by company legislation and the Accounting Standards Board.

Management Accounting is sometimes referred to as meeting the *internal* accounting needs of the organisation, as it is designed to help managers with decision making and planning. As such it often involves estimates and forecasts, and is not subject to the same regulatory framework as financial accounting. Chapter 11 explores some of the management accounting areas such as marginal costing and break-even analysis.

DID YOU KNOW?
The UK's Chartered Institute of Management Accountants, founded in 1919, has over 50,000 members.

1.5 Fundamental accounting concepts

Accounting procedures and practices have evolved over many centuries and are now known by the acronym GAAP (Generally Accepted Accounting Principles). There are many accounting concepts which underpin GAAP, and four of them have been identified as fundamental,[2] as follows:

Going concern concept: It is assumed that the organisation will continue to operate indefinitely.

[2] Accounting Standards Board (1990) Statement of Standard Accounting Practice (SSAP) 2, *Disclosure of Accounting Policies*, London

PAUSE FOR THOUGHT *This just means that when we draw up financial summaries, we don't assume that the organisation is in severe financial difficulties.*

Accruals concept: When calculating the profit or loss of an organisation, all income and related expenditure for a specified period should be included, not simply money paid or received. This is also known as the 'matching' concept.

PAUSE FOR THOUGHT *This means that, for example, if a summary of income and expenditure for a year is drawn up under financial accounting principles, all relevant revenues and costs must be included, not just the money paid or received. Consider a company which always summarises its finances according to calendar years. If by the end of 2000 electricity bills had been received for the period up to 31 October only, the summary must include an estimate of electricity used in November and December. Conversely, if in January 2000 rent had been paid in advance for the 18 months to 30 June 2001, the summary would include only the rent for the 12 months to 31 December 2000.*

Consistency concept: Accounting procedures used should be the same as those applied previously for similar items. This allows comparability of financial summaries over time.

PAUSE FOR THOUGHT *Accountants mustn't be consistently wrong, so they are allowed to change procedures if there are good reasons for doing so, provided an explanation of the change is given.*

Prudence concept: Accountants should be cautious in the valuation of assets or the measurement of profit. The *lowest* reasonable estimate of an asset's value should be taken, whilst a forecast loss would be included but not a forecast profit. This is also known as the 'conservatism' concept.

PAUSE FOR THOUGHT *The prudence concept is of paramount importance to users of the accounting information, as it ensures that the accounting summaries have not been drawn up on the basis of over-optimistic or speculative forecasts, and that foreseeable losses and expenses have been included.*

There is another principle to be considered which is so important that it over-rides the requirements of all other concepts. This is the need for the financial summaries to show a *true and fair view*. Consequently, if a *misleading* result is disclosed by following one of the four fundamental concepts, that concept must be abandoned.

An example is a company which bought a machine costing £5m. When it was bought, the company's directors forecast that it would last 5 years, and quite correctly showed a loss of value (depreciation) of £1m in its first year of ownership. By the end of the second year of ownership, it became clear that, due to greater than expected use, the machine had come to the end of its working life. Although *consistency* is a fundamental concept, it would not show a *true and fair view* to again show a loss of just £1m in the second year. The true and fair view overriding concept would require the full remaining £4m to be shown as a loss in value in the second year.

1.6 Assets, liabilities and capital
....

Much of the work of financial accountants consists of summarising financial information in accordance with generally accepted accounting principles. This information is derived from the double-entry bookkeeping system, which will be explained in detail in Chapters 2 and 3. The system is based on the relationship between the three key components of assets, liabilities and capital.

Assets: An 'official' definition of an asset, as contained in the Statement of Principles, is 'rights or other access to future economic benefits controlled by an entity as a result of past transactions or events'. Typical business assets are divided between *fixed assets*, which are expected to be retained by the business for at least a year and are of significant value, and *current assets*, which are constantly changing during the course of the business's activities.

Typical examples of *fixed assets* are:

➤ Land
➤ Buildings
➤ Motor vehicles
➤ Machinery
➤ Computers

Nearly all fixed assets will be subject to depreciation, a topic dealt with in Chapter 3. Another term used to describe the acquisition of fixed assets is *capital expenditure*, i.e. expenditure on assets contributing to the long-term capital accumulation of the organisation.

Typical examples of *current assets* are:

➤ Stock of unsold goods (also called inventories)
➤ Debtors (the amounts owed to the business by customers)
➤ Prepayments (amounts paid in advance for items such as rent)
➤ Bank balances (cash in the bank)
➤ Cash balances (cash held by the business, but not in the bank)

ACTIVITY 1.1
....

Make a list of any assets you own, with a rough estimate of their value. You could start by considering what you are wearing!

Answer

Your answer might include fixed assets, such as a car, motorbike or bicycle, clothes, watch, jewellery, etc., and current assets, such as cash and bank balances. Make a total of their estimated value.

Liabilities: The 'official' definition contained within the Statement of Principles is 'obligations of an entity to transfer economic benefits as a result of past transactions or events'. Typical business liabilities are divided between 'current' liabilities, which are expected to be paid within one year, and 'long-term' liabilities, which are expected to be paid after more than one year.

Typical examples of *current liabilities* are:

➤ Trade creditors (the amounts owed by the business to suppliers of goods)
➤ Accruals (amounts owing for expenses such as electricity, where the bills have not yet been received)
➤ Bank overdrafts

A typical example of a *long-term liability* is:

➤ A loan due for repayment in more than one year's time

ACTIVITY 1.2

Make a list of any liabilities you have, with a rough estimate of their value. Do you have a bank overdraft or a student loan?

Answer

Apart from an overdraft or a student loan, you might owe a credit card balance, rent, phone bills, etc.

Capital: This is also sometimes referred to as 'ownership interest', i.e. the interest which the owner or owners have in their business. The Statement of Principles defines it as 'the residual amount found by deducting all of the entity's liabilities from all of the entity's assets'.

ACTIVITY 1.3

Deduct the total of your liabilities which you found in Activity 1.2 from the total assets found in Activity 1.1.

Answer

If your assets exceed your liabilities, you have *positive* capital. If your liabilities exceed your assets, you have *negative* capital.

1.7 The accounting equation

As we have seen, we find the value of the owner's interest (capital) by deducting liabilities from assets. This equation can be represented in a number of different ways (for simplicity, we shall ignore long-term liabilities, and assume that assets exceed liabilities):

$$\text{Assets} - \text{Liabilities} = \text{Capital}$$

or

$$(\text{Fixed Assets} + \text{Current Assets}) - (\text{Current Liabilities}) = \text{Capital}$$

or

$$\text{Fixed Assets} + (\text{Current Assets} - \text{Current Liabilities}) = \text{Capital}$$

This final version of the formula is followed by accountants in the UK when preparing the financial summary of assets, liabilities and capital, which is known as a 'balance sheet'. We shall be looking at balance sheets in detail in Chapter 4.

ACTIVITY **1.4**

For each of the following transactions, show the effect (as pluses and minuses) on assets, liabilities and capital:

	Assets £	Liabilities £	Capital £
1 Owner starts business with £3,000 paid into a business bank account on 1 April			
2 Business buys machinery with cheque for £800 on 2 April			
3 Business buys office computer for £800 on credit from Lupin plc on 4 April			
4 On 5 April, business borrows £10,000 on loan from a bank. Money is paid into business's bank account			
5 Business pays Lupin plc £800 by cheque on 6 April			
6 Owner takes £100 from bank for personal spending money			
Summary (overall change)			

Answer

	Assets £	Liabilities £	Capital £
1 Owner starts business with £3,000 paid into a business bank account on 1 April	+ 3,000 (bank)		+ 3,000 (capital)
2 Business buys machinery with cheque for £800 on 2 April	+ 800 (machinery) − 800 (bank)		
3 Business buys office computer for £800 on credit from Lupin plc on 4 April	+ 800 (computer)	+ 800 (creditor: Lupin plc)	
4 On 5 April, business borrows £10,000 on loan from a bank. Money is paid into business's bank account	+ 10,000 (bank)	+ 10,000 (loan)	
5 Business pays Lupin plc £800 by cheque on 6 April	− 800 (bank)	800 (creditor: Lupin plc)	
6 Owner takes £100 from bank for personal spending money	− 100 (bank)		− 100 (capital)
Summary (overall change)	+ 12,900	+10,000	+ 2,900

PAUSE FOR THOUGHT

Applying the accounting equation, A − L = C, we see that the overall changes in assets (+ £12,900) and liabilities (+ £10,000) are matched by the change in capital (+ £2,900).

How does the value of capital change?

The ownership interest will change in value for a number of reasons, most obvious of which is if more capital is contributed by the owner, or capital is withdrawn by the owner. However, the other main reason is the business making either a *profit* or a *loss*. We calculate profit or loss by comparing a business's *income* with its *expenses*.

If income exceeds expenses:

➤ the business makes a profit, and the owner's capital increases.

If expenses exceed income:

➤ the business makes a loss, and the owner's capital decreases.

Income and expenses are defined as follows:

Income: The revenue generated by the business by selling its goods or services, plus any sundry income such as bank interest received.

Expenses: The expenditure made by a business related to the revenue generated within the same financial period. It is often referred to as *revenue expenditure*. The cost of fixed assets (*capital expenditure*) is not considered as an expense, as the asset lasts for several financial periods. However, an estimate is made, known as depreciation, of the proportion of the fixed asset's value used in the specific financial period. This loss in value is treated as an expense when calculating the profit or loss and is also deducted from the assets value in the balance sheet. See Figure 1.1.

figure 1.1
Capital expenditure and revenue expenditure

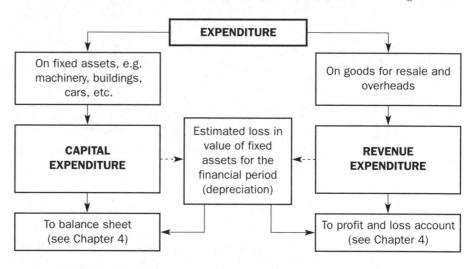

Remember that the accruals concept tells us to include *all* the income and expenses for a period, not just cash received or paid in that period.

The comparison of income and expenses leads us to another set of equations, the first of which is:

$$\text{Income} - \text{Expenses} = \text{Profit}$$

(assuming that income exceeds expenses).

This formula is represented in another main financial summary, the *profit and loss account*, which we shall be looking at in detail in Chapter 4.

If we combine the accounting equations for capital and profit, we see that the capital figure grows over a specific period (known, in algebraic terms, as from time zero to time one) as follows:

$$A_0 - L_0 = C_0$$

i.e. Total Assets minus Total Liabilities equal Capital at time zero.

If a profit is made during time one:

$$A_1 - L_1 = C_0 + (I_1 - E_1)$$

i.e. Total Assets at the end of time one minus Total Liabilities at the end of time one equal Capital at the start (time zero) plus the profit (Income less Expense) earned during time one.

The two financial summaries which have been referred to, the balance sheet and the profit and loss account, reflect this formula, as shown in Figure 1.2.

figure 1.2
How the accounting equation relates to the balance sheet and profit & loss account

Assets – Liabilities = Capital + (Income – Expenses)

Balance sheet   **Profit and loss account**

When, in the next chapter, we see how financial transactions are recorded by using the double-entry bookkeeping system, we are using a rearrangement of this formula, as follows:

$$A + E = L + C + I$$

where Assets and Expenses are seen to equal Liabilities, Capital and Income.

DID YOU KNOW?

You can remember this formula with the mnemonic 'All Elephants Like Choc Ices'.

1.8 Glossary

Accounting	The process of identifying, measuring and communicating economic information about an organisation or other entity, in order to permit informed judgements by users of the information
Accounting equation	The formula representing the relationship between a business's assets, liabilities and capital, usually expressed as A – L = C or, when extended to include income and expenses, A + E = L + C + I

Asset	Rights or other access to future economic benefits controlled by an entity as a result of past transactions or events
Balance sheet	A financial summary showing the assets, liabilities and capital at a specific date
Bookkeeping	The process of recording financial transactions
Capital	The value of the interest of the owner or owners in the business, found by deducting all of the organisation's liabilities from all of the organisation's assets
Capital expenditure	Another term for fixed assets
Current asset	An asset whose value constantly changes during the course of a business's activities
Current liability	A liability expected to be paid within one year of the date of the balance sheet
Depreciation	An estimate of the loss in value of a fixed asset
Double-entry bookkeeping	The system, first described by Luca Pacioli in 1494, which allows a logical record to be made of all the components of the accounting equation
Expense	The expenditure made by a business related to the revenue generated within the same financial period
Financial accounting	The day-to-day recording of an organisation's financial transactions and the summarising of those transactions to satisfy the information needs of various user groups in accordance with the regulatory framework
Fixed assets	Assets which are expected to be retained by the business for at least a year from the date of the balance sheet and are of a significant value. Most are subject to depreciation. Also referred to as capital expenditure
Fundamental concepts	Key principles underlying the preparation of financial summaries
Income	The revenue generated by the business by selling its goods or services, plus sundry income such as interest received
'In the red'	In the days before computers, banks used to use red ink to show overdrawn balances, hence you were 'in the red' if you had an overdraft
Liability	Obligations of an entity to transfer economic benefits as a result of past transactions or events
Management accounting	The internal accounting needs of an organisation, involving planning, forecasting and budgeting for decision-making purposes
Regulatory framework	The rules and regulations followed by financial accountants, imposed (in the UK) mainly by company legislation and the Accounting Standards Board

Revenue expenditure	Literally 'expenditure to gain revenue'. It includes goods bought for resale and overheads such as light and heat, wages and salaries, etc.
Stewardship	The trust placed in the managers of an organisation, who are acting on behalf of the owners
True and fair view	An overriding accounting concept, requiring financial summaries to reflect truth and fairness in their representation of the organisation's affairs

SELF-CHECK QUESTIONS

1 Financial accounting is:
   a Mainly concerned with forecasting the future
   b Used only by the management of the business
   c Used only by people outside the business
   d Used by people both inside and outside the business

2 The key aspects of accounting are:
   a Identifying, measuring and communicating economic information
   b Processing, recording and publishing financial information
   c Summarising, analysing and interpreting business information
   d Conveying inside information about the company to the owners

3 A steward is:
   a The accountant of the organisation
   b The owner of the organisation
   c A trusted person who manages an organisation for others
   d A security guard who patrols the organisation's premises

4 Which of the following is not a fundamental accounting concept?
   a Going concern
   b Conservatory
   c Prudence
   d Accruals

5 Fixed assets are assets which are:
   a Likely to last at least a year and are valuable
   b Not going to be depreciated
   c Unlikely to last a year
   d The unsold goods of the business

6 Current assets are assets which:
   a Keep their value over at least a year
   b Constantly change their value
   c Are depreciated
   d Sometimes change their value

7 Liabilities are usually divided between:
   a Urgent and non-urgent
   b Fixed and current
   c Current and long-term
   d Medium-term and long-term

8 A bank overdraft is usually classified as:
   a A current asset
   b A long-term liability
   c A current liability
   d Capital

9 The accounting equation can be shown as:
a Capital – Liabilities = Assets
b Capital + Assets = Liabilities
c Assets + Liabilities = Capital
d Assets – Liabilities = Capital

10 Which of the following will not result in a change in capital?
a A fixed asset bought by the business for £10,000
b A profit made by the organisation
c A loss made by the organisation
d The owner withdrawing £5,000 from the organisation

Further questions can be found on the accompanying website (www.booksites. net/black).

SELF-STUDY QUESTIONS

(Answers in Appendix 2)

Question 1.1

Using your knowledge of the accounting equation, fill in the shaded boxes in the following table (all figures in £):

	Assets	Liabilities	Capital
	£	£	£
1	25,630	14,256	
2		23,658	15,498
3	619,557	352,491	
4	69,810		14,863
5		21,596	35,462
6	36,520		24,510
7		65,342	86,290
8	114,785	17,853	
9	212,589		146,820
10		63,527	201,581
Totals			

Question 1.2

The annual report of a major public limited company included the following statement:

> Going concern
> The directors consider that the group and the company have adequate resources to remain in operation for the foreseeable future and have therefore continued to adopt the going concern basis in preparing the financial statements. As with all business forecasts the directors' statement cannot guarantee that the going concern basis will remain appropriate given the inherent uncertainty about future events.
>
> (Source: Tesco plc Annual Report)

a Explain why the going concern concept is of importance to a user of an annual report.
b Statement of Standard Accounting Practice (SSAP) 2, *Disclosure of Accounting Policies,* includes the 'going concern' concept as one of four fundamental accounting concepts. State and explain the other three concepts.
c Which concept can override other concepts, and why?

Question 1.3

Tesco plc and J. Sainsbury plc are the UK's largest retail supermarket groups. View (and print if possible) the latest available annual reports from the web sites of the two companies (http://www.tesco.co.uk and http://www.sainsburys.co.uk). Find the (group) balance sheets and profit and loss accounts of the two companies, and then complete the shaded boxes in this table:

	Tesco (£m)		J. Sainsbury (£m)	
	Latest year	Previous year	Latest year	Previous year
(from the balance sheets:)				
Total net assets (i.e. fixed and current assets, less liabilities)				
(from the profit and loss accounts:)				
Total sales for the year				
Operating profit				

Compare the two companies in terms of:

➤ their relative overall value as shown in the balance sheets for the latest year
➤ their relative dominance of the UK supermarket sector as revealed by their sales figures in the latest year
➤ their profitability as disclosed in the latest year's figures
➤ what the trends between the latest and previous years reveal about the progress of the two companies.

Further questions can be found on the accompanying website (www.booksites. net/black)

CASE STUDY
· · · · · · · · · · · ·

Marvin makes a career choice

Marvin always had an ambition to be a magician. As a child he took great delight in making his younger brothers and sisters disappear and he was often in demand to provide conjuring tricks at birthday parties. It was a natural career choice for him when, at the age of 21, he decided to leave college on 1 July 2000 and make his fortune in the world, setting up in business as a magician. He made the following payments in his first week out of college:

On 1 July he paid £3,000 for a glittering costume with a top hat and cloak, on 2 July he paid £2,000 for a special edition of a book, 'The ancient secrets of magic', and on 3 July he bought four packs of magicians' playing cards from Kazam Limited for £100 each. Marvin expected to use these items for many years. He paid cash from his own savings for the costume and the book, but he agreed that he would pay for the playing cards in a few weeks' time from the business bank account.

His first appearance as a magician was on 7 July at the Skittleborough Annual Flower Show, for which he was paid a fee of £750 by cheque, with which he opened a business bank account on the same day. He incurred £20 travel expenses which he again paid from his own savings.

1 Prepare a summary of Marvin's income and expenses for the week ended 7 July. Ignore any depreciation on Marvin's assets.

2 Draw up a list as at 7 July of Marvin's fixed assets and current assets, then deduct any current liabilities from the assets. What is Marvin's capital at that date? Show how you can prove that the capital figure is correct.

(Answers in Appendix 3)

References
....

Internet pages:
Tesco plc:
http://www.tesco.co.uk
J. Sainsbury plc:
http://www.sainsburys.co.uk
A list of the web sites of most, if not all, of the top 100 companies in the UK:
http://www.bized.ac.uk/listserv/companies/comlist.htm
Professional accountancy bodies:
Institute of Chartered Accountants in England and Wales:
http://www.icaew.co.uk
Chartered Institute of Management Accountants:
http://www.cima.org.uk
Chartered Association of Certified Accountants:
http://www.acca.org.uk
A web page with an academic discussion of accounting concepts:
http://les.man.ac.uk/IPA/papers/warnoc79.html

CHAPTER 2

Recording financial transactions

2.1 Introduction

In the previous chapter, the accounting equation showed us that

Assets + Expenses equals **Liabilities + Capital + Income**

Records of financial transactions of the vast majority of commercial organisations are made according to the *double-entry bookkeeping system*, which is based on this equation. The system is highly structured and logical and enables even the largest organisation to keep track of its financial position over time.

2.2 The principles of double-entry bookkeeping

As the name implies, *double-entry* bookkeeping requires each financial transaction to be recorded in two locations within the accounting records of the organisation. This is due to the recognition that there is a *dual aspect* to each transaction: that the organisation both receives and gives value when the transaction is made. For example, a business buying a machine with a cheque for £10,000 not only *receives* a machine costing £10,000 but also *gives* a cheque for £10,000. In terms of the accounting equation we can see that the increase in one asset (machine + £10,000) is matched by the decrease in another asset (bank balance – £10,000). If the business sold goods for £4,000 to a customer paying by cheque, the business both *gives* goods valued at £4,000 and *receives* a cheque for the same amount. The accounting equation stays in balance as the asset of the bank balance increases (+ £4,000) whilst income in the form of sales increases by the same amount.

ACTIVITY **2.1**
· · · · · · · · · · · · · ·

Look at the following transactions of Michael Shelton. How will they affect the accounting equation? Enter the changes to each component of the equation (as pluses and minuses) in the table below (or copy out the table if this book is not your property), and then show the overall effect on the accounting equation. (Note that all amounts are, for convenience, shown as whole pounds. In practice, of course, pence would be shown as well.)

1. January 1   Starts a business by opening a bank account with £4,000
2. January 2   Buys goods for resale with a cheque for £2,000
3. January 3   Sells goods for cash, £700
4. January 4   Pays wages £300 by cash
5. January 5   Buys stationery from Ink Stores valued at £700. Michael expects to pay for the stationery in a month's time
6. January 6   Buys a computer with a cheque, £1,000
7. January 7   Sells goods to Anna Butler for £820. Anna hopes to pay in two months' time
8. January 8   Michael pays a lottery win of £1,000 into the business bank account
9. January 9   Michael draws out £100 from the business bank account for his own use
10. January 10   Michael buys goods for resale costing £1,500 from Bettabuys, and intends to pay for them in a month's time

	Assets £	Expenses £	Liabilities £	Capital £	Income £
1					
2					
3					
4					
5					
6					
7					
8					
9					
10					

overall effect:

Answer

(all amounts in £s)

	Assets £	Expenses £	Liabilities £	Capital £	Income £
1	+ 4,000 (Bank)			+ 4,000	
2	− 2,000 (Bank)	+ 2,000 (Purchases)			
3	+ 700 (Cash)				+ 700 (Sales)
4	− 300 (Cash)	+ 300 (Wages)			
5		+ 700 (Stationery)	+ 700 (Creditors)		
6	+1,000 (Computer) − 1,000 (Bank)				
7	+ 820 (Debtor)				+ 820 (Sales)
8	+1,000 (Bank)			+ 1,000	
9	− 100 (Bank)			− 100	
10		+ 1,500 (Purchases)	+ 1,500 (Creditors)		

The overall effect of the 10 transactions is:

Assets £	Expenses £	Liabilities £	Capital £	Income £
+ 4,120	+ 4,500	+ 2,200	+ 4,900	+ 1,520
= + 8,620		= + 8,620		

PAUSE FOR THOUGHT

In transactions 1 and 8, Michael is increasing the value of his capital, but transaction 9 reduces this value. When an owner takes out money or goods from the organisation, it is classed as 'drawings'.

In transactions 2 and 10, because the goods are for resale, they are referred to as 'purchases'. Expenses such as stationery, petrol, etc., which are used up in running the business, are not classed as 'purchases', but might be entered as 'office expenses', 'motor expenses', etc.

In transaction 5, the stationery company is a creditor (a liability) until Michael pays the amount owing.

In transaction 6, the computer is a fixed asset, not an expense (see Chapter 1), as it is expected to last for several accounting periods and is of substantial value.

In transaction 7, Anna Butler is Michael's debtor (an asset of Michael) until she pays the amount she owes.

2.3 The double-entry bookkeeping system
....

The dual aspect of the accounting equation, as we have seen, applies to every financial transaction of the organisation, and this should be recorded by the business in the double-entry bookkeeping system.

The entries are made in a *ledger*, which is a collection of individual records known as *accounts*. There is no limit to the number of accounts which a business can open, but for convenience they tend to be grouped as follows:

Accounts grouped within:			
(the 'personal' ledgers)		(the 'impersonal' ledger)	
Sales (or Debtors) Ledger	Purchases (or Creditors) Ledger	General (or Nominal) Ledger	Cash Book (and Petty Cash Book)
contains:	contains:	contains:	contains:
The individual personal accounts of customers who buy on credit	The individual personal accounts of suppliers from whom we buy on credit	All other accounts, except bank, cash and petty cash	The bank account, cash account and petty cash account

Each account is split into two sides, a *debit* side and a *credit* side. The debit side is always on the left. The words Debit and Credit are often abbreviated to Dr and Cr. The accounting equation reflects these two sides, as follows:

Assets + Expenses = Liabilities + Capital + Income	
Accounts with more debit entries than credit entries	Accounts with more credit entries than debit entries

An account, in its simplest form, can be represented by two lines, forming a letter 'T'. Such accounts are often known as 'T accounts'. Looking back at Activity 2.1, the first transaction, where Michael Shelton starts a business by opening a bank account with £4,000, would be shown in T accounts as follows:

Bank account (part of the 'Cash Book')

(Debit side)	£	(Credit side)	£
Jan 1 M. Shelton's Capital	4,000		

M. Shelton's Capital account (part of the General Ledger)

(Debit side)	£	(Credit side)	£
		Jan 1 Bank	4,000

PAUSE FOR THOUGHT

The asset of the bank balance has increased. Therefore, based on the accounting equation, the account is debited. The owner's capital has also increased, so the capital account is credited. It is vital that you understand how the entries in the bank account (and cash account) are shown. The golden rule is:

Money paid IN to the bank appears on the DEBIT side
Money paid OUT of the bank appears on the CREDIT side

This is a mirror image of how you would see the details of the bank account shown on a bank statement, because the statement shows the state of the business's bank account in the bank's *ledger, not the business's. So every additional amount the business pays in increases the bank's liabilities, which are* credits *in the bank's ledger according to the accounting equation (i.e. the bank's creditors have increased). This is often confusing to accounting students, as if we have money in the bank, it is normal English usage to say we have a 'credit balance', even though the bank is our* debtor!

The T account entries for the next four of Michael Shelton's transactions are as follows. Note that, from now on, the words 'debit side' and 'credit side' will be omitted from the accounts, as will the word 'account' itself. Where several entries affect the same account they are shown within that one account rather than opening separate accounts for each entry.

January 2 Buys goods for resale with a cheque for £2,000
January 3 Sells goods for cash, £700
January 4 Pays wages £300 by cash
January 5 Buys stationery from Ink Stores valued at £700. Michael expects to
          pay for the stationery in a month's time

Michael Shelton's business

Cash Book

Bank

	£		£
Jan 1 M. Shelton's Capital	4,000	Jan 2 Purchases	2,000

Cash

	£		£
Jan 3 Sales	700	Jan 4 Wages	300

General Ledger

M. Shelton's Capital

	£		£
		Jan 1 Bank	4,000

Sales

	£		£
		Jan 3 Cash	700

Purchases

	£		£
Jan 2 Bank	2,000		

Wages

	£		£
Jan 4 Cash	300		

Stationery

	£		£
Jan 5 Ink Stores	700		

Purchases Ledger

Ink Stores

	£		£
		Jan 5 Stationery	700

PAUSE FOR THOUGHT

Notice that the Ink Stores transaction affects neither the bank nor cash accounts as it is on credit terms, with no payment yet being made.

ACTIVITY **2.2**

Complete the following ledger accounts with the remaining entries (from Activity 2.1) required for the transactions up to January 10. Copy out the accounts if this book is not your property. The transactions are:

January 6	Buys a computer with a cheque, £1,000
January 7	Sells goods to Anna Butler for £820. Anna hopes to pay in two months' time
January 8	Michael pays a lottery win of £1,000 into the business bank account
January 9	Michael draws out £100 from the business bank account for his own use
January 10	Michael buys goods for resale costing £1,500 from Bettabuys, and intends to pay for them in a month's time

Michael Shelton's business

Cash Book

Bank

	£		£
Jan 1 M. Shelton's Capital	4,000	Jan 2 Purchases	2,000

General Ledger

M. Shelton's Capital

	£		£
		Jan 1 Bank	4,000

Computer

	£		£

Sales

	£		£
		Jan 3 Cash	700

Purchases

	£		£
Jan 2 Bank	2,000		

Drawings

	£		£

Sales Ledger

Anna Butler

	£		£

Purchases Ledger

Bettabuys

	£		£

Answer

The following shows the ledger accounts and entries needed to record all transactions from January 1, including those for January 6 to 10.

Cash Book

Bank

	£		£
Jan 1 M. Shelton's Capital	4,000	Jan 2 Purchases	2,000
Jan 8 M. Shelton's Capital	1,000	Jan 6 Computer	1,000
		Jan 9 Drawings	100

Cash

	£		£
Jan 3 Sales	700	Jan 4 Wages	300

General Ledger

M. Shelton's Capital

	£		£
		Jan 1 Bank	4,000
		Jan 8 Bank	1,000

Computer

	£		£
Jan 6 Bank	1,000		

Sales

	£		£
		Jan 3 Cash	700
		Jan 7 Anna Butler	820

Purchases

	£		£
Jan 2 Bank	2,000		
Jan 10 Bettabuys	1,500		

Wages

	£		£
Jan 4 Cash	300		

Stationery

	£		£
Jan 5 Ink Stores	700		

Drawings

	£		£
Jan 9 Bank	100		

Sales Ledger

Anna Butler

	£		£
Jan 7 Sales	820		

Purchases Ledger

Ink Stores

	£		£
		Jan 5 Stationery	700

Bettabuys

	£		£
		Jan 10 Purchases	1,500

PAUSE FOR THOUGHT   *Each entry has the date, a brief description (a cross-reference to the account with the other side of the double-entry) and the amount. Try to record the information as neatly as possible, using a ruler where necessary.*

2.4 Balancing accounts

....

After entering numerous transactions, the ledger accounts may need to be 'balanced' to show the net value contained within them. At the end of a financial period this is referred to as 'closing off' the accounts. The procedure to balance an account is shown below.

Account with more debit entries than credit entries:

Motor expenses

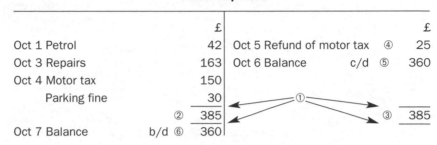

		£				£
Oct 1 Petrol		42	Oct 5 Refund of motor tax	④		25
Oct 3 Repairs		163	Oct 6 Balance	c/d ⑤		360
Oct 4 Motor tax		150				
Parking fine		30				
	②	385		③		385
Oct 7 Balance	b/d ⑥	360				

Account with more credit entries than debit entries:

Clifford Supplies

		£			£
Nov 10 Purchase returns		120	Nov 6 Purchases		487
Nov 11 Bank		367	Nov 9 Purchases		625
	④	487	Nov 11 Purchases		770
Nov 11 Balance	c/d ⑤	1,395			
	③	1,882		②	1,882
		360	Nov 12 Balance	b/d ①	1,000

Notes:

1. Draw in 'total lines' on both sides of the account, making sure there is enough room to write in two further lines of information underneath the last entry on the side with the lower overall value of entries.
2. The side with the greater value should then be totalled, with the amount shown within the total lines.
3. This value is repeated on the other side, on the same line.
4. The side with the smaller value is sub-totalled (not needed if there is only one entry recorded).
5. On the line below the sub-total (or the one entry), write the date of the balance and 'Balance c/d' (note that 'c/d' stands for 'carried down'), and the amount needed to increase the sub-total to equal the grand total.
6. On the opposite side to the 'Balance c/d' entry, write in below the total lines the entry date, 'Balance b/d' and the same amount as shown against 'Balance c/d' (note that 'b/d' stands for 'brought down'). It is usual to date this one day later than the balance c/d, as one period has closed and another one has started.

ACTIVITY **2.3**

Balance off the bank account of Michael Shelton at 10 January. (Copy out the account if this book is not your property.)

Bank

	£		£
Jan 1 M. Shelton's Capital	4,000	Jan 2 Purchases	2,000
Jan 8 M. Shelton's Capital	1,000	Jan 6 Computer	1,000
		Jan 9 Drawings	100

Answer

Bank

	£		£
Jan 1 M. Shelton's Capital	4,000	Jan 2 Purchases	2,000
Jan 8 M. Shelton's Capital	1,000	Jan 6 Computer	1,000
		Jan 9 Drawings	100
			3,100
		Jan 10 Balance c/d	1,900
	5,000		5,000
Jan 11 Balance b/d	1,900		

PAUSE FOR THOUGHT

Note that the b/d balance is not underlined, as it is the starting point for the following period's entries. Sometimes an opening balance might be described as 'b/f' (brought forward) if its corresponding closing balance from the previous period is not shown on the same page. Similarly a closing balance c/f (carried forward) does not have its corresponding opening balance for the following period shown on the same page.

2.5 A simple trial balance

Now that we know how to balance each account, we can perform a simple but essential check on the arithmetical accuracy of the entries we have made. This is known as a *trial balance*, and shows, at a specific date, every balance in every ledger account, listed under the headings 'debit' and 'credit'.

ACTIVITY **2.4**

Prepare a trial balance for Michael Shelton as at 10 January, by entering every balance from the T accounts shown on pages 21–23 in the appropriate column. Copy out the table if this book is not your property. The first two balances have been entered.

	Debit £	Credit £
Bank	1,900	
Cash	400	
	___	___
	___	___

Answer

	Debit £	Credit £
Bank	1,900	
Cash	400	
M. Shelton's Capital		5,000
Computer	1,000	
Sales		1,520
Purchases	3,500	
Wages	300	
Stationery	700	
Drawings	100	
Anna Butler (a debtor)	820	
Ink Stores (a creditor)		700
Betterbuys (a creditor)		1,500
	8,720	8,720

This proves that all the debit entries equal the total of all the credit entries, as they should under the accounting equation. It is not telling us that all the entries are accurate, as we may have omitted an entry completely, reversed entries, entered the wrong amount in the correct accounts or the correct amounts in the wrong accounts! However, the trial balance is an essential check to be made before proceeding to summarise the financial information as explained in Chapter 4.

2.6 Books of prime entry

The double-entry bookkeeping system, as we have seen, requires entries to be made within ledger accounts. Because of the mass of information generated by businesses, it is helpful to management to keep certain parts of the system within a number of self-contained areas, as follows:

➤ Bank and cash transactions within a cash book
➤ Small cash transactions within a petty cash book
➤ Invoices received or issued within day books
➤ Returns of goods within day books
➤ Specialised adjustments within a journal

These are known as 'books of prime entry' (or primary accounting records) as they show the first stage of the bookkeeping process prior to the posting of the information into the ledger accounts.

2.6.1 The cash book

The cash book is used to record the transactions affecting both the business's bank account and also its unbanked cash (notes and coins), shown within a cash account. Often, the two accounts are shown in what is known as a 'columnar' form, with two debit columns and two credit columns. Michael Shelton's cash book could be shown as follows:

Cash Book

	Cash £	Bank £		Cash £	Bank £
Jan 1 Capital		4,000	Jan 2 Purchases		2,000
Jan 3 Sales	700		Jan 4 Wages	300	
Jan 8 Capital		1,000	Jan 6 Computer		1,000
			Jan 9 Drawings		100

The advantage of this layout is that details of all the cash and bank transactions are within the same part of the ledger.

2.6.2 The petty cash book

Most organisations spend cash on low value items such as tea and coffee, postage stamps, window cleaning, etc. These items are considered too immaterial (i.e. insignificant) to be left within the main cash book, so they are given their own book within the system, known as the petty cash book, which contains the petty cash account.

This is usually operated under an *imprest
system*, where the petty cash has a 'float' of
a predetermined amount, which is topped
up at regular intervals. For example,
assume that in Michael Shelton's business, a cash float of £80 was decided upon
on 8 January as a typical amount to cover a week's petty cash expenditure. Firstly,
£80 would be transferred from the 'main' cash account within the cash book
(though it may, alternatively, have been drawn out from the bank account):

Cash Book ('cash' columns only)

	£		£
Jan 3 Sales	700	Jan 4 Wages	300
		Jan 8 Transfer to Petty Cash	80

The petty cash book is then opened. This book looks different from the cash
book seen earlier as it has only one account within it (petty cash) whereas the
cash book has two (cash and bank). Also, because the vast majority of the items
are expenses and therefore credit entries, there is usually no separate column on
the debit side for the date or details of amounts received. Using a 'typical'
week's petty cash expenditure for illustration and assuming that the cash float
is topped up at the start of the following week, the petty cash book for Michael
Shelton is as follows:

Petty Cash Book

£/p			£/p
80.00	Jan 8	Transfer from Cash Book	
	Jan 9	Window cleaning	9.50
	Jan 10	Refreshments	2.35
	Jan 11	Bus fares	2.55
	Jan 12	Parcel tape	3.65
	Jan 13	Postage stamps	21.20
	Jan 14	Advertising – local newspaper	32.55
		Total expenditure for the week	71.80
		Balance c/d	8.20
80.00			80.00
8.20	Jan 15	Balance b/d	
71.80		Transfer from Cash Book	
80.00			

During the week, £71.80 has been spent from the opening cash float of £80. At
the start of the following week, the float must be 'topped up' by drawing the
total of the previous week's expenditure from the main cash account, and

transferring it to the petty cash to again make up the £80. The imprest system is a useful control against fraud, as the person responsible for the petty cash would normally have to present evidence of the expenditure (vouchers, receipts, etc.) to the person controlling the main cash book when requesting the top-up for the petty cash float.

ACTIVITY **2.5**

From the following details, write up the petty cash book of Maggie Pepper:

October 1	Petty cash book opened with a float of £100
October 2	Repair to office chair £13.50
October 3	Bought milk for office £4.80
October 4	Bought raffle tickets from local charity £5
October 5	Paid £35.90 for a train ticket
October 6	Paid a car parking charge of £4.50
October 7	Paid a laundry bill of £7.80. Petty cash balance to be shown at the end of this day
October 8	Petty cash float topped up

(Copy out the following if this book is not your property.)

Maggie Pepper: Petty Cash Book

£/p   £/p

Answer

Maggie Pepper: Petty Cash Book

£/p			£/p
100.00	Oct 1	Transfer from Cash Book	
	Oct 2	Repair to office chair	13.50
	Oct 3	Milk	4.80
	Oct 4	Raffle tickets	5.00
	Oct 5	Train ticket	35.90
	Oct 6	Car parking	4.50
	Oct 7	Laundry	7.80
		Total expenditure for the week	71.50
		Balance c/d	28.50
100.00			100.00
28.50	Oct 8	Balance b/d	
71.50		Transfer from Cash Book	
100.00			

2.6.3 Day books

In Activity 2.1, only three of the transactions were on *credit terms*, where there was a delay between the date on which goods were bought or sold and the date of paying or receiving the amounts due. It is vital to keep the individual personal accounts of debtors and creditors (as seen with the ledger accounts for Anna Butler – a debtor, and Ink Stores and Bettabuys – both creditors), so that the business knows at any time to whom it owes money and who owes it money. However, it is often unnecessary to show every individual purchase and sale in the relevant account in the general ledger. Even a moderately sized business may generate many hundreds or thousands of invoices over a financial period, so it makes sense to show them in separate books known as day books. There will be four day books:

➤ Purchases
➤ Sales
➤ Purchase Returns (or 'Returns Out')
➤ Sales Returns (or 'Returns In')

At intervals, totals are transferred from the day books to the relevant accounts within the general ledger, thus reducing the number of entries within the ledger accounts.

The day books are also useful for resolving queries, as they provide a chronological list of all invoices issued or received and goods returned to or by the business. They also have a role to play in the creation of control accounts (see Chapter 3).

ACTIVITY **2.6**
....

Wayne Allan's business recorded the following transactions during the week ended 7 July. Show how they would appear in the day books, the personal ledgers (sales ledger and purchases ledger) and the general ledger.

Jul 7	Invoices received from T. Rogers £300, P. Cox £800, J. Wall £450
Jul 10	Invoices sent to L. Kenwood £790, A. Gardiner £980, L. Kerr £340
Jul 11	Invoice received from P. Cox £100, and invoice sent to L. Kerr, £490
Jul 12	Wayne Allan returned goods worth £125 to P. Cox
Jul 13	A. Gardiner returned goods to Wayne Allan which cost £50
Jul 14	Wayne Allan paid the amount owing to P. Cox, and L. Kerr paid in full.

Answer

Wayne Allan's business

Purchases Day Book

		£
Jul 7	T. Rogers	300
	P. Cox	800
	J. Wall	450
Jul 11	P. Cox	100
		1,650

Sales Day Book

		£
Jul 10	L. Kenwood	790
	A. Gardiner	980
	L. Kerr	340
Jul 11	L. Kerr	490
		2,600

Purchase Returns Day Book

		£
Jul 12	P. Cox	125
		125

Sales Returns Day Book

		£
Jul 13	A. Gardiner	50
		50

Purchase Ledger

T. Rogers

		£
	Jul 7 Invoice	300

P. Cox

	£		£
Jul 12 Purchases Returns	125	Jul 7 Invoice	800
Jul 14 Bank	775	Jul 11 Invoice	100
	900		900

J. Wall

	£		£
		Jul 7 Invoice	450

Sales Ledger

L. Kenwood

	£		£
Jul 10 Invoice	790		

A. Gardiner

	£		£
Jul 10 Invoice	980	Jul 13 Sales Returns	50

L. Kerr

	£		£
Jul 10 Invoice	340	Jul 14 Bank	830
Jul 11 Invoice	490		
	830		830

General Ledger

Sales

	£		£
		Jul 14 Sales Day Book	2,600

Purchases

	£		£
Jul 14 Purchases Day Book	1,650		

Purchase Returns

	£		£
		Jul 14 Purchase Returns Day Book	125

Sales Returns

	£		£
Jul 14 Sales Returns Day Book	50		

Cash Book

Bank account

	£		£
Jul 14 L. Kerr	830	Jul 14 P. Cox	775

The day books take the detail out of the general ledger accounts, as only the totals of the invoices or returns are shown. It is vital that full records are still maintained within the personal ledgers. Note that the day book totals are transferred into the general ledger at the last day of the period, 14 July.

2.6.4 The journal

Occasionally there may be adjustments or corrections to the financial information recorded within the ledger system. Journal entries show which accounts are to be debited and which to be credited (always in that order), with a simple explanation for the entries, known as a 'narrative'.

ACTIVITY **2.7**

Assume that the following errors were made when entering the transactions of Wayne Allan in Activity 2.6:

➤ The invoice (£300) from T. Rogers was credited to P. Bodger's account
➤ The invoice from J. Wall was entered in the Purchases day book and J. Wall's ledger account as £540 instead of £450

Answer

The Journal

	Dr £	Cr £
1. Debit P. Bodger	300	
Credit T. Rogers		300
– Correction of misposting to P. Bodger's account		
2. Debit J. Wall	90	
Credit Purchases		90
– Error in amount posted to J. Wall's account and Purchases day book		

The journal is not used very often, but is useful for explaining the reasons for making essential changes to ledger accounts.

2.7 Computerised accounts

As would be expected, most businesses use computers for some or all of their accounting needs. The bookkeeping system described in this chapter forms the basis of accounting software programs. These programs give the following advantages:

➤ speed
➤ accuracy of calculation
➤ integration of functions, avoiding duplication of effort
➤ reduction in costs of professional accountancy services
➤ provision of detailed financial reports for management
➤ provision of summarised financial information complying with the regulatory framework

References are given at the end of this chapter to the web sites of a number of leading accounting software suppliers. Some might let you download 'demo' accounting programs for evaluation with no obligation to purchase them. Alternatively, try searching the Internet for freeware or shareware accounting software. If possible, download one of these programs, respecting any copyright, and see how they work by entering Michael Shelton's transactions from Activity 2.1. There are many more features available on these programs than can be utilised by this simple example, but it should give you the confidence to explore these further.

2.8 Glossary

Account	The individual record contained within the ledger
Balancing	The process of inserting a closing balance into the ledger account to show the net value of the account at a specific date
Books of prime entry	The location of the first stage of the bookkeeping process, i.e. the Cash Book, Petty Cash Book, Day Books and Journal
Cash book	The book containing the bank account and cash account. Part of the general (impersonal) ledger
Closing off	Balancing accounts at the end of a financial period
Credit	The right-hand side of a ledger account. Liability, capital and income accounts have credit balances. Abbreviated to Cr
Creditor	A supplier of goods or services who is owed money by the business
Debit	The left-hand side of a ledger account. Asset and expenses accounts have debit balances. Abbreviated to Dr
Debtor	A customer or client who owes an amount to the business
General ledger	The impersonal ledger containing accounts for capital and types of assets, expenses, liabilities and income

Impersonal ledger	The general (or nominal) ledger
Imprest system	A method of controlling petty cash by keeping a 'float' which is topped up at intervals
Journal	A book of prime entry used to record the correction of errors and other adjustments between ledger accounts
Ledger	A collection of individual records known as accounts
Nominal ledger	Another name for the general ledger
Personal ledgers	The Sales (Debtors) and Purchases (Creditors) ledgers, containing the individual accounts of customers and suppliers who trade on credit terms
Petty cash	Small items of expenditure, usually shown in a separate book
Posting	A word used to describe the entering of information in the double-entry system
Purchases	The name of an account in the general ledger which records goods bought for resale
T account	Simple representation of the layout of a ledger account
Trial balance	A list of all the account balances, divided between debit and credit balances at a specific time. If the total debit balances equal the total credit balances, the trial balance is said to 'agree' and shows that the arithmetic of all the entries is correct. It is not a perfect check of overall accuracy

SELF-CHECK QUESTIONS

1   A business sells goods for £1,000 paid into its bank account. The entries to be made are:
    a   Debit Sales   Credit Bank
    b   Debit Stock   Credit Bank
    c   Debit Bank   Credit Sales
    d   Debit Bank   Credit Purchases

2   Goods bought for resale will be debited to the
    a   Stock Account
    b   Office Expenses Account
    c   Sales Account
    d   Purchases Account

3   When the owner takes out cash from the business for personal use it is referred to as:
    a   Drawings
    b   Wages
    c   Capital
    d   Salary

4   Creditors are:
    a   Customers who pay cash
    b   Customers who owe money to the business
    c   Suppliers who are owed money by the business
    d   Suppliers who have been paid by the business

5 Which of the following is a personal ledger?
  a General ledger
  b Purchases ledger
  c Cash book
  d Balance sheet

6 The Cash Book contains which of the following accounts?
  a Petty Cash and Bank
  b Drawings and Bank
  c Bank and Cash
  d Capital and Cash

7 A T account is:
  a The account of all debtors whose names begin with the letter T
  b The account which shows the cost of office refreshments
  c The account of a golfer
  d A simple representation of the layout of an account

8 C/d and B/d are abbreviations for:
  a Carried down and Brought down
  b Carried down and Balance down
  c Correctly drawn and Badly drawn
  d Current deposit and Bank deposit

9 A trial balance is:
  a A perfect check on the bookkeeping system
  b A check on the accuracy of the bookkeeping entries
  c A check on the arithmetical accuracy of the bookkeeping entries
  d A way of proving that the business has made a profit

10 A business operates an imprest system with a cash float of £150 topped up at
   the start of every week. During a week it spends £90 on petty cash items.
   How much will be transferred from the main cash account at the start of the
   following week?
   a £150
   b £90
   c £240
   d £60

Further questions can be found on the accompanying website (www.booksites.net/black).

SELF-STUDY QUESTIONS

(Answers in Appendix 2)

Question 2.1

Balance the following accounts at 31 December, bringing down balances on 1 January.

Sales Account

		£			£
12 Dec	Cash repaid to customer	65	17 Dec	Cash received	84,000
			22 Dec	Sales day book	125,600

Bank charges account

		£			£
12 Oct	Charges	112	13 Dec	Refund due to bank error	26
12 Nov	Charges	145			

Question 2.2

For each of the following transactions, show the effect (as pluses and minuses) on assets, expenses, liabilities, capital and income.

	Assets £	Expenses £	Liabilities £	Capital £	Income £
1 The business pays a cheque of £100 for phone charges					
2 The business pays a creditor £250					
3 The owner takes out £100 in cash from the business					
4 Goods are sold to a debtor for £900					
5 Petrol is bought on credit for £60					
Summary (overall change)					

Question 2.3

For each of the following transactions, show the effect (as pluses and minuses) on assets, expenses, liabilities, capital and income.

	Assets £	Expenses £	Liabilities £	Capital £	Income £
1 The owner pays in £6,000 to start the business's bank account					
2 The business pays wages of £250 by cheque					
3 Goods are bought for £400 on credit from Goff Limited					
4 Goods are sold on credit to Plod plc for £510					

	Assets £	Expenses £	Liabilities £	Capital £	Income £
5 A computer is bought for £600 with a cheque					
6 Stationery is bought for £50 with a cheque					
Summary (overall change)					

Question 2.4

From the following transactions of Rachel Roberts, write up a cash book showing cash and bank transactions and T accounts for all other transactions. Balance off the bank and cash accounts only, then extract a trial balance at 7 October.

Oct 1 Started the business by paying £9,000 into the business bank account and also providing £100 as an opening cash balance

Oct 1 Bought goods for resale with a cheque for £4,000 and paid £60 in cash for stationery

Oct 2 Sold goods for £600 cheque and £280 cash

Oct 3 Paid a cheque for £30 for advertising and a cheque for £45 for printing

Oct 4 Paid rent by cheque, £100

Oct 5 Sold goods for £700 cheque and £130 cash

Oct 6 Paid wages £260 cash. Owner withdrew £400 from the bank for personal use

Oct 7 A customer was given a refund by cheque £40 for faulty goods returned into the business.

Question 2.5

Casper Peabody's business recorded the following transactions during the week ended 7 May. Show how they would appear in the day books, the personal ledgers (sales ledger and purchases ledger) and the general ledger.

May 1 Invoices received from C. Moss £630, J. Carter £419 and A. McKeane £330

May 2 Invoices sent to K. Palfreyman £199 and L. Patel £870

May 3 Invoice received from A. Iqbal £560 and A. McKeane £210

May 4 Casper Peabody returned goods worth £80 to J. Carter

May 5 L. Patel returned goods to Casper Peabody which cost £62

May 6 Casper Peabody paid the amount owing to J. Carter, and L. Patel paid in full

May 7 Casper Peabody returned goods worth £40 to A. Iqbal

Question 2.6

Lara Kelly recorded the following petty cash transactions during the week ended 20 October.

Oct 14 Started the week with the normal cash float of £200.00. Paid £25.56 travel expenses

Oct 15 Paid £14.29 for window cleaning
Oct 16 Paid £18.45 for train fares
Oct 17 Paid £40 for new kennel for guard dog, and £19 for dog food
Oct 18 Paid postage £2.65
Oct 19 Made a loan of £10 to Hiram Decker, a member of staff
Oct 20 Paid £23.85 for window cleaning

The cash float was topped up at the start of the following week.

Show the petty cash book for the week, balance the book at the end of the week, carry down the balance and show the cash float being topped up at the start of the following week.

Question 2.7

Show how the following errors would be corrected by means of journal entries in the books of Paul Pascoe:

a £400 received from Andrew Cheung which should have been posted to his account in the Sales Ledger but was entered in Andrew Young's account.

b A cheque for £40 paid for stationery which was entered on the debit side of the bank account in the cash book and the credit side of the stationery account.

c An invoice for £200 for goods for resale received from a supplier, Dingle Dynamics, was omitted entirely from the books.

Further questions can be found on the accompanying website (www.booksites. net/black).

CASE STUDY
• • • • • • • • • • • •

Marvin buys rabbits!

Marvin the magician (see Chapter 1's case study) entered his second week of business and was offered fees to appear as an entertainer at three parties during the week. Realising that he had no rabbits to pull out of his top hat, he contacted the United Rabbit Corporation, which agreed, on 8 July, to supply six white rabbits at a cost of £40 each on the condition that Marvin treated them kindly and fed them well. On the same day, Amalgamated Carrots plc supplied several sacks of rabbit food at a total cost of £250. Both companies sent Marvin invoices. Marvin built a rabbit hutch from scrap materials at no cost.

On 10 July, Marvin travelled to William Green's party, which was a success, and he was paid £100 in cash. Travel expenses cost £15 cash. On 11 July he paid a cheque for £18 for cleaning his costume, which became soiled after handling the rabbits. On 12 July he paid £9 for a train ticket in cash, and travelled to Violet Cartwright's party, which was also successful, and he received a cheque for £120. On 13 July he performed at Jasper Peter's party which was only partly successful, since a child felt sorry for the rabbits and let them all escape. They were never seen again. Marvin gave an invoice to Mr and Mrs Peter for £250 for his magic act at the party.

On 14 July, he returned the unused rabbit feed to Amalgamated Carrots plc, which gave him a credit of £60. He paid the United Rabbit Corporation invoice by cheque and also paid Kazam Limited's account for the playing cards bought in the first week.

1 Enter the first week's transactions in a cash book and T accounts. Day books and a petty cash book are not required. The transactions (as shown in Chapter 1's case study) were:

July 1 Bought costume £3,000, using own capital

July 2 Bought ancient book £2,000, using own capital

July 3 Bought playing cards £400, by invoice from Kazam Limited

July 7 Received £750 for magic show and opened a bank account. Paid £20 travel expenses, using own savings

2 Enter the second week's transactions into the cash book and T accounts.

3 Balance all the accounts at 14 July, and carry the balances down at 15 July.

4 Prepare a trial balance as at 14 July.

(Answers in Appendix 3)

References

Internet pages:

Accounting software developers:

Dosh:

http://www.dosh.co.uk

MYOB:

http://www.myob.com

Pegasus:

http://www.pegasus.co.uk

Sage:

http://www.sage.com

Tas Books:

http://www.tassoftware.com

Business and Accounting Software Developers Association:

http://www.basda.org

CHAPTER 3

Applying controls and concepts to financial information

3.1 Introduction
. . . .

In Chapter 1, four fundamental accounting concepts were identified: *Going Concern*, *Accruals*, *Consistency* and *Prudence*, plus the overriding concept of the *true and fair view*. Every business needs to prepare periodic summaries of their finances, and this chapter looks at how the concepts affect the way in which these summaries are prepared. We also look at accounting control over accuracy and completeness of data. In the previous chapter we have already seen two types of control – the trial balance and the imprest system of petty cash. This chapter looks at two further aspects of control over the accuracy and completeness of data within the bookkeeping system prior to preparing the financial summaries: bank reconciliation statements and control accounts. The way in which accounting concepts affect what appears within financial summaries is also explained.

3.2 Cash flow statements and beyond
. . . .

The double-entry bookkeeping system described in Chapter 2 records the business's assets, expenses, liabilities, capital and income. From time to time, a business needs to summarise its financial position by comparing its income with its expenditure over a specific period, in a statement known as a *profit* and *loss account*, and by summarising its assets and its liabilities (and therefore its capital) at the end of that period, in a statement known as a *balance sheet*.

What must be understood at the outset is that these two key financial summaries are *accounting* summaries – and must therefore comply with the fundamental concepts. It could be argued that all a business needs to understand its financial position is a summary of its cash and bank accounts – a cash flow statement. Many individuals, after all, look at their bank balance and the amount of cash in their purses or wallets as a guide to how affluent they are. However, for a business to understand fully its financial position it is also vital to know:

> how much is owed to or by the business by customers, suppliers and lenders
> the values of unsold stocks of goods
> whether all the expenses for the period have been included
> whether some of the expenses paid in the period relate to a future period
> whether fixed assets have lost value during the period
> how much profit or loss has been made
> what overall assets and liabilities the business has accumulated, not just those bought in the current period.

None of this information would be disclosed by a cash flow statement.

3.3 Bank reconciliation statements

Another factor which should be considered by a business before relying on the information contained within bank statements is whether the statements reconcile with the business's own record of the bank account as shown in the cash book. Usually there are items in the bank statements which have not yet been recorded in the cash book, such as bank charges, standing orders and direct debits, and items in the cash book which are not yet shown in the bank statement, such as unpresented cheques (i.e. cheques not yet banked by the recipients). A reconciliation should be made to agree the two versions of the account.

ACTIVITY **3.1**

Julia Ronson is trying to reconcile her business's bank statements with the bank account details as shown in the business's cash book. She had previously reconciled the opening balance at 1 November, and has subsequently received the following bank statement for the month of November:

Grimley's Bank plc Higglethorpe Branch
Julia Ronson Current Account No. 563428974

	Debits £	Credits £	Balance £
Nov 1 Opening balance			563.21 CR
Nov 3 Cheque 563121	48.23		514.98 CR
Nov 5 Standing order: Water company	20.00		494.98 CR
Nov 9 Cheque 563123	145.23		349.75 CR
Nov 15 Bank credit		600.52	950.27 CR
Nov 19 Bank charges	8.62		941.65 CR
Nov 24 Cheque 563124	621.56		320.09 CR
Nov 27 Cheque 563125	453.62		133.53 DR
Nov 30 Bank credit		704.26	570.73 CR
Nov 30 Direct debit: HP Finance	30.00		540.73 CR

The details of the bank account as contained in her cash book are as follows:

Cash Book

Bank

		£			£
Nov 1	Opening balance b/f	563.21	Nov 1	Lotty Miller Fashions	48.23
Nov 12	Cash to bank	600.52	Nov 6	Garry Hill Ltd	263.25
Nov 29	Netta Muskett Ltd	704.26	Nov 7	Lilly Trotter	145.23
		1,867.99	Nov 23	UK Gas plc	621.56
			Nov 24	Modaphone plc	453.62
			Nov 26	Kibbley Limited	65.32
					1,597.21
			Nov 30	Closing balance c/d	270.78
		1,867.99			1,867.99
Dec 1	Opening balance b/d	270.78			

Reconcile the bank statement details with the cash book as at 30 November.

Answer

First, we compare items shown in the bank statement with those shown in the cash book, by placing a tick against each one in each record. This leaves the standing order, the bank charges and the direct debit unticked in the statement, and the entries on 6 and 26 November unticked in the cash book.

We must then update the cash book for the three items unticked in the statement, as follows:

Bank

		£			£
Nov 1	Opening balance b/f	563.21	Nov 1	Lotty Miller Fashions	48.23
Nov 12	Cash to bank	600.52	Nov 6	Garry Hill Ltd	263.25
Nov 29	Netta Muskett Ltd	704.26	Nov 7	Lilly Trotter	145.23
		1,867.99	Nov 23	UK Gas plc	621.56
			Nov 24	Modaphone plc	453.62
			Nov 26	Kibbley Limited	65.32
					1,597.21
			Nov 30	Closing balance c/d	270.78
		1,867.99			1,867.99
Dec 1	Opening balance b/d	270.78	Nov 5	Water company	20.00
			Nov 19	Bank charges	8.62
			Nov 30	HP Finance	30.00
					58.62
			Dec 1	Revised balance c/d	212.16
		270.78			270.78
Dec 1	Revised balance b/d	212.16			

PAUSE FOR THOUGHT

As we are adjusting the 1 December balance for the omitted entries, that date is used for both the c/d and b/d revised balances.

Then we reconcile the revised balance with the statement balance:

	£	£
Balance as per bank statement		540.73 In hand
Less unpresented cheques:		
Garry Hill Ltd	263.25	
Kibbley Limited	65.32	
		(328.57)
Balance as per cash book		212.16 In hand

PAUSE FOR THOUGHT *Because debits and credits in the bank statement are reversed when shown in the cash book, it is better to avoid referring to bank balances as 'debit' or 'credit' balances. Use 'in hand' or 'overdrawn' to avoid confusion. Note also that brackets have been placed around the £328.57 figure. This is common practice to show an amount which is deducted from the figure immediately above it.*

3.4 Control accounts

In the previous chapter, we saw how the two 'personal' ledgers, the sales ledger and the purchases ledger, contain the individual accounts of all the debtors and creditors of the business. Even a relatively small business may have hundreds of such accounts, whilst large companies may have many thousands, most of them within the sales ledger. With computer packages, the information can be processed speedily and efficiently. Information entered in, for example, a customer's invoice will automatically adjust the balance on that customer's sales ledger account. Where the system is non-computerised, it is possible to confirm the overall accuracy of the personal ledger entries by producing control (or 'total') accounts. These work on the simple principle that if you can produce one account which summarises the totals of all the thousands of individual entries which appear in a personal ledger, then the closing balance on that one account should be the same as the total of all the individual account balances within the personal ledger (see Figure 3.1). If they don't agree, one or more errors are present and must be rectified.

The 'control' operates due to the fact that the 'summarised totals' do not come from the personal ledger itself but from the appropriate book of prime entry. As these totals are used within the bookkeeping system to complete the double-entry recording (e.g. by the total of the purchases day book being posted to the debit of the purchases account in the general ledger), the successful reconciliation of the control account with the total of the individual personal ledger accounts proves the arithmetical accuracy of that part of the system.

figure 3.1

Control accounts

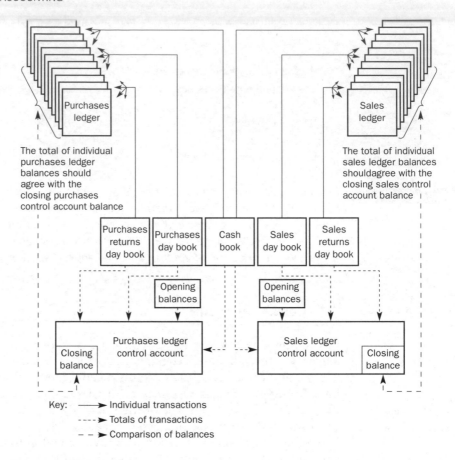

Key: ──────► Individual transactions
 ----► Totals of transactions
 ─ ─ ► Comparison of balances

The main entries, and their source, which would be found in a typical sales ledger control account are shown below.

Sales Ledger Control Account

Debit entries	(Source)	Credit entries	(Source)
Opening debtors[1]	Previous closing balance	Sales returns (Returns inwards)	Sales returns day book
Total credit sales	Sales day book	Cash and cheques received from debtors[2]	Cash book
		Closing debtors	(Balancing figure to be compared with total of individual balances in sales ledger)

[1] There may also be some credit balances within the sales ledger brought forward, resulting from over-payments, duplicated payments or a customer returning goods after having paid for them.
[2] Any discounts allowed to customers would be shown separately (see Chapter 4), as would bad debts written off (see Chapter 5).

A typical purchases ledger control account would contain the following main entries:

Purchases Ledger Control Account

Debit entries	(Source)	Credit entries	(Source)
Purchases returns (Returns outwards)	Purchases returns day book	Opening creditors[1]	Previous closing balance
Cash and cheques paid to creditors[2]	Cash book	Total credit purchases	Purchases day book
Closing creditors	(Balancing figure to be compared with total of individual balances in purchases ledger)		

[1] There may also be some debit balances within the purchases ledger brought forward, resulting from over-payments, duplicated payments or the company returning goods to the supplier after having paid for them.
[2] Any discounts received from suppliers would be shown separately (see Chapter 4).

Control accounts have a number of advantages for management:

➤ Total debtors and creditors figures can be produced at any time by balancing the control accounts. This avoids the need to calculate every individual balance within the personal ledgers.

➤ Fraud can be prevented if the person responsible for compiling and checking the control accounts is a supervisor unconnected with the day-to-day bookkeeping procedures. This also provides an independent check on the quality and accuracy of the accounting records.

➤ Errors within a double-entry bookkeeping system can be located to a specific ledger, which it avoids unnecessary effort.

➤ The control accounts themselves can be brought within the double-entry bookkeeping system as part of the general ledger, with the debtors' and creditors' individual accounts in the personal ledgers then being treated as detailed, 'subsidiary' records outside the system. This has the great advantage of summarising all the sales ledger and purchases ledger information within just two ledger accounts, with the balances on these accounts providing the debtors and creditors figures for the trial balance.

ACTIVITY 3.2

The following totals were extracted from the books of prime entry of Davinia Draycott for November:

	£
Cheques received from debtors	297,640
Cheques paid to creditors	216,900
Goods returned by customers	130
Goods returned to suppliers	650

	£
Invoices issued to customers	316,595
Invoices received from suppliers	284,100

At 1 November, opening debtors were £47,210 and opening creditors were £14,600. At 30 November, the individual balances within the sales ledger totalled £66,035 and the individual balances within the purchases ledger totalled £82,750.

When Davinia extracted a trial balance as at 30 November, there was a difference of £1,600. Assuming that the entries in the general ledger and cash book were correct, which personal ledger contained the error? Draw up control accounts for each personal ledger to find out.

Answer

Sales Ledger Control Account

	£		£
Opening debtors	47,210	Sales returns	130
Total sales invoices	316,595	Cheques received	297,640
		Closing debtors (balancing figure)	66,035
	363,805		363,805

This ledger appears to be arithmetically correct, as the balance on the control account is the same as the total of the individual ledger balances.

Purchases Ledger Control Account

	£		£
Purchases returns	650	Opening creditors	14,600
Cheques paid	216,900	Total purchase invoices	284,100
Closing creditors (balancing figure)	81,150		
	298,700		298,700

As the total of the individual sales ledger is £82,750 and the control account balance is £81,150, the error must be within this ledger.

3.5 Accounting adjustments

Once the bank reconciliation is completed and the control accounts agree with the personal ledgers, we can progress to consider the various accounting adjustments which are needed to comply with accounting concepts prior to preparation of the financial summaries of the business.

These summaries are prepared in relation to a *financial period*, which can be as short or long as suits the business.

DID YOU KNOW?

Businesses set up as limited companies (see Chapter 7) have to comply with Acts of Parliament known as the Companies Acts, which set out detailed accounting requirements.

However, it is usual for *annual* summaries to be prepared for taxation purposes or to comply with legislation. These are referred to as being for the *financial year*. The financial year need not be a calendar year, but usually ends on the last day of a month, e.g. 31 March.

PAUSE FOR THOUGHT

Seasonal businesses traditionally choose a 'quiet' month to end their financial year so that their busiest trading time is not disrupted by the need to obtain accounting information. Many retail fashion stores choose February or March to end their financial year (i.e. the time between the January sales and the new spring collections appearing).

3.5.1 Unsold stock

This is stock which the business has bought during the period which is unsold at the end of the period and carried forward to the next period. In the general ledger, we show the information in a 'Stock account'. This records *only* information relating to opening and closing stock, not goods bought during the period (which are shown in the purchases account in the general ledger). Due to the *prudence concept*, stock is valued at the *lower of cost and net realisable value*,[1] which in simple terms means either what the stock cost the business or the value it might fetch if for some reason (damage, changing fashions, etc.) it is anticipated that it could only be sold at a price less than cost (see Chapter 5 for further explanation of this). Stock is never valued at normal selling price, as that would anticipate a profit, which is unacceptable under the prudence concept.

EXAMPLE 3.1
. . . .

Bulk Buys, which has a financial year ending on 28 February, had opening unsold stock of £90,000 on 1 March 2000 and £70,000 unsold stock a year later on 28 February 2001. Show the entries in the Stock account.

General Ledger

Stock

		£			£
1/3/00	Opening stock b/f	90,000	28/2/01	P & L account	90,000
28/2/01	P & L account	70,000	28/2/01	Closing stock c/d	70,000
		160,000			160,000
1/3/01	Opening stock b/d	70,000			

PAUSE FOR THOUGHT

'P & L account' stands for 'Profit and Loss Account', the financial summary of income and expenditure (see Section 3.6.1 of this chapter).

Note that we use the abbreviation 'b/f' for 'brought forward' where we don't see the other side of the double entry on the same page. Similarly, we would use 'c/f' (carried forward) instead of c/d for a closing balance where the balance is transferred to a different page.

[1] Accounting Standards Board (1990) Statement of Standard Accounting Practice (SSAP) 9, *Stocks and Long Term Contracts*, London

In a trial balance prepared at the end of a financial period, it is usual to see the opening stock (i.e. the balance brought forward) as a debit entry representing the opening asset of unsold stock. The value of closing stock then appears as a note (usually the first) to the trial balance. The way in which stock values are shown in the financial summaries is explained later in this chapter. The accruals concept is relevant here, as by transferring values of unsold goods into the financial summaries, we are ensuring that the income from the sale of goods is matched only by the cost of those goods, and excludes the value of any *unsold* stock at the end of the period.

3.5.2 Accruals and prepayments

At the end of the financial period there are likely to be some expenses which are owing, other than normal 'trade creditors'. Often the bills have not been received, so an estimate must be made. Conversely, some expenses may have been paid in advance for a future period, in which case we extract the 'prepayment' from the current period.

We have to make sure that the expenses shown in the financial summary cover only the stated period, neither more nor less than that. This is due to the application of the *accruals concept*, which states that *all* income and related expenditure for a specified period should be included, not simply money paid or received.

Adjustment for accruals

EXAMPLE **3.2**
. . . .

Bulk Buys paid £4,000 for electricity during the year to 28 February 2001. The last bill paid was for the quarter ended 31 December 2000. Average bills for the winter quarter are £1,500.

Electricity

	£		£
(to 31/12/00) Bank	4,000	28/2/01 P & L account	5,000
28/2/01 Accrual c/d	1,000		
	5,000		5,000
		1/3/01 Accrual b/d	1,000

PAUSE FOR THOUGHT

A quarter of a year is three months, but we need only an extra two months (January and February) to complete the information for the financial year. We therefore estimate how much electricity would be used (2/3 × £1,500) and insert this into the account as an accrual. The accrual is then brought down as a liability (credit balance) at the start of the new accounting period. £5,000 will be shown as the electricity expense for the year, whilst a liability of £1,000 is shown in the balance sheet.

*Remember: **A**dd **A**ccruals to expenses!*

EXAMPLE **3.3**

Adjustment for prepayments

Bulk Buys paid £9,000 on 1 March 2000 for rent for the nine months to 30 November 2000 and £6,000 on 30 November 2000 for the half-year to 31 May 2001.

Rent

		£		£
1/3/00	Bank (9 months)	9,000	28/2/01 P & L account	12,000
30/11/00	Bank (6 months)	6,000	28/2/01 Prepayment c/d	3,000
		15,000		15,000
1/3/01	Prepayment b/d	3,000		

PAUSE FOR THOUGHT

If a financial summary is drawn up for a year, then it must show 12 months' information, not 9 or 15! The £15,000 paid during the year ended 28 February 2001 is for 15 months' rent, so we must take out the 'extra' three months, which is shown as a prepayment to be carried down as an asset (debit) balance at the start of the new accounting period. £12,000 is shown as the expense for rent in the profit and loss account, whilst £3,000 will be shown as an asset in the balance sheet.

*Remember: **RE**duce expenses by the p**RE**payment!*

ACTIVITY **3.3**

Claudia Grimaldi completed her first year of business on 31 December 2000. During the year she paid an insurance premium of £2,400 by cheque on 1 October to insure a building for a twelve-month period from that date.

During the year 2000, she also paid three quarterly telephone bills on 1 April, 1 July and 1 October of £120, £180 and £240 respectively. Future bills are expected to keep increasing at the same rate as previously.

Show the insurance account and telephone account in the general ledger for the year ended 31 December 2000, showing the balances to be transferred to the profit and loss account and the balances brought down at the start of the following year.

Answer

Insurance

		£		£
1/10/00	Bank	2,400	31/12/00 P & L account	600
			31/12/00 Prepayment c/d	1,800
		2,400		2,400
1/1/01	Prepayment b/d	1,800		

Telephone

		£		£
1/4/00	Bank	120	31/12/00 P & L account	840
1/7/00	Bank	180		
1/10/00	Bank	240		
		540		
31/12/00	Accrual c/d	300		
		840		840
			1/1/01 Accrual b/d	300

The profit and loss account will show insurance and telephone expenses for the year of £600 and £840 respectively, whilst the balance sheet at 31 December 2000 will record an asset of £1,800 (the insurance prepayment) and a liability of £300 (the telephone accrual).

3.5.3 Depreciation

All fixed assets, with the exception of most freehold land, are subject to depreciation. Depreciation is defined as

> The measure of the cost or revalued amount of the economic benefits of the tangible fixed asset that have been consumed during the period. Consumption includes the wearing out, using up or other reduction in the useful economic life of a tangible fixed asset whether arising from use, effluxion of time or obsolescence through either changes in technology or demand for the goods and services produced by the asset.[2]

DID YOU KNOW?

'Tangible' means 'capable of being touched', i.e. 'physical' assets such as cars, machinery, buildings, etc.

'Effluxion of time' means the same as 'the passage of time'.

'Obsolescence' is the process of becoming obsolete.

Due to the accruals and prudence concepts, accountants have to make an estimate of the amount of depreciation which has been suffered by fixed assets during the financial period. This is then included within the profit and loss account as an expense. This estimate is based on three components, the last two of which are 'best guesses':

➤ The cost of the fixed asset, which is easily determined if purchased from an outside supplier. However, any installation costs incurred to bring the asset into a working condition should also be included as part of the cost. For example, if a factory wall had to be dismantled and rebuilt to allow the installation of a large machine, the building costs would be included as part of the cost of the fixed asset. If the fixed asset is built by the business itself, then labour costs and other directly attributable costs would be included as part of the cost of the asset.

➤ The useful economic life of the asset, which is the estimate of how long the fixed asset will continue to provide economic benefits to the organisation.

➤ The residual value, which is the estimate, based on prices prevailing at the date of acquiring the asset, of the value which the asset may have at the end of its useful economic life. In many cases, it is assumed that the asset will have no residual value.

For example, a welding robot is bought by a car manufacturer for £200,000 on 1 January 2000. It costs £40,000 to install the robot and it is expected to be used for a period of 10 years, after which it is expected to be sold to an industrial museum for £4,000.

➤ The cost is £240,000 (£200,000 + £40,000).
➤ The useful economic life is 10 years.
➤ The estimated residual value is £4,000.

[2] Accounting Standards Board (1999) Financial Reporting Standard (FRS) 15, *Tangible Fixed Assets*, London

A variety of methods can be used to calculate the amount of depreciation to be allocated to a specific financial period. The two most common methods are the straight line method and the reducing balance method.

The straight line method

This assumes that depreciation occurs evenly over the life of the asset, so the asset is written off in equal instalments over its useful economic life. In fact it is sometimes called the equal instalment method. Straight line depreciation is used by most businesses for the vast majority of fixed assets. The formula for calculating depreciation under this method is

$$\frac{\text{Cost} - \text{Estimated residual value}}{\text{Useful economic life in years}}$$

The welding robot (see above) would be depreciated over 10 years at

$$(£240,000 - £4,000)/10 = £23,600 \text{ p.a.}$$

ACTIVITY 3.4

Bulk Buys bought a forklift truck for £30,000 on 1 March 1998. It was estimated to last for 5 years, when it would be worth about £4,000. What is the annual depreciation under the straight line method?

Answer

$$\text{Annual depreciation} = \frac{(\text{Cost} - \text{Residual value})}{\text{Useful economic life in years}}$$
$$= (30,000 - 4,000)/5 = £5,200 \text{ p.a.}$$

The reducing balance method

This assumes higher depreciation in earlier years than in later years and is used where it is clear that greater economic benefits are provided by assets when new than when they become older – perhaps as a result of general wear causing them to become more prone to breakdown or less capable of producing a high-quality product. The method (sometimes called the 'diminishing balance' method) works by applying a given (or calculated) percentage to the net book value (i.e. cost less accumulated depreciation up to the date of the calculation).

DID YOU KNOW?

The depreciation rate under the straight line method can also be expressed as a percentage. For example, 20% p.a. straight line depreciation means equal instalments over 5 years, 25% p.a. straight line is over 4 years, etc.

PAUSE FOR THOUGHT

It is rare for students to be asked to calculate the percentage used for the reducing balance method! However, the formula is

$$r = 1 - n\sqrt{\frac{s}{c}}$$

where r = percentage, n = useful life, s = residual value and c = original cost.

ACTIVITY 3.5

Bulk Buys paid £12,000 for a car for a sales manager on 1 March 1999. The depreciation rate is 40% p.a. Show the depreciation on a reducing balance basis.

Answer

Cost	12,000
Depreciation: Year 1 (40% × £12,000)	4,800
	7,200
Depreciation: Year 2 (40% × £7,200)	2,880
	4,320
Depreciation: Year 3 (40% × £4,320)	1,728
	2,592

etc., until sold or scrapped.

Bookkeeping for depreciation

Depreciation is an expense – a loss – to the business, so the depreciation for the financial period will be included within the profit and loss account. The value of the fixed asset, as adjusted for depreciation, will be included on the balance sheet. Fixed assets are not shown individually, but grouped into classes of assets, for example *Land and buildings*, *Machinery*, *Motor vehicles*, *Fixtures and fittings*, etc. The process of charging depreciation is known as 'making a provision', or *providing* for depreciation, and the bookkeeping requires separate provision accounts to be opened for each class of assets.

PAUSE FOR THOUGHT

If a company has leasehold *premises (buildings which it doesn't own, but for which it has paid an amount to the owner for the right to use them over a defined period), the term 'amortisation' is used rather than 'depreciation'. Amortisation is derived from two French words,* à mortir, *meaning 'to the death', as the cost of the lease is being reduced to zero over its life, usually by the straight line method. For example, if a business paid £50,000 for the right to use a building over 20 years, it would be* amortised *at the rate of £2,500 p.a. over that time.*

ACTIVITY **3.6**

Show the ledger accounts required to record the bookkeeping entries for Bulk Buys in Activities 3.4 and 3.5 above, for the first three years of the assets' lives.

Answer

Forklift truck

	£		£
1/3/00 Cost	30,000	28/2/01 Balance c/d	30,000
1/3/01 Balance b/d	30,000	28/2/02 Balance c/d	30,000
1/3/02 Balance b/d	30,000	28/2/03 Balance c/d	30,000
1/3/03 Balance b/d	30,000		

Car

	£		£
1/3/99 Cost	12,000	28/2/00 Balance c/d	12,000
1/3/00 Balance b/d	12,000	28/2/01 Balance c/d	12,000
1/3/01 Balance b/d	12,000	28/2/02 Balance c/d	12,000
1/3/02 Balance b/d	12,000		

Provision for depreciation on forklift truck

	£		£
28/2/01 Balance c/d	5,200	28/2/01 P & L account	5,200
28/2/02 Balance c/d	10,400	1/3/01 Balance b/d	5,200
		28/2/02 P & L account	5,200
	10,400		10,400
		1/3/02 Balance b/d	10,400
28/2/03 Balance c/d	15,600	28/2/03 P & L account	5,200
	15,600		15,600
		1/3/03 Balance b/d	15,600

Provision for depreciation on car

	£		£
28/2/00 Balance c/d	4,800	28/2/00 P & L account	4,800
28/2/01 Balance c/d	7,680	1/3/00 Balance b/d	4,800
		28/2/01 P & L account	2,880
	7,680		7,680
28/2/02 Balance c/d	9,408	1/3/01 Balance b/d	7,680
		28/2/02 P & L account	1,728
	9,408		9,408
		1/3/02 Balance b/d	9,408

PAUSE FOR THOUGHT *Every balance carried down at the end of each financial period will appear in the balance sheet at that date. For example, the car will be shown in the balance sheet at 28 February 2002 at cost £12,000, less depreciation £9,408, leaving a 'net book value' of £2,592. Each of the items marked 'P & L account' will be shown as an expense (loss) in the profit and loss account for that financial period, for example £1,728 will be shown in the profit and loss account for the year ended 28 February 2002 as 'Depreciation on Car'.*

3.6 The financial summaries

We can now consider the way in which the two key financial summaries, the profit and loss account and balance sheet, are presented. Let's recall the various stages we have passed through to reach this point (see Figure 3.2).

3.6.1 The profit and loss account

Also known as the income, or revenue, statement, this summary of all the income and expenditure for the financial period is part of the double-entry bookkeeping system but, unlike all other accounts, is not usually split into debit and credit sides but is shown in a 'vertical' or 'columnar' format. In many mainland European countries, however, it is normal practice to show expenses on the debit side and income on the credit side. In the UK, the normal layout for a trading business's profit and loss account is shown below, using invented data for illustration.

figure 3.2
Stages in reaching
balance sheet and
profit and loss
account

| Enter all financial transactions in the double-entry bookkeeping system |

↓

| Check the arithmetical accuracy of the bookkeeping by extracting and agreeing a trial balance |

↓

| Check that the relevant banking transactions have been included by reconciling the bank's records with those contained in the cash book |

↓

| Check the overall arithmetical accuracy of the personal ledgers by extracting and agreeing purchase ledger and sales ledger control accounts |

↓

| Insert accruals and prepayments into the relevant ledger accounts |

↓

| Calculate depreciation on fixed assets and enter details in provisions for depreciation |

ABC & Co
Profit and loss account for the year ended 30 June 2001[1]

	£	£
Sales[2]		500,000
Less **Cost of goods sold**		
Opening Stock at 1 July 2000	15,000	
Add Purchases[3]	230,000	
	245,000	
Less Closing stock at 30 June 2001	(45,000)	
		(200,000)[4]
Gross profit[5]		300,000
Less **Expenses**[6]		
Wages	45,000	
Rent and rates	23,000	
Depreciation[7]	32,000	
(other expenses listed...)	80,000	
		(180,000)
Net profit[8]		120,000

Notes:

1 Sometimes this statement is referred to as the 'Trading and Profit and Loss Account', as the first section leading to the Gross Profit is known as the 'Trading Account'. However, the modern style of heading usually omits the reference to 'Trading'.

2 All the sales for the period, whether paid for or not.

3 All the goods bought for resale in the period, whether paid for or not.

4 This figure (and the expenses figure of £180,000 below it) is derived from the details contained in the inner column. Brackets are usually placed around figures which are deducted from the figure immediately above.

5 Gross profit is the profit from trading before overhead expenditure is deducted.

6 All the relevant expenditure, adjusted where necessary for accruals and pre-payments.

7 Only the depreciation charged for this financial period.

8 Net profit is sometimes referred to as *operating profit*. It is the profit after all expenses have been deducted.

3.6.2 The balance sheet

This summary of all the assets, liabilities and capital balances at the end of the financial period is not part of the double-entry bookkeeping system but is, like the trial balance, a list of balances remaining within the accounts at a specific time. As with the profit and loss account, many countries show the balance sheet in a two-sided 'account' format but, in the UK, the normal layout for a balance sheet is as follows, again using invented data for illustration:

ABC & Co
Balance sheet as at 30 June 2001[1]

	Cost	Depreciation[2]	Net book value[3]
	£	£	£
Fixed assets[4]			
Land and buildings	153,600	42,500	111,100
Motor vehicles	65,000	17,500	47,500
Fixtures	15,100	8,300	6,800
	233,700	68,300	165,400
Current assets[5]			
Stock		45,000	
Debtors		23,000	
Prepayments		4,000	
Bank		2,000	
Cash		600	
		74,600	
Less **Current liabilities**			
Creditors	33,000		
Accruals	5,200		
		(38,200)	
Net current assets[6]			36,400[7]
Total net assets			201,800

	£	£

Capital

	£	£
Opening balance, 1 July 2000	146,700	
Add Net profit[8]	120,000	
	266,700	
Less Drawings	(64,900)	
Closing balance, 30 June 2001		201,800

Notes:

1 The balance sheet is always dated as the last day of the financial period, never for the year ended ... .
2 All the depreciation on that class of assets, not just the depreciation for that financial period.
3 These three headings refer only to the 'Fixed Assets' section.
4 There are other acceptable ways of showing this information, e.g.:

Land and buildings at cost	153,600
Less Accumulated depreciation	42,500
	111,100

etc.
5 Shown in 'increasing order of liquidity', so the most liquid asset, cash, is shown at the end. 'Liquidity' simply means the ability to be converted into cash.
6 Also known as 'working capital'.
7 As with the profit and loss account, figures in the right-hand columns are derived from the details contained in the inner columns.
8 The net profit for the year, as shown in the profit and loss account (see p. 54).

3.7 Glossary

Accrual	An expense owing at the end of a financial period where the bill has not yet been received
Amortisation	The equivalent of depreciation, as applied to leasehold premises
B/f	Abbreviation for 'brought forward', used where we don't see the other side of the double-entry of an opening account balance on the same page
Balance sheet	The financial summary which records assets, liabilities and capital at the end of a financial period
Bank reconciliation statement	A statement prepared to reconcile the information appearing in the bank account in the business's cash book with the bank statements showing the bank's records of the account
C/f	Abbreviation for 'carried forward', used where we don't see the other side of the double-entry of a closing account balance on the same page
Cash flow statement	A summary of all the inflows and outflows of cash and bank transactions during a period

Control accounts	Total accounts summarising all the individual transactions in the purchases ledger and sales ledger to check on accuracy and completeness
Depreciation	The loss in value of a fixed asset over time
Financial period	The period, often a year, used as the time interval for summarising financial information
Gross profit	The difference between income from sales and the cost of the goods sold, before overhead expenditure has been deducted
In hand	A bank balance with a positive balance (a debit balance in the business's books, but a credit balance in the bank's ledger)
Net profit	Also called *operating profit*, this is the gross profit plus any sundry income, less overhead expenditure
Operating profit	Another term for *net profit*, usually seen in the profit and loss account of a limited company (see Chapter 7)
Overdraft	A bank balance with a negative balance (a credit balance in the business's books, but a debit balance in the bank's ledger)
Prepayment	An expense paid in one financial period where the benefits are not received until some future period
Profit and loss account	The financial summary which records the income and expenditure for a financial period
Provision	An amount set aside out of profits where the amount cannot be determined with accuracy, e.g. a provision for depreciation
Reducing balance method	A method of calculating depreciation using the assumption that the loss in value is greater in the early years than in the later years of the asset's life
Residual value	The estimate of value at the end of a fixed asset's useful economic life
Stock	The value of unsold goods, also known as an inventory
Straight line method	A method of calculating depreciation using the assumption that the loss in value occurs evenly over the life of the asset
Tangible fixed asset	A fixed asset with physical properties, such as land, machinery, cars, etc.
Trading account	The first section of the profit and loss account, where the gross profit is calculated. Sometimes included as part of the description of that statement, i.e. *Trading and profit and loss account*
Unpresented cheque	A cheque sent to a creditor by the business but not yet banked by that creditor
Useful economic life	The estimate of how long a fixed asset will be of use to the business
Working capital	Another term for net current assets, the difference between current assets and current liabilities on the balance sheet

1   A cash flow statement shows:
   a The profit of a business
   b The money coming in to and going out of a business
   c The income and expenditure of a business
   d The assets and liabilities of a business

2   On checking a bank statement against the bank account details in the cash
   book, you find that a direct debit for rates has not been entered in the cash
   book. Do you:
   a Debit the bank account and credit the rates account
   b Debit the rates account and credit the bank account
   c Debit the rates account and credit the bank statement
   d Not enter the direct debit as it affects only the bank statement

3   A credit balance may appear on a sales ledger account because:
   a A supplier has overpaid
   b A sales invoice has been duplicated
   c A customer may have returned goods after paying for them
   d The business has repaid an overpayment by a customer

4   Which of the following represent advantages of control accounts?
   a They can make it harder to find total debtors and creditors figures
   b They can help in finding spelling mistakes
   c They can help in locating errors to a specific ledger
   d They can help to find if a payment for rent has been posted to the rates
      account

5   Relating to the opening and closing stock for a financial period, which of the
   following is true?
   a Both figures are shown in the profit and loss account but only the opening
      stock is shown in the balance sheet
   b Only the opening stock is shown in the profit and loss account, but both
      figures are shown in the balance sheet
   c Both figures are shown in the profit and loss account but only the closing
      stock is shown in the balance sheet
   d Only the closing stock is shown in the profit and loss account, but both
      figures are shown in the balance sheet

6   If a business has paid gas bills totalling £34,000 during a financial period but
   owes £3,000 for gas by the end of the period, what will be the opening
   balance in the gas account at the start of the following period?
   a £37,000 credit
   b £3,000 debit
   c £31,000 debit
   d £3,000 credit

7   A business paid a £720 subscription to a trade magazine on 30 June 2000, for
   the two years to 1 July 2002. The business's financial year ends on 30
   November 2000. What relevant figures for subscriptions will be shown in the
   financial summaries for that period?
   a £150 in the profit and loss account, £570 prepayment in the balance sheet
   b £720 in the profit and loss account, nil in the balance sheet

    c £360 in the profit and loss account, £360 prepayment in the balance sheet

    d £1,440 in the profit and loss account, £720 prepayment in the balance sheet

8 A business buys a car which costs £15,000. This price includes £500 for insurance and £60 for road tax. The business's name was painted on the side of the car at an additional cost of £160. The car is expected to be in use for 5 years, after which time it will have an estimated value of £4,600. What is the annual depreciation if the straight line method is used?

    a £2,000

    b £2,112

    c £1,968

    d £2,080

9 A machine is bought for £18,000, plus £3,000 installation costs. It is to be depreciated on a reducing balance basis using a rate of 60% p.a. What is the depreciation to be charged in the second year of the asset's ownership?

    a £12,600

    b £4,320

    c £5,040

    d £8,400

10 Cost of Sales equals:

    a Opening stock plus purchases plus closing stock

    b Opening stock less purchases plus closing stock

    c Closing stock plus purchases less opening stock

    d Opening stock plus purchases less closing stock

Further questions can be found on the accompanying website (www.booksites.net/black).

SELF-STUDY QUESTIONS

(Answers in Appendix 2)

Question 3.1

a Explain the need for, and give examples of, controls within a bookkeeping system.

b From the following information, produce sales ledger and purchase ledger control accounts, showing the closing debtors and creditors in the relevant accounts.

	£
Opening creditors	92,100
Opening debtors	86,250
Opening credit balances on the sales ledger	370
Cheques paid to suppliers	472,450
Cheques received from debtors	577,800
Goods returned by 'credit' customers	3,200
Goods returned to suppliers	770
Sales invoices issued	610,200
Purchase invoices received	463,750

Question 3.2

a Explain how the *accruals concept* affects the information to be disclosed within a profit and loss account.

b Write up the relevant general ledger accounts of Polly Harris for the year ended 30 April 2001 for the following information:

(i) She had opening unsold stock of £50,000 and £60,000 unsold stock a year later.

(ii) She paid £4,000 for telephone charges during the year for 10 months' usage, but the final two months are owing. The next quarter's bill is expected to be £1,350.

(iii) She paid £15,000 at the very start of the year for rent for the first six months and then paid £22,500 on 1 November 2000. The monthly rent did not change during the period.

Question 3.3

a Define *depreciation* and explain its relevance to fundamental accounting concepts.

b Show the relevant fixed asset accounts and provision for depreciation accounts for the following information for each of the three financial years ending 31 December 2002.

	£
Machinery at cost, 1 January 2000	65,000
Computers at cost, 1 January 2000	20,000
Motor cars at cost, 1 January 2001	45,000
Estimated residual value of machinery after five years' useful economic life	5,000
Estimated residual value of computers after four years' useful economic life	nil

Basis of depreciation: machinery and computers – straight line
Basis of depreciation: motor cars – 40% on reducing balance

c Show how the information relating to fixed assets and depreciation would appear in the profit and loss account for the year ended 31 December 2002 and the balance sheet as at that date.

Question 3.4

From the following information relating to Louise Jones, prepare the profit and loss account for the year ended 30 November 2001 and a balance sheet as at that date. Pay special attention to clarity and neatness when drawing up the information.

	£
Accountancy	350
Accruals at 30 November 2001	130
Advertising	285
Bank balance (asset)	3,600
Bank charges (an expense)	74
Cash balance	120
Closing stock	12,400
Creditors at end of period	8,140
Debtors at end of period	7,384
Depreciation for the year on fixtures and fittings	800
Depreciation for the year on motor van	1,600
Drawings	7,500

Fixtures and fittings at cost	11,400
Light and heat	1,030
Motor van at cost	8,900
Motor expenses	518
Net profit for the year	?
Opening stock	7,224
Opening capital balance at 1 December 2000	23,652
Postage and printing	390
Prepayments at 30 November 2001	200
Purchases	49,600
Rent and rates	2,900
Repairs	810
Sales	75,972
Telephone and insurance	619
Total depreciation on fixtures and fittings at 30 November 2001	4,200
Total depreciation on motor van at 30 November 2001	4,800
Wages	11,590

Further questions can be found on the accompanying website (www.booksites. net/black).

CASE STUDY
....

Esmeralda appears, then disappears

The busiest time for any children's entertainer is Christmas, and Marvin (see previous case studies) was finding that as the year progressed he was in great demand. He felt he needed an assistant so decided to employ Esmeralda, who had previously been chief inventor at Kaboosh Limited, a company manufacturing equipment for magic tricks and novelties. As a leaving present, that company had given her a 'disappearing lady' apparatus. Being unsentimental about such things, she promptly sold it to Marvin on 1 December 2000 for £2,000. Esmeralda started to appear (and disappear) as part of Marvin's magic act.

After two months in her new job Esmeralda persuaded Marvin to diversify by buying in items made by her former employers and selling them at the children's parties to the parents and guests.

During January 2001, Marvin received a letter from his bank, asking for financial summaries for his first six months in business. January is a quiet month for him, so he spent some time producing the following information:

Cash and cheques received

	£
Sales of novelties bought from Kaboosh Ltd	2,500
Appearance fees as entertainer	18,320

Cash and cheques paid

Kaboosh Ltd for novelties to be sold	1,500
Wages	1,200
Kazam Limited for playing cards	400
Travel expenses	2,600
Rabbits and rabbit food, less returns (expenses)	430
Cleaning	140
Esmeralda for 'disappearing lady' apparatus	2,000
Marvin's drawings	11,890

Other information

Cash balance at 31 December 2000	560
Bank balance at 31 December 2000	120
Total invoices received from Kaboosh Ltd up to 31 December 2000	1,700
Stock of unsold novelties at cost price at 31 December 2000 (N.B.: no 'opening stock')	80
Amounts owing from customers for novelties	350
Other fixed assets still owned at 31 December 2000:	
Costume at cost	3,000
Magic book at cost	2,000
Opening capital (see case study in Chapter 2)	5,020

Notes:

1 The costume, the magic book and the playing cards are to be grouped as 'Magician's equipment' and depreciated at 20% p.a. (i.e. over 5 years), straight line method, with no residual value. Note that the period here is only six months!

2 The 'disappearing lady' apparatus is to be depreciated at 40% p.a. on the reducing balance method. The full six months' depreciation is to be deducted, even though it was owned for only part of that time.

3 Marvin owed £100 wages to Esmeralda at 31 December, and had paid £50 in December for a train ticket which was going to be used in January.

Prepare, as neatly as possible, Marvin's profit and loss account for the six months to 31 December 2000, and a balance sheet as at that date. Note that in the profit and loss account, gross profit on novelties should be calculated first and the fees added to that before deducting the expenses.

(Answers in Appendix 3)

Reference
•••••••••••••

A discussion on 'cash flow'
'Net income v. cash flow: If I'm making so much money, why am I so broke?'
http://www.ohiosbdc.org/osbdc/research/5001.html

CHAPTER **4**
....

The profit and loss account and balance sheet

Objectives
....

When you have read this chapter you will be able to:

➤ Appreciate that accounting is not an exact science

➤ Understand and apply the profit and loss account layouts for manufacturing, trading and service businesses

➤ Be aware of the use of the appropriation account by partnerships and limited companies

➤ Understand the place of the profit and loss account and balance sheet within the bookkeeping system and be aware that they can be shown in an 'account' format as well as in vertical or columnar style

➤ Be aware that limited companies publish financial summaries which must follow prescribed formats

➤ Draw up a detailed profit and loss account and balance sheet from a trial balance, adjusting for such items as accruals, prepayments and depreciation

4.1 Introduction
....

In the previous chapter we saw how the financial summaries reflect the application of accounting concepts to financial information. The two key summaries we have already encountered are the *profit and loss account*, showing income and expenses for a financial period, and the *balance sheet* showing assets, liabilities and capital at the end of the financial period. In this chapter we look in more detail at these, showing how the statements can be made more meaningful for different types of business organisations and also how they link with the double-entry bookkeeping system. We also address some specific problem areas.

4.2 What is 'profit'?
....

Profit is ascertained by comparing income with expenses which, according to the accruals (matching) concept, must reflect all the relevant transactions for the financial period, not just those which represent cash and cheques received or paid. Although this appears quite straightforward, jokes are sometimes made about accountants who, when asked by a business owner what profit their business has made, would reply 'How much would you like it to be?', implying that by skilful accounting surgery the final figures could be as high or low as suited the needs of the business. Indeed one author went so far as to suggest that 'Every company in the country is fiddling its profits. Every set of published accounts is based on books which have been gently cooked or completely roasted.'[1] Because some of the information (such as depreciation) found in the financial summaries relies on estimates, it is true to say that accounting is not an exact science. However, in the last 30 years, and particularly since the formation of the Accounting Standards Board in 1990, the UK regulatory framework has tightened in a concerted attempt to overcome the real anxieties expressed by users regarding the reliability of financial information. For many years, all limited companies had to appoint an independent auditor to report on whether the financial summaries reflected a *true and fair view* of the company's affairs. In recent times, however, this requirement for a compulsory audit has been removed from small companies, though they can opt to appoint an independent auditor if they wish.

4.3 The format of the profit and loss account

The format of the profit and loss account will vary depending upon whether the organisation is:

➤ a manufacturing business (i.e. making the goods they sell),
➤ a trading business (i.e. buying goods for resale), or
➤ a service business (i.e. selling a service for a fee).

There will be further differences depending upon whether the organisation has been structured as:

➤ a sole trader (i.e. a one-person business),
➤ a partnership (two or more owners of the business), or
➤ a limited company (a business with shareholders).

Figure 4.1 shows the various components within the profit and loss account for each type of business.

Note that the statement as a whole is referred to as the *profit and loss account* despite the fact that it might contain up to four separate accounts. It is permissible to include the names of each of the accounts (other than the appropriation account) within the title, so for a manufacturing business you could

figure 4.1
Components of the profit and loss account

| Component | Type of organisation | | | | | |
	Manufacturing	Trading	Service	Sole trader	Partnership	Limited company
Manufacturing account	✓	✗	✗	✓ (if manufacturing)		
Trading account	✓		✗	✓ (if trading)		
Profit and loss account	✓			✓		
Appropriation account	✓ (but not if a sole trader)			✗	✓	

[1] Griffiths, I. (1986) *Creative Accounting*, 1st edition, London: Waterstone & Co.

call the statement the 'manufacturing, trading and profit and loss accounts' rather than simply the 'profit and loss account'. However, nearly all UK limited companies use the simplified heading in their published financial information.

4.3.1 Manufacturing businesses

Companies which manufacture the products which they sell will have specific costs relating to the manufacturing process, which are summarised in a separate account before being transferred into the trading account. The expenses are allocated as follows.

➤ *Direct costs*, which can be readily identified with the items being produced. For example, in a ship-building company, the cost of metal and the other fittings used to construct the ship, plus the wages paid to the metalworkers and fitters, are direct costs. In a sweet factory, direct costs would be the cost of sugar, colourings and other ingredients. Another name for direct costs is *prime costs*.

➤ *Indirect costs* are all other manufacturing expenses which cannot be directly associated with the items being produced. These could include the rent of a shipyard or factory, the wages paid to supervisors, the cost of running the staff canteen, etc.

More information regarding the classification of costs is given in Chapter 11, *An introduction to management accounting*.

ACTIVITY 4.1

During the year to 31 December 2001, Bert Bodlington incurs the following costs in his factory, which produces cakes for sale to hotels and restaurants:

	£
Flour	63,250
Sugar	23,580
Chocolate	12,560
Cream	3,562
Wages to factory workers	74,120
Wages owed to factory workers	6,300
Factory rent and rates	12,500
Factory light and heat	8,543
Wages to supervisors	26,100
Depreciation of factory machinery	9,910
Stock of raw materials on 1 January 2001	12,400
Stock of raw materials on 31 December 2001	11,500
Partly completed stock (work-in-progress) on 1 January 2001	1,540
Partly completed stock (work-in-progress) on 31 December 2001	640

Prepare the manufacturing account for the year ended 31 December 2001.

Answer

Bert Bodlington
Manufacturing Account for the year ended 31 December 2001

	£	£
Raw materials		
Opening stock at 1 January 2001	12,400	
Add Purchases of raw materials	102,952	
	115,352	
Less Closing stock at 31 December 2001	(11,500)	
Cost of raw materials		103,852
Other direct costs:		
Production labour		80,420
Prime cost of production		184,272
Indirect factory costs:		
Rent and rates	12,500	
Light and heat	8,543	
Wages to supervisors	26,100	
Depreciation of factory machinery	3,910	
		51,053
		235,325
Add Opening work-in-progress	1,540	
Less Closing work-in-progress	(640)	
		900
Total factory production cost c/d		236,225

PAUSE FOR THOUGHT *The manufacturing account summarises all the factory costs for the period (including those not yet paid for, such as the accrued wages), dividing them between direct and indirect and adjusting for opening and closing stocks of raw materials and work-in-progress. The 'c/d' on the last line indicates that this figure is taken into the next section, the trading account, to form part of the 'cost of sales' to be compared with the sales revenue.*

4.3.2 The trading account

The trading account calculates the *gross profit* of the organisation for the financial period by comparing the total sales revenue with the cost of the goods sold. In a business which does not make the products it sells, the layout of the trading account (using invented figures) would be as follows:

(name of trader)
Trading account for the year ended 30 June 2002

	£	£
Sales		600,000
Less **Cost of goods sold**		
Opening stock at 1 July 2001	35,000	
Add Purchases	460,000	
	495,000	
Less Closing stock at 30 June 2002	(52,000)	
		(443,000)
Gross profit		157,000

In a manufacturing business, the total factory production cost is 'brought down' as part of the cost of goods sold.

ACTIVITY **4.2**
· · · · · · · · · · · · · · ·

Bert Bodlington (see Activity 4.1), in addition to his own manufactured cakes, buys in speciality wedding cakes from another manufacturer. He provides the following further information for the year ended 31 December 2001:

	£
Sales to hotels and restaurants for the year	488,060
Purchases from Gretna Cake plc during the year	25,670
Stock of cakes on 1 January 2001	36,709
Stock of cakes on 31 December 2001	29,670

Prepare the trading account for the year ended 31 December 2001.

Answer

Bert Bodlington
Trading account for the year ended 31 December 2001

	£	£
Sales		488,060
Less **Cost of goods sold**		
Opening stock at 1 January 2001	36,709	
Add Purchases	25,670	
Total factory production cost b/d	236,225	
	298,604	
Less Closing stock at 31 December 2001	(29,670)	
		(268,934)
Gross profit		219,120

PAUSE FOR THOUGHT *Total factory production cost is 'b/d' from the manufacturing account (see Activity 4.1).*
In a manufacturing business, there are likely to be three different types of stock at the start and end of the financial period: raw materials, work-in-progress (partly completed goods) and finished goods. The first two stock types appear in the manufacturing account, the last in the trading account, but all three closing stock figures would appear in the balance sheet.

4.3.3 Service businesses

An organisation which does not buy or make goods for resale is known as a 'service' business. Neither a manufacturing nor a trading account would be appropriate in this case. Instead, the financial summary starts with the fees earned from the services provided, any sundry income is added to this and then overhead expenses are deducted to calculate net profit, as in the example of an architect (using invented figures) which follows.

Len Corbusier, Architect
Profit and loss account for the year ended 30 April 2002

	£	£
Fees – professional services		192,410
Add Bank interest received		120
		192,530
Less Expenses		
Assistants' wages	65,310	
Secretarial wages	19,640	
Stationery	7,296	
Travel and accommodation	17,630	
Telephone charges	3,260	
Office rent and rates	14,633	
Depreciation of motor car	4,000	
Depreciation of office fittings	2,500	
Sundry expenses	3,400	
		(137,669)
Net profit		54,861

Trading and manufacturing companies also have to calculate their net profit, in which case the format of the profit and loss account would follow that of the architect given above, with 'Gross profit' being substituted for 'Fees for professional services'.

DID YOU KNOW?

Net profit is also known as 'Operating profit', and all limited companies would describe it as such in their published profit and loss accounts (see Chapter 7).

ACTIVITY **4.3**
....

Show the combined manufacturing, trading and profit and loss accounts of Bert Bodlington (see Activities 4.1 and 4.2) for the year ended 31 December 2001, assuming that the office expenses totalled £110,320 and other administration expenses (including depreciation) totalled £68,471.

Answer

Bert Bodlington
Profit and loss account for the year ended 31 December 2001

	£	£
Raw materials		
Opening stock at 1 January 2001	12,400	
Add Purchases of raw materials	102,952	
	115,352	
Less Closing stock at 31 December 2001	(11,500)	
Cost of raw materials		103,852
Other direct costs:		
Production labour		80,420
Prime cost of production	c/f	184,272

	b/f	184,272
Indirect factory costs:		
Rent and rates	12,500	
Light and heat	8,543	
Wages to supervisors	26,100	
Depreciation of factory machinery	3,910	
		51,053
		235,325
Add Opening work-in-progress	1,540	
Less Closing work-in-progress	(640)	
		900
Total factory production cost c/d		236,225
Sales		488,060
Less **Cost of goods sold**		
Opening stock at 1 January 2001	36,709	
Add Purchases	25,670	
Total factory production cost b/d	236,225	
	298,604	
Less Closing stock at 31 December 2001	(29,670)	
		(268,934)
Gross profit		219,126
Less **expenses**		
Office expenses	110,320	
Administration expenses (including depreciation)	68,471	
		(178,791)
Net profit		40,335

If Bert didn't manufacture products, the statement would start with the 'Sales' figure and then 'Cost of goods sold' (excluding the factory production cost) would be deducted to arrive at the gross profit.

PAUSE FOR THOUGHT

Many students have difficulties in knowing which numbers are entered in which columns. In Bert's profit and loss account above, there are two columns. The right-hand column has the summarised totals, which are derived from the detail placed in the inner column. Sometimes you see a third column (e.g. see the answer to Activity 4.4 on page 74), where further detail is given to analyse the information in the second column. So the information flows like this:

Ist inner column (A)   2nd inner column (B)   Outer column (C)

(Breakdown of figure in column B)

(Breakdown of figure in column C)

(Summarised total of figures in columns A and B)

4.3.4 The appropriation account

The appropriation account follows on immediately after the net profit or loss shown on the last line of the profit and loss account. Whilst it is not relevant where the business has a sole owner, for a partnership its function is to reflect the financial implications of the partnership agreement by allocating profits or losses between partners. For a limited company it shows deductions for taxation liabilities, dividends and transfers to reserves. Figure 4.2 shows the basic layout, but these topics are covered in detail in Chapter 7.

figure 4.2
Appropriation accounts

(a) Assume that Bert Bodlington (see Activity 4.3) has a partner, Betty Worthingdene, and that they have agreed to share profits in the ratio 3:2. The appropriation account follows on directly after the 'net profit' as shown in the profit and loss account:

(Bodlington and Worthingdene)

	£	£
Net profit (as in profit and loss account)		40,335
Divided as follows:		
Bert Bodlington (3/5)	24,201	
Betty Worthingdene (2/5)	16,134	
		40,335

If the partnership agreement includes other financial implications such as salaries to partners, etc., these would also be shown.

(b) Assume that Bert Bodlington set up his business as a limited company (i.e. a separate legal entity with shareholders). The company is subject to taxation on its profits, might declare a dividend to transfer profit to shareholders, and will keep any surplus profit as a 'reserve' within the company. As with the partnership example shown above, a limited company appropriation account follows on directly after the net profit, as shown below (using estimated figures for taxation and dividends):

(Bodlington Limited)

	£
Net profit (as in profit and loss account)	40,335
<u>Less</u> Taxation	(10,230)
Net profit after taxation	30,105
<u>Less</u> Dividends	(14,000)
Retained profit for the year, added to reserves	16,105

4.4 The balance sheet
··························

This is the summary of a business's assets, liabilities and capital, reflecting the accounting equation $A - L = C$. It shows all the balances carried down within ledger accounts at the end of the financial period, though 'interim' balance sheets could be produced at any time. The basic contents of the balance sheet are similar, whether the business is in the manufacturing, trading or service sectors. However, if the business is structured as either a partnership or a limited company, additional items of information will be given, as shown in Figure 4.3. This is covered in more detail in Chapter 7.

figure 4.3

Balance sheets for different forms of business organisations

	Business type		
	Sole trader	Partnership	Limited company
Balance sheet heading			
Fixed assets	✓	✓	✓
Current assets	✓	✓	✓
Current liabilities (Creditors due for payment within one year)	✓	✓	✓, with taxation and dividends owing included in this heading
Long-term liabilities (Creditors due for payment after more than one year)	✓ (if any)	✓ (if any)	✓ (if any)
Capital account	✓	✓ (one for each partner)	✗
Partners' current accounts*	✗	✓ (one for each partner if maintained)	✗
Share capital*	✗	✗	✓
Reserves*	✗	✗	✓

* explained in Chapter 7

4.5 Alternative formats: 'horizontal' layout
···

The financial statements presented within this chapter have all been produced following the *vertical or columnar* style of presentation, which is followed by the vast majority of UK organisations. Remember that the profit and loss account (though not the balance sheet) is part of the double-entry bookkeeping system, so even though that account might not be shown as being split between debit and credit sides, each entry within it will have been transferred from the debit or credit side of a general ledger account. Figure 4.4 shows how this works in a typical general ledger 'expense' account.

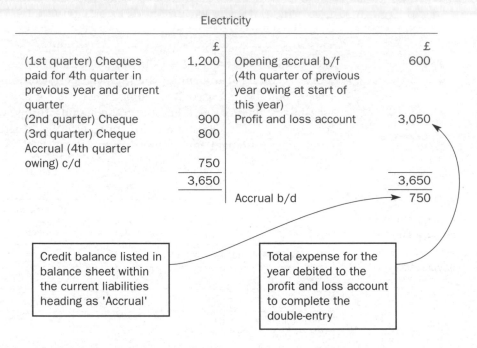

figure 4.4
Typical general ledger 'expense' account showing how profit and loss account and balance sheet figures are derived

In many countries, the position of the profit and loss account within the 'double-entry' system is reinforced by presenting the information in a 'horizontal' style, divided into a conventional debit and credit side. For example, the architect's profit and loss account seen earlier could be rearranged on a horizontal basis, as follows:

Len Corbusier, Architect
Profit and loss account for the year ended 30 April 2002

	£		£
Assistants' wages	65,310	Fees – professional services	192,410
Secretarial wages	19,640	Bank interest received	120
Stationery	7,296		
Travel and accommodation	17,630		
Telephone charges	3,260		
Office rent and rates	14,633		
Depreciation of motor car	4,000		
Depreciation of office fittings	2,500		
Sundry expenses	3,400		
	137,669		
Net profit for the year	54,861		
	192,530		192,530

PAUSE FOR THOUGHT *It is clear that there is neither more nor less information than in the vertical style, but advocates of the vertical style argue that the data flows more logically as 'Income less Expenses = Profit', which accords with the accounting equation seen in Chapter 1.*

Similarly, the balance sheet could be shown in a horizontal format (usually with assets on the left and liabilities and capital on the right), but it is *not* part of the double-entry system. Like the trial balance it is merely a list of balances as at a specific date.

4.6 Published profit and loss accounts and balance sheets

Businesses operating with sole owners or as partnerships do not have to publish their financial summaries – in fact, the only people likely to see them are the owners themselves, their accountants, the tax authorities and possibly their bankers. Members of the public have no right of access to the information. For limited companies, however, one of the drawbacks of this form of business organisation is that their summarised financial information must be made available to the public. Although there are some restrictions on the amount of information which small and medium-sized companies have to divulge, larger companies (including all plc's – public limited companies) must publish an annual report including their profit and loss account and balance sheet. Bearing in mind that many plc's are extremely complicated multinational conglomerates conducting millions of transactions each year, how can this mass of information be made informative and readable?

The answer is that the data is summarised into main headings via the double-entry bookkeeping system and is also presented according to a specified *format* as laid out in the UK Companies Act. This ensures that the reporting company complies with not only UK law but also that of the European Union, as the UK Companies Acts have incorporated the relevant legislation ensuring that companies throughout Europe follow broadly the same format when presenting their profit and loss account and balance sheet. We shall be looking in more detail at limited companies in Chapter 7.

> **DID YOU KNOW?**
> *BP Amoco plc is one of the world's largest petroleum companies, with sales in 1998 totalling $83,732,000,000 ($83bn). The company's published profit and loss account contained only 19 lines of information on half a page!*

4.7 Odds and ends

There is a handful of minor points which need to be covered when considering the presentation of a fully detailed profit and loss account. These are:

➤ Sales returns and purchase returns (also known as 'Returns inwards and outwards')

➤ Carriage inwards and outwards, which is the cost of transporting goods into or out of the business

➤ Discounts allowed and received, which represent amounts deducted from debtors' and creditors' accounts for prompt payment of amounts owing

Work carefully through Activity 4.4 to see how these items are shown within the profit and loss account.

ACTIVITY **4.4**
··············

Errol Lewis sells fruit and vegetables from a market stall and also has a home delivery service, selling on credit but offering a 2% discount for prompt payment. Sometimes he pays an extra carriage charge for fresh strawberries to be flown in during winter months. During the year ended 30 November 2001 he records the following income and expenses:

	£
Sales	75,968
Sales returns (poor quality goods returned by customers)	405
Purchase of produce	32,710
Purchase returns (over-ripe bananas returned to supplier)	620
Carriage inwards (air freight of strawberries)	2,150
Carriage outwards (home delivery costs)	3,752
Assistants' wages	6,530
Rent and rates	3,520
Advertising	265
Depreciation of weighing scales	50
Accountant's fees	350
Bank interest and charges	600
Sundry expenses	3,600
Discount received from suppliers for prompt payment	240
Discount allowed to customers for prompt payment	320
Note: Opening stock of produce at 1 December 2000	3,680
Note: Closing stock of produce at 30 November 2001	3,420

Prepare Errol Lewis's profit and loss account for the year ended 30 November 2001.

Answer

Errol Lewis
Profit and loss account for the year ended 30 November 2001

	£	£	£
Sales		75,968	
Less Sales returns		(405)	
			75,563
Less **Cost of goods sold**			
Opening stock at 1 December 2000		3,680	
Add Purchases	32,710		
Carriage inwards	2,150		
	34,860		
Less Purchase returns	(620)		
		34,240	
	c/f	37,920	75,563

	b/f	37,920	75,563
Less Closing stock at 31 December 2001		(3,420)	
			34,500
Gross profit			41,063
Add Discount received			240
			41,303
Less **expenses**			
Assistants' wages		6,530	
Carriage outwards		3,752	
Rent and rates		3,520	
Advertising		265	
Depreciation of weighing scales		50	
Accountant's fees		350	
Bank interest and charges		600	
Discount allowed		320	
Sundry expenses		3,600	
			(18,987)
Net profit			22,316

PAUSE FOR THOUGHT *To accommodate the extra detail, a third column has been added. The right-hand column provides the summarised information, with the detail being shown in the inner columns as required (see p. 69).*

4.8 From the trial balance to the profit and loss account and balance sheet

We are now ready to see how a detailed profit and loss account and balance sheet can be prepared from the trial balance. Remember that the trial balance is the summary of all the balances within the double-entry bookkeeping system at a specific date and therefore includes the 'ingredients' needed to produce the two financial summaries. Figure 4.5 shows how they fit in to the overall structure of the double-entry bookkeeping system.

DID YOU KNOW?
The profit and loss account and balance sheet, when produced at the end of a financial period, are often called the 'final' accounts, even though, strictly speaking, the balance sheet is not an 'account', being outside the double-entry bookkeeping system.

The next two activities explain in detail the procedures to be followed when preparing the profit and loss account and balance sheet from a trial balance.

figure 4.5
**The production of the
profit and loss
account and balance
sheet from the
double-entry
bookkeeping system**

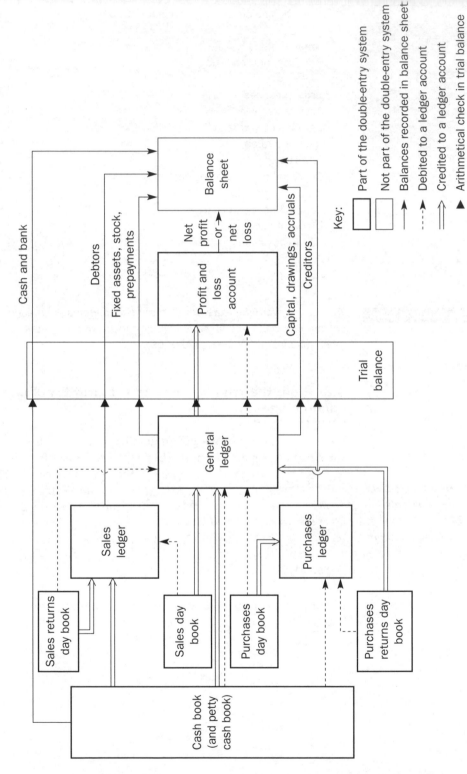

ACTIVITY **4.5**
. . . .

From the following trial balance, prepare the profit and loss account of
Charlie Owen for the year ended 30 April 2001:

	Dr £	Cr £
Bank	3,800	
Capital at 1 May 2000		22,154
Carriage outwards	2,400	
Carriage inwards	6,850	
Cash	250	
Creditors		27,600
Debtors	35,200	
Discount allowed	420	
Discount received		386
Electricity	4,000	
Motor cars – cost	22,000	
Motor cars – depreciation to 1 May 2000		13,200
Office fittings – cost	20,000	
Office fittings – depreciation to 1 May 2000		10,800
Opening stock at 1 May 2000	90,000	
Owner's drawings	25,000	
Purchases	204,000	
Purchases returns		4,500
Rent	15,000	
Sales returns	3,920	
Sales		416,200
Wages and salaries	62,000	
	494,840	494,840

Notes:

1 Closing stock at 30 April 2001 was £110,000.
2 Electricity of £1,000 is to be accrued at the year-end.
3 Rent of £3,000 has been prepaid at the year-end.
4 Depreciation on the office fittings is calculated over 5 years on the straight line method, assuming a residual value of £2,000.
5 Depreciation on the car is calculated at 60% using the reducing balance method.

Answer

Before constructing the profit and loss account we need to follow a series of steps.

Step 1
Read through the trial balance items, making a mental note of possible problem areas – these could include the treatment of the carriage in and out, the discount allowed, etc.

Step 2
Read through the notes, and write in the adjustments needed for accruals and prepayments against the relevant trial balance items. These appear as follows:

| Electricity | (11000) | 1,000 |
| Rent | (–3000) | 15,000 |

Step 3

Using the information in Notes 4 and 5, calculate the year's depreciation charge. The 'workings' (which should be shown as a note to the answer) would be as follows:

Motor cars

Cost	22,000
Less depreciation to 1 May 2000	(13,200)
Net book value at 1 May 2000	8,800
Depreciation @ 60% × 8,800	(5,280)

Office fittings

(Cost – Residual value)/5
= (£20,000 – £2,000)/5
= £18,000/5 = £3,600

We can then write this into the trial balance as follows:

| Motor cars: depreciation to 1 May 2000 (+5,280) | | 13,200 |
| Office fittings: depreciation to 1 May 2000 (+3,600) | | 10,800 |

Note that only the bracketed figures appear in the year's profit and loss account, but the total depreciation of £18,480 and £14,400 will be shown in the balance sheet.

Step 4

Start the profit and loss account by writing the heading at the top of a new page, drawing three columns about 3 cm wide on the right-hand side. The 'trading account' is the first part of the summary, ending with the gross profit. Remember the sequence **'Sales – Cost of goods sold = Gross profit'**. Tick items in the trial balance as you enter them.

Step 5

Complete the summary by entering the remaining items of income and expenses, adjusting for the accrual and prepayment. Don't forget to include only the current year's depreciation. The completed profit and loss account is shown below:

Charlie Owen

Profit and loss account for the year ended 30 April 2001

	£	£	£
Sales		416,200	
Less Sales returns		(3,920)	
			412,280
Less Cost of goods sold			
Opening stock at 1 May 2000		90,000	
Add Purchases	204,000		
Carriage inwards	6,850		
	210,850		
Less Purchases returns	(4,500)		
		206,350	
c/f		296,350	412,280

		b/f	296,350	412,280
Less Closing stock at 30 April 2001			(110,000)	
				186,350
Gross profit				225,930
Add Discount received				386
				226,316
Less expenses				
Carriage outwards			2,400	
Discount allowed			420	
Electricity			5,000	
Depreciation: motor cars			5,280	
Depreciation: office fittings			3,600	
Rent			12,000	
Wages and salaries			62,000	
				(90,700)
Net profit				135,616

PAUSE FOR THOUGHT

The trial balance items left unticked represent the assets, liabilities and capital (including 'drawings', which are deducted from the owner's capital) at the end of the period, which are all entered into the balance sheet (see Activity 4.6).

ACTIVITY **4.6**

Construct the balance sheet for Charlie Owen (see Activity 4.5). Use the layout shown on page 55.

Answer

Charlie Owen
Balance sheet as at 30 April 2001

	Cost	Depreciation	Net book value
	£	£	£
Fixed assets			
Office fittings	20,000	14,400	5,600
Motor cars	22,000	18,480	3,520
	42,000	32,880	9,120
Current assets			
Stock		110,000	
Debtors		35,200	
Prepayments		3,000	
Bank		3,800	
Cash		250	
		152,250	
Less Current liabilities			
Creditors	27,600		
Accruals	1,000		
		(28,600)	
Net current assets			123,650
Total net assets			132,770

Capital

Opening balance, 1 May 2000	22,154	
Add Net profit	135,616	
	157,770	
Less Drawings	(25,000)	
Closing balance, 30 April 2001		132,770

4.9 Glossary

Appropriation account	An additional part of the profit and loss account, inserted after the net profit or loss, showing, for a partnership, the financial implications of the partnership agreement or, for a limited company, tax and dividend deductions and reserve transfers
Auditor	An independent accountant who reports on whether the financial summaries reflect a true and fair view of a business's affairs
Columnar layout	*see* Vertical layout
Direct costs	Costs which can be readily identified with the items being produced, for example sugar in a biscuit factory
Final accounts	A name given to the profit and loss account and balance sheet when prepared at the end of a financial period
Horizontal layout	A traditional account format used for the profit and loss account and balance sheet by many mainland European and other countries. Nowadays, it is very unusual in the UK
Indirect costs	All manufacturing costs other than direct costs, e.g. the rent of a biscuit factory
Loss	An excess of expenses over income
Manufacturing account	The first part of a manufacturing company's profit and loss account, showing total factory production cost
Prime costs	Another name for direct costs
Profit	An excess of income over expenses
Profit and loss account	The part of the financial summary which shows the net profit or loss of the organisation. It can be used to describe the whole summary, including manufacturing and trading accounts
Published accounts	Condensed versions of a limited company's final accounts following specified formats laid down by the Companies Acts, and complying with European legislation
Total factory production cost	All the costs, direct and indirect, of producing the goods manufactured in the period
Trading account	The first part of the profit and loss account for a business which buys in goods for resale. It shows the gross profit

Vertical layout	The presentation of the financial summaries in columns, where the information is read from top to bottom in logical sequence, irrespective of whether it represents debit or credit balances
Work-in-progress	Partly completed stock

SELF-CHECK QUESTIONS

1 Profit is calculated by:
   a Comparing assets with liabilities
   b Comparing assets with expenses
   c Comparing income and expenses
   d Comparing income with liabilities

2 An independent auditor is:
   a An independent accountant who prepares the financial summaries
   b An independent accountant who reports if financial summaries show a true and fair view
   c An accountant employed by a business to check if the financial summaries of that business show a true and fair view
   d An independent accountant who reports if the financial summaries are totally accurate

3 The profit and loss account of a partnership which manufactures the goods it sells will include:
   a Manufacturing, trading, profit and loss and appropriation accounts
   b As (a) but without the appropriation account
   c As (a) but with a partnership account
   d Only the trading account

4 For a soft drinks factory, direct costs could include:
   a The cost of machinery used to liquidise oranges
   b Depreciation of a bottle washing machine
   c Factory rent
   d Flavourings

5 Which of the following headings does not appear in a manufacturing account?
   a Prime cost of trading
   b Total factory production cost
   c Raw materials
   d Indirect factory costs

6 A company has opening stock £3,900, closing stock £2,800, purchases £18,650, carriage inwards £850 and purchases returns £1,600. What is its cost of goods sold?
   a £22,200
   b £12,200
   c £19,000
   d £17,300

7 In a manufacturing company which also buys completed goods for resale, 'Cost of goods sold' is found by the formula:
   a Opening stock of raw materials + Purchases + Factory production cost – Closing stock of raw materials
   b Opening stock of finished goods + Purchases + Factory production cost – Closing stock of finished goods
   c Opening stock of finished goods + Purchases – Factory production cost – Closing stock of finished goods

   d Opening stock of finished goods + Purchases + Factory production cost +
      Closing stock of finished goods
8 A horizontal layout for a profit and loss account is:
   a The same as a columnar format
   b Where the information is read from top to bottom
   c Where the account has debit and credit sides
   d A special format which is easier to use by drunken accountants
9 Which of these is not an expense?
   a Carriage inwards
   b Carriage outwards
   c Discount allowed
   d Discount received
10 Which type of business organisation has to publish its profit and loss account?
   a Public limited company
   b Partnership
   c Architect
   d Sole trader

Further questions can be found on the accompanying website (www.booksites.
net/black).

SELF-STUDY QUESTIONS

(Answers in Appendix 2)

Question 4.1

From the following information, prepare suitable profit and loss accounts for
each organisation.

Name Type of business Year ended	Amber Manufacturer 30 April 2001 £	Blue Trader 31 May 2002 £	Cerise Service provider 30 June 2003 £
Sales	253,620	184,162	–
Closing stock :			
finished goods	13,671	10,700	
raw materials	9,641	–	–
work-in-progress	32,040	–	–
Purchases (finished goods)	–	65,210	–
Carriage inwards	–	360	–
Sales returns	–	580	–
Discount allowed	840	320	160
Carriage outwards	–	240	–
Purchases returns	–	2,600	–
Raw materials purchased	52,450	–	–
Opening stock:			
finished goods	12,634	12,700	–
raw materials	8,320	–	–
work-in-progress	35,620	–	–
Fees from clients	–	–	85,400
Factory indirect expenses	89,322	–	-
General office expenses	34,600	54,923	21,500
Depreciation: factory	6,000	–	–
Depreciation: office	3,600	2,300	1,600
Discount received	114	120	–
Production labour	47,653	–	–

Question 4.2

From the following information, produce the profit and loss account of Wesley Timpson for the year ended 30 November 2002.

	£
Bank interest received	140
Carriage inwards	6,200
Carriage outwards	900
Closing stock, 30 November 2002	16,822
Depreciation on office furniture for the year	2,500
Depreciation on computers for the year	900
Depreciation on motor cars for the year	4,500
Discount allowed	533
Discount received	640
Light and heat	5,230
Opening stock, 1 December 2001	15,684
Postage and stationery	2,710
Purchase returns	2,910
Purchases	124,100
Sales returns	2,350
Sales	245,610
Sundry office expenses	3,571
Telephone	1,499
Wages and salaries	47,231

Question 4.3

From the following trial balance and notes relating to Betta Buys, prepare a profit and loss account for the year to 28 February 2002, and a balance sheet as at that date.

	Dr £	Cr £
Bank	960	
Cash	250	
Shop fittings – cost	30,000	
Shop fittings – depreciation to 1 March 2001		10,400
Motor car – cost	12,000	
Motor car – depreciation to 1 March 2001		4,800
Sales		425,000
Purchases	204,000	
Opening stock at 1 March 2001	90,000	
Rent	15,000	
Electricity	4,000	
Debtors	35,200	
Creditors		27,600
Wages and salaries	62,000	
Owner's drawings	25,000	
Capital		10,610
	478,410	478,410

Notes;
1 Closing stock is £70,000.
2 Electricity of £1,000 is to be accrued at the year-end.
3 Rent of £3,000 has been prepaid at the year-end.
4 Depreciation on the shop fittings is calculated over 5 years on the straight line method, assuming a residual value of £4,000.
5 Depreciation on the car is calculated at 40% using the reducing balance method.

Question 4.4

Helen Thorne, a retail jeweller, extracted the following trial balance for her business as at 31 May 2001.

	Dr	Cr
	£	£
Sales of jewellery		324,650
Sales returns	1,250	
Opening stock, 1 June 2000	34,500	
Purchases	168,220	
Discount received		690
Discount allowed	1,520	
Insurance	5,900	
Assistants' wages	33,100	
Telephone and e-mail	5,200	
Light and heat	6,230	
Security guards' wages	12,400	
Repairs to premises	3,970	
Amortisation of leasehold premises to 1 June 2000		18,000
Depreciation of safe to 1 June 2000		4,800
Depreciation of shop fittings to 1 June 2000		10,200
Rent and rates	17,000	
Sundry expenses	3,940	
Leasehold premises, at cost	60,000	
Safe, at cost	12,000	
Shop fittings, at cost	34,000	
Debtors	3,400	
Creditors		19,670
Bank overdraft		2,380
Cash in hand	520	
Website maintenance expenses	1,430	
Publicity and advertising	9,740	
Opening capital, 1 June 2000		58,630
Owner's drawings	24,700	
	439,020	439,020

Notes:
1 Closing stock at 31 May 2001, £27,880.
2 Security guards were owed £400 wages at 31 May 2001 and £200 was owing for telephone and e-mail.

3 £900 of the charge for maintaining the company web site was paid on 1 January 2001 to cover a year from that date.

4 Depreciation is to be calculated as follows:

 (i) leasehold premises are amortised in equal instalments over a 20-year period,

 (ii) the safe is depreciated at 40% p.a. by the reducing balance method,

 (iii) the shop fittings are depreciated at 10% p.a. by the straight line method, assuming no residual values.

Prepare Helen Thorne's profit and loss account for the year ended 31 May 2001 and a balance sheet as at that date.

Further questions can be found on the accompanying website (www.booksites. net/black).

CASE STUDY
. . . .

Marvin makes magic

During the second half of his first year in business, Marvin (see previous case studies) decided to supplement his income by manufacturing and selling magic sets. This was in addition to his fees as an entertainer and any profit made by selling bought-in novelties from Kaboosh Limited. He rented a workshop on 1 March 2001 and employed his assistant Esmeralda's seven brothers and sisters as production workers. At the end of his first year of business, 30 June 2001, he produced the following trial balance:

	Dr	Cr
	£	£
Appearance fees as entertainer		34,300
Cleaning	280	
Cost of machinery used in workshop	3,600	
Cost of magician's equipment	5,400	
Cost of disappearing lady apparatus	2,000	
Light and heat of workshop	2,400	
Other workshop expenses	4,100	
Production wages paid to Esmeralda's brothers and sisters	5,620	
Purchase of materials used to manufacture magic sets	15,621	
Purchases of novelties bought-in from Kaboosh Limited	3,400	
Rabbit expenses	430	
Sales of novelties and magic sets		45,821
Marvin's drawings	19,720	
Opening capital		5,020
Creditor – Kaboosh Limited		240
Travel to performance venues	5,510	
Bank balance	660	
Cash in hand	40	
Wages to assistant (Esmeralda)	12,400	
Workshop costs: rent and rates	4,200	
	85,381	85,381

At the end of the year, the following further information was provided:

➤ Closing stock of materials used to manufacture magic sets was valued at £6,320 and closing stock of bought-in novelties was valued at £2,400. All the manufactured magic sets were sold in the year. There was no work-in-progress at the year-end.

➤ £200 was owed to Grimstock, one of the workers on the production line, whilst £100 was owed for light and heat.

➤ One-seventh of the rent and rates had been prepaid for the following financial period. Marvin was owed £200 at the year-end by Mrs Featherskew for a party fee. This had not been shown in Marvin's accounting records.

➤ Depreciation for the year on the magician's equipment totalled £1,080, and depreciation for the year on the disappearing lady apparatus was £800. Depreciation on the workshop machinery was to be calculated on the straight line method over 6 years, assuming a residual value of £600. A full year's depreciation was to be charged, even though the machinery had been owned for less than a year.

Prepare Marvin's manufacturing, trading and profit and loss accounts for the year ended 30 June 2001, and a balance sheet as at that date.

(Answer in Appendix 3)

References
• • • • • • • • • • • • • •

BP-Amoco financial report
http://bpamoco.saltmine.co.uk/reports/ara/accounts/income/index.htm
Leading audit firms:
http://www.kpmg.co.uk
http://www.arthurandersen.com
http://www.pricewaterhousecoopers.co.uk

CHAPTER 5

A further look at assets and liabilities

Objectives
....

When you have read this chapter you will be able to:
➤ Make adjustments when fixed assets are sold
➤ Understand and apply the key methods of stock valuation
➤ Understand why provisions for doubtful debts are needed and make adjustments for bad and doubtful debts
➤ Distinguish between current and long-term liabilities

5.1 Introduction
....

In this chapter we look at some further aspects of key components found within the balance sheet, answering such questions as 'what happens if fixed assets are sold?', 'how is stock valued?' and 'what if customers don't pay their debts?'. We look at these in the order in which the relevant items would be found on the balance sheet: fixed assets; current assets; current liabilities; long-term liabilities.

5.2 Sales of fixed assets
....

In Chapter 3 we saw how all fixed assets, with the exception of most freehold land, is subject to depreciation (*amortisation* in the case of leasehold land and buildings). Depreciation recognises the loss in value of a fixed asset due to various factors including wearing out, usage or becoming obsolete due to changes in technology. When an asset reaches the end of its useful life, the business has the following choices:

➤ Scrap the asset, in which case it may have a scrap value, e.g. an old machine may contain recyclable metal and components. Alternatively the item may be simply thrown away (also known as 'writing it off').
➤ Part-exchange the asset, where any value given for the old asset is used partly to pay for a replacement asset.
➤ Sell the asset at the market value.

Whatever happens to the asset, it will have a 'book' value in the business's ledger which is usually the cost of the asset less all the depreciation charged to the date of sale. Often companies do not depreciate assets in the year of sale, but policy varies from business to business. Whatever the eventual fate of the asset being disposed of, a calculation must be made of the profit or loss, by comparing the book value with the disposal proceeds. This is done by creating a disposal of fixed assets account and transferring to it:

➤ the asset's cost from the relevant fixed asset account,
➤ the total depreciation from the relevant depreciation account, and
➤ the proceeds (or part exchange value) of disposal.

The balance is either a profit (proceeds > net book value) which is added to gross profit in the profit and loss account, or a loss (net book value < proceeds) shown as an expense in the profit and loss account.

PAUSE FOR THOUGHT   *Strictly speaking, a profit or loss on a sale of asset should be described as an over- or under-provision for depreciation over the asset's life. This is because depreciation is an estimate and it is only when the asset is disposed of that the exact amount of depreciation can be known.*

ACTIVITY **5.1**

Amy has been in business as a commercial photographer for several years. At 1 January 2000 her fixed assets and accumulated depreciation balances were as follows:

	Cost	Accumulated depreciation
	£	£
Pintax camera	650	450
Tripod	125	100
Darkroom equipment	1,600	1,300
Hunda car	5,000	3,600

During the year to 31 December 2000, the following transactions occurred:

➤ The Pintax camera was exchanged for a Fujitsu 200XL costing £800. A £100 part-exchange allowance was given, and the balance was paid by cheque.
➤ The tripod was thrown away and not replaced.
➤ The darkroom equipment was sold for £200 and not replaced.
➤ The Hunda car was sold in March for £1,600. A Kamari estate was bought in May for £7,000.

Cameras are depreciated at 10% p.a. straight line method and cars at 25% straight line method. It is Amy's policy not to depreciate assets in the year of sale, but to charge a full year's depreciation in the year of purchase, even if bought part way through the year.

Show the entries required to record the above in Amy's general ledger and profit and loss account for the year ended 31 December 2000 and her balance sheet as at that date.

Answer

Even without knowing anything about bookkeeping, we can use common sense to work out if a profit or loss was made, as follows:

➤ The Pintax camera had a net book value of £200 (£650 – £450) but fetched only £100 in part-exchange, therefore a loss of £100.

➤ The tripod had a net book value of £25 (£125 – £100) but had no value when it was scrapped, therefore a loss of £25.

➤ The darkroom equipment had a net book value of £300 (£1,600 – £1,300) when it was sold for £200, therefore a loss of £100.

➤ The Hunda car had a net book value of £1,400 (£5,000 – £3,600) but was sold for £1,600, a profit of £200.

The entries in the general ledger as shown below take the cost and depreciation on the 'disposed' assets out of the relevant fixed asset and depreciation accounts into a 'disposal of assets' account (one account can be used for all disposals). The new fixed assets are added into the relevant asset accounts, with depreciation calculated in the usual way.

General Ledger

Cameras account

		£			£
Jan 1	Balance b/f (cost) (Pintax)	650	Dec 31	Disposal of fixed assets account	650
Dec 31	Cost – Fujitsu 200XL:			Balance c/f	800
	Bank	700			
	Part-exchange (disposal of assets account)	100			
		1,450			1,450

Tripod account

		£			£
Jan 1	Balance b/f (cost)	125	Dec 31	Disposal of fixed assets account	125
		125			125

Darkroom equipment account

		£			£
Jan 1	Balance b/f (cost)	1,600	Dec 31	Disposal of fixed assets account	1,600
		1,600			1,600

Cars account

		£			£
Jan 1	Balance b/f (cost) (Hunda)	5,000	Dec 31	Disposal of fixed assets account	5,000
May 1	Bank (Kamari)	7,000		Balance c/f	7,000
		12,000			12,000

Provision for depreciation on cameras account

	£		£
Dec 31 Disposal of fixed assets account	450	Dec 31 Balance b/f	450
Balance c/f	80	P & L account*	80
	530		530

* The depreciation on the new camera (10% × £800)

Provision for depreciation on tripod account

	£		£
Dec 31 Disposal of fixed assets account	100	Dec 31 Balance b/f	100

Provision for depreciation on darkroom equipment account

	£		£
Dec 31 Disposal of fixed assets account	1,300	Dec 31 Balance b/f	1,300

Provision for depreciation on cars account

	£		£
Dec 31 Disposal of fixed assets account	3,600	Dec 31 Balance b/f	3,600
Balance c/f	1,750	P & L account*	1,750
	5,350		5,350

* The depreciation on the new car (25% × £7,000)

Disposal of fixed assets account

	£		£
Dec 31 Transfer cost of disposed assets:		Dec 31 Transfer depreciation on disposed assets:	
Cameras	650	Dep'n on cameras	450
Tripod	125	Dep'n on tripod	100
Darkroom equipment	1,600	Dep'n on darkroom equipment	1,300
Cars	5,000	Dep'n on car	3,600
	7,375	Dec 31 Proceeds of disposals:	
		Cameras account	100
		Bank (re darkroom)	200
		Bank (re car)	1,600
			7,350
		Profit and loss account:	
		Overall loss on disposal*	25
	7,375		7,375

* This is the balancing figure on the account. If there had been a balance on the opposite side it would have indicated an overall profit.

Profit and loss account for the year ended 31 December 2000 (extracts)

	£	£
Gross profit		?
Less **Expenses** (including):		
Loss on disposal of fixed assets	25	
Depreciation on camera	80	
Depreciation on car	1,750	

Balance sheet as at 31 December 2000

Fixed assets	Cost	Depreciation	Net book value
	£	£	£
Camera	800	80	720
Car	7,000	1,750	5,250
	7,800	1,830	5,970

PAUSE FOR THOUGHT

The balance sheet shows only the fixed assets owned at the end of the year (the new camera and car), all other assets having been disposed of. If fully detailed final accounts are required, then a summary of the changes of each category of fixed asset would be given as a note. This would be shown as follows:

	Cameras	Tripod	Darkroom equipment	Cars	Total
	£	£	£	£	£
Cost, 1 January 2000	650	125	1,600	5,000	7,375
Additions in the year	800	–	–	7,000	7,800
	1,450	125	1,600	12,000	15,175
Less disposals	(650)	(125)	(1,600)	(5,000)	(7,375)
Cost, 31 December 2000	800	–	–	7,000	7,800
Depreciation, 1 January 2000	450	100	1,300	3,600	5,450
Provision for the year	80			1,750	1,000
	530	100	1,300	5,350	7,280
Less depreciation on disposed assets	(450)	(100)	(1,300)	(3,600)	(5,450)
Depreciation, 31 December 2000	80	–	–	1,750	1,830
Net book value, 31 December 2000	720	–	–	5,250	5,970
Net book value, 1 January 2000	200	25	300	1,400	1,925

5.3 Stock valuation

5.3.1 The importance of the valuation

From a financial accounting viewpoint, the key date for valuing stock is the end of the financial year, as the valuation affects the cost of goods sold calculation in the 'trading account' part of the profit and loss account and also the current assets total in the balance sheet. If stock is overvalued it will increase this year's profit but reduce next year's, as the closing stock of one period is of course the opening stock of the next. Balance sheet values will also be distorted. How then should stock be valued? The relevant accounting standard, SSAP 9,[1] states that 'stock is to

[1] Accounting Standards Board (1990) Statement of Standard Accounting Practice (SSAP) 9, *Stocks and Long-Term Contracts*, London

be stated at the total of the lower of cost and net realisable value of the separable items of stock or of groups of similar items'. It also contains these definitions:

➤ *Cost*: '... that expenditure which has been incurred in the normal course of business in bringing the product to its present location and condition ...'.
➤ *Net realisable value*: '... the estimated proceeds from the sale of items of stock less all further costs to completion and less all costs to be incurred in marketing, selling and distributing directly related to the items in question.'

The prudence concept requires us to be cautious in valuing assets and we would never anticipate a profit by valuing stock at its selling price. The only exception is where the likely selling price (after deducting relevant costs to enable the stock to be sold) is less than the cost price, in which case the SSAP 9 definition is applied. This may happen in cases such as where stock has deteriorated in some way or is unfashionable.

Another problem is deciding what can be included as 'cost'. It might be as simple as looking up an invoice and reading off the price paid. For example the owner of a bicycle shop with four Speedwing Racers in stock is probably able to find their purchase price quite easily, but in many cases the price paid cannot be matched to actual goods, perhaps due to the physical nature of the stock.

ACTIVITY **5.2**

A retailer of pet fish looks in the fish tank at the end of his first financial year, 31 December, and counts 500 goldfish. All the fish are bought from the same supplier, but prices change frequently. Details of stock purchases and sales are as follows:

		Number	Cost of each fish	Sales at end of month
		(*fish*)	£	(*fish*)
Jan 1	Purchases	350	2	—
Mar 1	Purchases	600	3	300
Jul 1	Purchases	800	4	550
Oct 1	Purchases	700	5	1,000
Dec 1	Purchases	650	6	750
Dec 31	(Closing stock)	500	?	

What value should be placed on the closing stock?

Answer

We can't tell by looking at them! Goldfish don't swim around with price labels on them, and it would be very difficult to look at one goldfish and say with certainty when it was bought. What has to be done is to apply a *theoretical* method of valuation, such as FIFO, LIFO or AVCO.

5.3.2 FIFO, LIFO and AVCO

FIFO stands for *First In, First Out*, LIFO for *Last In, First Out*, and *AVCO* for *Average Cost*. Each of these methods of stock valuation is theoretical and does not necessarily reflect the way in which stock physically moves through the business, so a cake shop could use FIFO without getting into trouble with the health and hygiene regulations! AVCO can be either *periodic* or *perpetual*: periodic means that the average is calculated at intervals (e.g. once a year or quarterly); perpetual requires recalculation every time a price change is recorded. Refer to the web site listed under 'References' at the end of the chapter for further details.

In times of rising prices, using FIFO will result in a higher stock value than the other methods (the latest prices being applied to closing stock). LIFO would result in the earliest and lowest prices being used. This would result in a low stock value and also a lower profit figure as stock values are part of the 'Cost of Sales' calculation. Low profits would result in low tax payments, which is why the UK tax authorities do not allow LIFO to be used for the calculation of taxable profits.

> **DID YOU KNOW?**
> Although banned in the UK, LIFO is allowed by tax authorities in many countries, including the USA.

ACTIVITY **5.3**

Use the FIFO method to value the goldfish at 31 December (see previous activity).

Answer

Use a 'price grid' to establish which fish are, in theory, sold at which prices.

Purchase price	£2	£3	£4	£5	£6
January Purchases	350				
March Purchases		600			
Sub-total	350	600			
March Sales (FIFO)	(300)				
July Purchases			800		
Sub-total	50	600	800		
July Sales (FIFO)	(50)	(500)			
October Purchases				700	
Sub-total	—	100	—	700	
October Sales (FIFO)		(100)	(800)	(100)	
December Purchases					650
Sub-total	—	—	—	600	650
December Sales (FIFO)				(600)	(150)
December Closing stock	—	—	—	—	500

Closing stock = 500 × £6 = £3,000

ACTIVITY 5.4

Use the LIFO method to value the goldfish at 31 December.

Answer

Use another 'price grid' to establish which fish are, in theory, sold at which prices.

Purchase price	£2	£3	£4	£5	£6
January Purchases	350				
March Purchases		600			
Sub-total	350	600			
March Sales (LIFO)		(300)			
July Purchases			800		
Sub-total	350	300	800		
July Sales (LIFO)			(550)		
October Purchases				700	
Sub-total	350	300	250	700	
October Sales (LIFO)		(50)	(250)	(700)	
December Purchases					650
Sub-total	350	250	—	—	650
December Sales (LIFO)		(100)			(650)
December Closing stock	350	150	—	—	—

Closing stock = (350 × £2 = £700) + (150 × £3 = £450), total £1,150

ACTIVITY 5.5

Use the AVCO method (perpetual inventory) to value the goldfish at 31 December.

Answer

Use a third 'price grid' to establish which fish are, in theory, sold at which prices.

	Fish in stock	Price (£)	Value (£)	Average (£)
January Purchases	350	2	700	
March Purchases	600	3	1,800	
Sub-total	950		2,500	
Average (£2,500/950 fish)				2.632
March Sales	(300)	2.632	(790)	
July Purchases	800	4	3,200	
Sub-total	1,450		4,910	
Average (£4,910/1,450 fish)				3.386
July Sales	(550)	3.386	(1,862)	
October Purchases	700	5	3,500	
Sub-total	1,600		6,548	
Average (£6,548/1,600 fish)				4.093
October Sales	(1,000)	4.093	(4,093)	
December Purchases	650	6	3,900	
Sub-total	1,250		6,355	
Average (£6,355/1,250 fish)				5.084
December Sales	(750)	5.084	(3,813)	
December Closing stock	**500**	**5.084**	**2,542**	

PAUSE FOR THOUGHT

Closing stock using each of the three methods is:
FIFO £3,000
LIFO £1,150
AVCO £2,542

ACTIVITY **5.6**

Calculate the gross profit for the year, using each of the three stock valuation methods. Assume that each goldfish is sold for £10, and that no goldfish died during the year.

Answer

	FIFO £		LIFO £		AVCO £	
Sales (2,600 × £10)		26,000		26,000		26,000
Less Cost of sales						
Opening stock	—		—		—	
Purchases*	13,100		13,100		13,100	
	13,100		13,100		13,100	
Less Closing stock	(3,000)		(1,150)		(2,542)	
		(10,100)		(11,950)		(10,558)
Gross profit		15,900		14,050		15,442

* (350 × £2) + (600 × £3) + (800 × £4), etc.

5.4 Bad and doubtful debts

The next current asset listed after 'Stock' in the Balance Sheet is 'Debtors', which is the total of all the individual customers' account balances within the sales ledger at the balance sheet date. Because accountants need to be prudent (cautious, conservative, realistic, etc.), they must be reasonably sure that the total shown in the balance sheet represents 'good' debts (i.e. those they think will pay their debts), as there can also be:

➤ bad debts – where there is no possibility of the customer paying, and
➤ doubtful debts – where there is uncertainty whether the debt can be paid.

5.4.1 Bad debts

Bad debts are the nightmare of any business – the customer has been sold goods or services and doesn't pay for them. It is an extreme step to consider a debt as bad, and is usually the culmination of a long drawn-out process involving reminders, threats of legal action, solicitors' letters, etc. The bad debts are 'written off' to the profit and loss account, i.e. they are shown as a loss to the business, and the customer's sales ledger account is closed. Sometimes, miracles happen and a debt previously written off is then paid. In that case, the amount is added to profit as a 'bad debt recovered'.

ACTIVITY **5.7**

Tarquin Micawber owed £650 to The Crisp n' Tasty Pizza Company. Despite many reminders and phone calls, Tarquin refused to pay. The company has now received a letter from Peru saying 'Having a lovely time – not coming back! Tarquin'. The company has reluctantly decided to write off the debt at 31 December 2000. Total debts at that date, including Tarquin's, amounted to £6,950.

Show the entries required in the pizza company's ledger and the relevant extracts from the financial summaries.

Answer

Sales Ledger
Tarquin Micawber's account

2000	£	2000	£
Jan 1 Opening debtor	650	Dec 31 Bad debts account	650

General Ledger
Bad debts account

2000	£	2000	£
Dec 31 Bad debts account	650	Dec 31 Profit and loss account	650

Profit and loss account for the year ended 31 December 2000 (extract)

(Expenses include:)	£
Bad debt written off	650

Balance sheet as at 31 December 2000 (extract)

(Current assets include:)	£
Debtors	6,300

(Notice that there is no reference to the bad debt on the balance sheet. The amount is no longer a balance within the sales ledger so cannot be included as a debtor.)

ACTIVITY **5.8**

Two years later, on 1 December 2002, the managing director of the Crisp n' Tasty Pizza Company gets another letter from Peru. It states 'Made a fortune selling Peruvian marmalade. Cheque enclosed. Sorry! Tarquin.'
What entries would be made in the company's books?

Answer

Cash Book

Bank account

2002	£		£
Dec 1 Tarquin Micawber:			
Bad debt recovered	650		

General Ledger

Bad debt recovered account

2002	£	2002	£
Dec 31 Profit and loss account	650	Dec 1 Cash book	650

Profit and loss account for the year ended 31 December 2002 (extract)

(added to the gross profit as sundry income:)

	£
Bad debt recovered	650

(No relevant entries in the balance sheet)

Once the bad debt was written off, Tarquin's sales ledger account was closed. Two years later, there is no reason to reopen it as there is no indication that Tarquin will be sold any more goods by the pizza company.

5.4.2 Doubtful debts

Some debts are neither good nor bad – there is an element of doubt as to whether or not they will be paid. Reasons include:

➤ disputes over quality of goods or services,
➤ unresolved queries such as duplicated invoices,
➤ temporary financial difficulties of a customer,
➤ customers whose debts have been outstanding for an unduly long period.

The major difference between doubtful debts and bad debts is that if a debt is considered doubtful there is still some hope that the customer will pay, so the sales ledger account is kept 'alive'. However, due to the prudence concept, an amount of profit is transferred to a provision to recognise the potential loss if the debt eventually turns bad. This provision is adjusted up or down in subsequent years, depending upon whether there are more or less doubtful debts to be provided for by the end of the financial period.

DID YOU KNOW?

A provision for doubtful debts is also known as either a provision for bad debts or a provision for bad and doubtful debts! They all mean the same thing: a provision against the future possibility of a debt becoming bad. They must never be confused with 'bad debts', which are written off as a loss.

The provision can be either:

➤ specific (relating to actual amounts owing by named customers), or
➤ general (a percentage of total debts is provided for, after bad debts have been written off).

ACTIVITY **5.9**

Assume that the Texas Tea company's doubtful debts were as follows:

2000 (no doubtful debts)
2001 Total doubtful debts = £6,900
2002 Total doubtful debts = £8,200
2003 Total doubtful debts = £7,800

What provision would be needed in each year?

Answer

➤ In 2000 there is no provision.

➤ In 2001 a provision of £6,900 is created (show £6,900 as an expense in the profit and loss account and deduct £6,900 from total debtors in the balance sheet).

➤ In 2002 the provision needs to be increased by £1,300 (show £1,300 as an expense in the profit and loss account and deduct £8,200 from total debtors in the balance sheet).

➤ In 2003 the provision needs to be decreased by £400 (show £400 as income in the profit and loss account and deduct £7,800 from total debtors in the balance sheet).

Note that there are no entries needed in the debtors' accounts in the sales ledger. The 'Provision for doubtful debts' account in the General Ledger for the years 2001–2003 would be as follows:

General Ledger

Provision for doubtful debts account

		£			£
31/12/01	Balance c/d	6,900	31/12/01	P & L account	6,900
31/12/02	Balance c/d	8,200	1/1/02	Balance b/d	6,900
			31/12/02	P & L account	1,300
		8,200			8,200
31/12/03	P & L account	400	1/1/03	Balance b/d	8,200
	Balance c/d	7,800			
		8,200			8,200
			1/1/04	Balance b/d	7,800

PAUSE FOR THOUGHT

90% of all accountancy students have difficulty understanding how provisions work! Look very carefully at the amounts either coming out of the profit and loss account (2000: £6,900, 2001: £1,300) or going back into the profit and loss account (2002: £400). What do you notice? Apart from the first year, you do not need to take out all the provision in each year – you are just 'fine tuning' it to make sure that the closing balance on the provision equals the total of doubtful debts at the balance sheet date. Re-read this activity and then see if you can apply its principles to the next one.

ACTIVITY **5.10**

Barker & Co., a company which started on 1 January 2000, had identified the following balances on its sales ledger:

As at 31 December:	2000 £	2001 £	2002 £
Total debtors including:	49,310	39,551	37,690
Bad debts:			
Carl Fraudmeister	2,500		
Lola Noepay	560		
Frank Leebroke		630	
Owen Millions			1,700
Doubtful debts:			
Luke Ivenocash	300		
Linda Safiver	2,600	1,600	1,200
Adam Disgrace		1,700	
Robin Cash			1,800

Show the entries required in Barker & Co.'s sales and general ledgers, and relevant extracts from the financial summaries for each of the three years.

Answer

Sales Ledger
Carl Fraudmeister

	£		£
31/12/00 Balance b/f	2,500	31/12/00 Bad debts account	2,500

Lola Noepay

	£		£
31/12/00 Balance b/f	560	31/12/00 Bad debts account	560

Frank Leebroke

	£		£
31/12/01 Balance b/f	630	31/12/01 Bad debts account	630

Owen Millions

	£		£
31/12/02 Balance b/f	1,700	31/12/02 Bad debts account	1,700

General Ledger
Bad debts account

	£		£
31/12/00 Carl Fraudmeister	2,500	31/12/00 P & L account	3,060
Lola Noepay	560		
	3,060		3,060
31/12/01 Frank Leebroke	630	31/12/01 P & L account	630
31/12/02 Owen Millions	1,700	31/12/02 P & L account	1,700

Provision for doubtful debts account

	£		£
31/12/00 Balance c/d	2,900	31/12/00 P & L account	2,900
31/12/01 Balance c/d	3,300	1/1/01 Balance b/d	2,900
		31/12/01 P & L account	400
	3,300		3,300
31/12/02 P & L account	300	1/1/02 Balance b/d	3,300
31/12/02 Balance c/d	3,000		
	3,300		3,300
		1/1/03 Balance b/d	3,000

Profit and loss account for the year ended 31 December 2000

	£	£
Expenses include:		
Bad debts written off		3,060
Increase in provision for doubtful debts		2,900

Balance sheet as at 31 December 2000

	£	£
Current assets include:		
Debtors (49,310 – 3,060)*	46,250	
Less Provision for doubtful debts	(2,900)	
		43,350

*This calculation would not be shown on the balance sheet.

Profit and loss account for the year ended 31 December 2001

	£	£
Expenses include:		
Bad debts written off		630
Increase in provision for doubtful debts		400

Balance sheet as at 31 December 2000

	£	£
Current assets include:		
Debtors (39,551 – 630)	38,921	
Less Provision for doubtful debts	(3,300)	
		35,621

Profit and loss account for the year ended 31 December 2002

	£	£
Added to gross profit:		
Decrease in provision for doubtful debts		300
Expenses include:		
Bad debts written off		1,700

Balance sheet as at 31 December 2002

	£	£
Current assets include:		
Debtors (37,690 – 1,700)	35,990	
Less Provision for doubtful debts	(3,000)	
		32,990

5.5 Current and long-term liabilities

Current liabilities can also be called 'Creditors due for payment within one year', and this description is always given if the balance sheet has been prepared for a limited company. The main creditors found within this section are:

➤ Trade creditors, being amounts owed for goods or services
➤ Accruals, which are expenses owing at the end of a financial period where the bills have not yet been received
➤ Bank overdrafts.

In addition, for a limited company, there will be:

➤ Taxation due on the profits on the year (this is not relevant to a sole trader or partnership as the individual owners are responsible for meeting the tax on profits)
➤ Proposed dividends, which is the amount expected to be paid to shareholders as a return on the capital invested by them.

Long-term liabilities are also referred to as 'Creditors due for payment after more than one year', and again, this term would be used if a limited company's balance sheet is being prepared. This heading refers mainly to loans due for repayment after more than 12 months from the balance sheet date. The term 'debenture' is often used to describe such a loan in the case of limited companies.

5.6 Glossary

AVCO	*Average Cost*, a method of stock valuation which applies average prices to value closing stock. 'Perpetual valuation' requires constant updating of the average when prices change; 'periodic valuation' changes only at intervals, e.g. annually
Bad debts	Debts where there is no hope of collecting the amount due
Cost of stock	Expenditure incurred on stock to bring it to its present location and condition
Current liability	A creditor due for payment within one year of the balance sheet date
Debenture	A name often given to a loan repayable by a limited company
Doubtful debts	Debts where there is uncertainty as to whether the amount due will be paid, but the business has not given up hope of payment
FIFO	*First In First Out*, a method of stock valuation which assumes that the earliest stock acquired is the first to be used, resulting in closing stock being valued at most recent prices
Good debts	Debts which are expected to be paid in the normal course of business
LIFO	*Last In First Out*, a method of stock valuation which assumes that the most recently acquired stock is the first to be used, resulting in closing stock being valued at earliest prices. Not allowed by the UK tax authorities
Long-term liability	A creditor due for payment after more than one year of the balance sheet date
Net realisable value	Selling price of stock, after deducting all relevant costs to enable it to be sold

Profit or loss on sale of fixed asset	Another way of describing an over- or under-provision for depreciation over the life of a fixed asset
Provision	An amount set aside out of profits to reduce the value of an asset, due to factors such as wear and tear (provision for depreciation) or uncertainty of value (provision for doubtful debts)
Provision for bad debts	Another term for a provision for doubtful debts
Provision for doubtful debts	An amount of profit set aside to cover the possibility of some debts becoming bad in the future
Provision for bad and doubtful debts	Another term for a provision for doubtful debts
Theoretical valuation methods	Stock valuation methods such as FIFO and LIFO which assume that stock moves through the business in a particular way

SELF-CHECK QUESTIONS

1 A business sells an asset on 1 January for £8,000. The asset was bought exactly three years previously for £24,000 and depreciation was charged at 30% p.a. on the reducing balance method. What is the profit or loss on disposal?
   a £5,600 profit
   b £232 profit
   c £232 loss
   d £16,000 loss

2 A profit on the disposal of a fixed asset can also be described as:
   a An over-provision for depreciation on the asset
   b An increase in fixed assets on the balance sheet
   c An increase in the bank balance
   d An under-provision for depreciation on the asset

3 What is the effect of overvaluing closing stock on the current year's profit?
   a Decreases the gross profit and net profit
   b Increases the gross profit but decreases net profit
   c Decreases the gross profit but increases net profit
   d Increases the gross profit and net profit

4 Applying the FIFO method of stock valuation in a period of rapidly rising prices will result in:
   a Stock valued at low prices
   b Stock valued at high prices
   c Stock valued at average prices
   d Stock valued at selling prices

5 Why can't LIFO be used to compute profits for tax purposes in the UK?
   a It results in low profits which would mean low tax payments to the government
   b It would result in high profits and tax payments, and the government doesn't want to be greedy

   c It would mean that businesses would always have old stock and the
government wants to discourage this

   d The government wants to be different from the USA, which allows the use
of LIFO

6 A company bought 50 dresses at £40 each. Normal selling price is £60 each
but the dresses are now thought to be old-fashioned and have to be shortened
at a cost of £5 each. What should be their total value as part of closing stock?

   a £2,750

   b £3,000

   c £2,000

   d £1,750

7 What is a bad debt?

   a A debt where there is some hope of getting paid

   b A debt where there is no hope of getting paid

   c A debt which is doubtful

   d A debt where the customer has gone abroad

8 Graham Pickle is owed £400 by Harvey Willow. Graham now regards Harvey as
a bad debtor. What will be the effect of writing off the debt as bad?

   a No effect on profit, but debtors decrease

   b The bank balance goes down and the profits decrease

   c Profit decreases, as do current assets

   d Profit decreases, but no effect on the balance sheet

9 A business starts its year with £800 in a provision for doubtful debts. At the
end of the year, debtors total £12,000 of which £600 are considered doubtful.
What is the effect on the P & L account and balance sheet?

   a £200 is added to profit and the balance sheet shows Debtors less provision
as £11,400

   b £600 is deducted from profit and the balance sheet shows Debtors less
provision as £11,400

   c £1,400 is deducted from profit and the balance sheet shows Debtors less
provision as £10,600

   d £800 is added to profit and the balance sheet shows Debtors less provision
as £11,400

10 A long-term liability is:

   a A creditor due for payment within 12 months

   b A liability where it is not known when it is to be repaid

   c A creditor due for payment after more than 12 months

   d The same as an accrual

Further questions can be found on the accompanying website (www.booksites.
net/black).

**SELF-STUDY
QUESTIONS**

(Answers in Appendix 2)

Question 5.1

Straits Liners is a shipping company which at 1 January 2005 owned the following vessels:

➤ SS Invisible, bought for £450,000 on 1 July 2000

➤ SS Submersible, bought for £600,000 on 1 August 2001

➤ SS Outrageous, bought for £900,000 on 1 March 2002

All the ships are depreciated over 5 years on the straight line basis, assuming a residual value of 25% of cost price, with a full year's depreciation in the year of purchase but no depreciation in the year of sale. During the year ended 31 December 2005, the following events occurred:

> SS Invisible disappeared in the Bermuda Triangle and was considered lost.
> SS Submersible was part-exchanged for a new ship, SS Implausible, on 3 October. The cost of the new ship was £700,000. £200,000 was given in part-exchange, with the balance paid by cheque.
> SS Outrageous was still owned at 31 December 2005.

Show all the relevant entries in the profit and loss account for the year ended 31 December 2005 and in the balance sheet as at that date. Show all workings.

Question 5.2

Martha started business on 1 October 2000 buying and selling computer mouse mats. Each year in October she placed an order for mats with the North Caledonian Mouse Mat Company. During her first four years of trading, Martha's purchases and sales of mouse mats were as follows:

Year ended 30 September	Purchases	Sales
2001	120,000 @ 70p	100,000
2002	120,000 @ 90p	100,000
2003	120,000 @ £1.10	140,000
2004	120,000 @ £1.30	100,000

a   Calculate the value of stock on 30 September 2004, using each of the following stock valuation methods:
> FIFO (First In, First Out)
> LIFO (Last In, First Out)
> AVCO (Average Cost)
b   Explain why, in the UK, FIFO is used in preference to LIFO.

Question 5.3

Trimmings plc manufactures textiles which are sold to fashion designers to be made into garments.

Although the majority of patterns in stock at 31 May 2001 were likely to be sold at prices significantly above the manufacturing cost, the company accountant is concerned about the following product lines:

1   Orange Lace. Manufacturing cost £9,000. This stock has been on a shelf since 1990. The accountant believes that the only way of selling it would be to shred and bundle it (at a cost of £500) and sell it as industrial cleaning wipes for an anticipated price of £2,000.
2   Injured Turtles. Originally printed to meet a high demand for garments linked to a popular television series, there is no further demand for the textile in this country. Stocks cost £16,000, and the only possible source of revenue would be to export the material at a cost of £750 for use as dusters in Guatemala. Administration costs to handle the sale are estimated at £650, and the sale price is estimated at £4,000.

a   Explain what is meant by the term 'stock is valued at the lower of cost and net realisable value'.
b   Explain, with reasons, how each of the above product lines should be accounted for in the annual accounts of the company for the year ended 31 May 2001.

Question 5.4

Bickley Brothers sell luxury picnic hampers from their prestigious shop in London. When the firm's accountant draws up the list of sales ledger balances at its year-end, 31 May 2002, the following information is revealed:

	£
Total balances	13,525
This total includes the following customer who is considered a bad debt:	
Lord Fitztightly	2,400
and a further number of doubtful debtors, amounting to	3,500

Bickley Brothers had an opening balance of £3,000 on its provision for doubtful debts at 1 June 2001.

On 31 May 2003, the business had total sales ledger balances of £17,630. Of that total, one customer, Lady Agapanthus, owes £600 which is considered to be irrecoverable. £3,200 of debts is considered doubtful at that date.

a   Explain the difference between bad and doubtful debts.
b   Show the relevant extracts from the profit and loss accounts for each of the years ended 31 May 2002 and 31 May 2003 and the balance sheets ended on those dates.
c   What would be the effect on the profit and loss account for the year ended 31 May 2004 and the balance sheet as at that date if Lord Fitztightly pays the amount he owed on 1 December 2003?

Further questions can be found on the accompanying website (www.booksites. net/black).

CASE STUDY
·············

Esmeralda doesn't disappear, so Chiquita appears

Marvin (see previous case studies) is now entering the second year of his business and things appear to be going well. His fame is spreading and he was invited to appear on 1 July 2001 at a special royal command performance. As the highlight of his act was the 'disappearing lady' trick, he was highly embarrassed when, after saying the 'magic words' and tapping the correct number of times with his wand, the curtains drew back to reveal Esmeralda in a close embrace with a stagehand. Marvin was so furious that as soon as the show was over he not only sacked Esmeralda but also closed his magic set factory (thereby putting Esmeralda's seven brothers and sisters, the factory's only employees, out of work). Immediately, all the factory's stock was sold at cost and the factory machinery was sold at its net book value. During the following six months, the following events occur:

➤   The disappearing lady apparatus was sold on 1 August 2001 for £1,000. Its net book value at 30 June 2001 was £1,200 (cost £2,000 less 40% p.a. reducing balance depreciation). One month's depreciation is to be charged prior to calculating the profit or loss on disposal.

> Marvin takes on a new assistant, Chiquita, who was previously employed as a sales ledger clerk at Kaboosh Limited. She will perform in a new 'saw the lady in half' routine (for which a new prop costing £3,000 was bought on 1 September 2001) as well as supervising the collection of Marvin's debtors. She immediately prepares a report on the sales ledger, showing that at 31 August he was owed £900, including £200 from a Mrs Featherskew who was a 'bad' debtor, and £150 from Crispin Fairbright whose cheque had been returned three times marked 'no funds available – refer to drawer' and was to be considered doubtful.

a Calculate the profit or loss on disposal of the 'disappearing lady' apparatus

b Explain the effect on Marvin's profit and assets of classifying debts as 'bad' or 'doubtful'.

(Answers in Appendix 3)

References
••••••••••••••

For further details on accounting standards, including SSAP 9 *Stocks and Long-Term Contracts*:

Black, Geoff (2000) *Students' Guide to Accounting and Financial Reporting Standards*, 7th edition, Harlow: Financial Times/Prentice Hall

For an interesting slide show on stock valuation, US-style:

http://nersp.nerdc.ufl.edu/~acadian/legacct/class4/slide1.htm (and subsequent slides). Note that the term 'inventory' is used in the US for stock.

CHAPTER 6

Revision chapter (1)

Objectives

When you have read this chapter you will be able to:

➤ Consolidate your knowledge gained in previous chapters

➤ Prepare a detailed profit and loss account and balance sheet from a trial balance with appropriate adjustments

➤ Understand how *extended* trial balances can help the process of preparing financial summaries

6.1 Introduction

Having got this far, you may be feeling rather overwhelmed by the amount of information and explanations you have had to absorb. This chapter, whilst hardly 'light relief', is included to give you a chance to consolidate your knowledge – it is roughly the half-way stage of the book. The only new topic introduced is the idea of an 'extended' trial balance which can speed up the process of producing the profit and loss account and balance sheet.

The following section requires you to prepare the financial summaries from a detailed trial balance with several adjustments. Work through the question before checking the answer.

6.2 Revision question

Abigail Harvey's trial balance at 31 May 2001 was as follows:

	Dr £	Cr £
Advertising	18,563	
Bad debts	5,835	
Bank overdraft		14,852
Bank interest paid	5,231	
Capital at 1 June 2000		100,000
Cash in hand	650	
Creditors		24,510
Debtors	16,540	
Delivery expenses to customers	4,230	
Depreciation on fixtures and fittings, at 1 June 2000		6,503
Depreciation on motor cars, at 1 June 2000		26,800

Drawings	67,500	
Electricity	6,420	
Fixtures and fittings (cost)	24,210	
Insurance	2,640	
Loan interest (half year)	2,400	
Long-term 6% loan (repayable in 2009)		80,000
Motor cars (cost)	65,920	
Provision for doubtful debts at 1 June 2000		2,000
Purchases	478,000	
Rent and rates	5,900	
Sales		626,220
Stock at 1 June 2000	87,355	
Sundry expenses	13,700	
Telephone	11,240	
Wages and salaries	64,551	
	880,885	880,885

Notes:

1 Stock at 31 May 2001 was valued at £84,800.
2 Depreciation is to be provided as follows:
   Motor cars at 40% p.a. on reducing balance
   Fixtures and fittings at 10% on cost
3 Sales includes a receipt of £2,000 from Wem Garage for the sale of a car which was bought two years previously at a cost of £6,000. No entries relating to the disposal of the car have been made, and the car has been fully depreciated for the two years prior to sale.
4 At 31 May 2001 £1,300 was owed for electricity, and £200 of the insurance was prepaid. The second half-year's loan interest is owing.
5 The provision for doubtful debts is to be increased by £500.

Prepare Abigail Harvey's profit and loss account for the year ended 31 May 2001 and her balance sheet as at that date. Show all relevant workings.

6.3 Answer to revision question

Methodology

Before constructing the profit and loss account and balance sheet we need to follow a series of steps.

Step 1

Read through the trial balance items, making a mental note of possible problem areas – these could include the treatment of the delivery expenses, the loan interest and the provision for doubtful debts. This enables you to get an overall 'feel' of the problem. You could also write in 'T' for trading account, 'P & L' for profit and loss account and 'B/S' for balance sheet against relevant items, though this is not essential.

Step 2

Read through the notes, and write in the adjustments needed for notes 3, 4 and 5 against the relevant trial balance items. These will appear as follows:

Sales (– £2,000)		626,220
Depreciation on motor cars, at 1 June 2000 (– £3,840)*		26,800
Electricity (+ £1,300)	6,420	
Insurance (– £200)	2,640	
Loan interest (half year) (+ £2,400)	2,400	
Motor cars (cost) (– £6,000)	65,920	
Provision for doubtful debts at 1 June 2000 (+ £500)		2,000

* The depreciation on the car which was sold, first year £2,400, second year £1,440.

Step 3

Using the information in notes 2 and 3, calculate the year's depreciation charge and the loss on disposal of the car. Ledger accounts are not required, unless specifically asked for. The 'workings' would be as follows:

Motor cars:

	£	£
At cost per trial balance		65,920
Less cost of car sold		(6,000)
		59,920
Depreciation at 1 June 2000	26,800	
Less depreciation on car sold	(3,840)	
		22,960
'Reduced' value to be depreciated at 40%		36,960
Depreciation for the year (40% x 00,000)		14,784
Accumulated depreciation (for balance sheet)		
(22,960 + 14,784)		37,744

Profit or loss on disposal of car

	£
Cost of car sold	6,000
Less depreciation to date of sale	(3,840)
Net book value at date of sale	2,160
Proceeds of sale	(2,000)
Loss on disposal	160

Fixtures and fittings:
Depreciation for the year 10% × £24,210 = £2,421
Accumulated depreciation (for balance sheet) £6,503 + £2,421 = £8,924

Step 4

Draw three columns each about 3 cm wide on the right-hand side of two sheets of A4 paper. Sometimes it is not necessary to have a third column in the profit and loss account, but it is useful to draw it, just in case it is needed. Write in the heading and then start compiling the 'trading account' part of the profit and loss account, leading to the gross profit (no manufacturing account is required in this question). Continue with the rest of the profit and loss account, leading to the net profit or loss, making sure that all the adjustments previously noted have been made. Then complete the balance sheet.

The answer

Abigail Harvey
Profit and loss account for the year ended 31 May 2001

	£	£
Sales		624,220
Less **Cost of goods sold**		
Opening stock at 1 June 2000	87,355	
Add Purchases	478,000	
	565,355	
Less Closing stock at 31 May 2001	(84,800)	
		(480,555)
Gross profit		143,665
Less **Expenses**		
Wages and salaries	64,551	
Advertising	18,563	
Bad debts written off	5,835	
Bank interest paid	5,231	
Delivery expenses to customers	4,230	
Depreciation on fixtures and fittings	2,421	
Depreciation on motor cars	14,784	
Electricity	7,720	
Increase in provision for doubtful debts	500	
Insurance	2,440	
Loan interest	4,800	
Loss on disposal of motor car	160	
Rent and rates	5,900	
Telephone	11,240	
Sundry expenses	13,700	
		(162,075)
Net loss		(18,410)

Note that we didn't need to use the 'third column' in this example.

Abigail Harvey
Balance sheet as at 31 May 2001

	Cost	Depreciation	Net book value
	£	£	£
Fixed assets			
Motor vehicles	59,920	37,744	22,176
Fixtures	24,210	8,924	15,286
	84,130	46,668	37,462
Current assets			
Stock		84,800	
Debtors	16,540		
Less Provision for doubtful debts	(2,500)		
		14,040	
Prepayments		200	
Cash		650	
		99,690	
***Less* Current liabilities**			
Creditors	24,510		
Accruals	3,700		
Bank overdraft	14,852		
		(43,062)	
Net current assets			56,628
			94,090
Less **Long-term liability**			
6% Loan (repayable 2009)			(80,000)
Total net assets			14,090
Capital			
Opening balance, 1 June 2000		100,000	
Less Net loss		(18,410)	
		81,590	
Less Drawings		(67,500)	
Closing balance, 31 May 2001			14,090

6.4 Extended trial balances

Many accountants use a technique known as an 'extended' trial balance to summarise all the trial balance adjustments. Further columns show the profit and loss account entries (with the balance of profit or loss shown) and also the balance sheet figures. This format is useful where spreadsheets and computerised accounting methods are used. The extended trial balance for Abigail Harvey (see previous question) would be shown as in Figure 6.1. Look carefully at the format and see if you can trace back all the adjustments shown.

figure 6.1

**Abigail Harvey
extended trial
balance as at
31 May 2001**

Abigail Harvey Extended Trial balance as at 31 May 2001

(All figures in £s)	Trial balance		Adjustments		Profit and Loss Account		Balance Sheet	
	Dr	Cr	Dr	Cr	Dr	Cr	Dr	Cr
Advertising	18,563				18,563			
Bad debts	5,835				5,835			
Bank overdraft		14,852						14,852
Bank interest paid	5,231				5,231			
Capital at 1 June 2000		100,000						100,000
Cash in hand	650						650	
Creditors		24,510						24,510
Debtors	16,540						16,540	
Delivery expenses to customers	4,230				4,230			
Depreciation on fixtures and fittings, at 1 June 2000		6,503		2,421				8,924
Depreciation on motor cars, at 1 June 2000		26,800	3,840	14,784				37,744
Drawings	67,500						67,500	
Electricity	6,420		1,300		7,720			
Fixtures and fittings (cost)	24,210						24,210	
Insurance	2,640			200	2,440			
Loan interest (half year)	2,400		2,400		4,800			
Long-term 6% loan (repayable in 2000)		80,000						80,000
Motor cars (cost)	65,920			6,000			59,920	
Provision for doubtful debts at 1 June 2000		2,000		500				2,500
Purchases	478,000				478,000			
Rent and rates	5,900				5,900			
Sales		626,220	2,000			624,220		
Stock at 1 June 2000	87,355				87,355			
Sundry expenses	13,700				13,700			
Telephone	11,240				11,240			
Wages and salaries	64,551				64,551			
	880,885	880,885						
Closing stock (to profit and loss)				84,800		84,800		
Closing stock (to balance sheet)			84,800				84,800	
Accruals				3,700				3,700
Prepayments			200				200	
Increase in provision for doubtful debts			500		500			
Depreciation on cars for the year			14,784		14,784			
Loss on sale of car			160		160			
Depreciation on fixtures and fittings for the year			2,421		2,421			
			112,405	112,405				
Net loss for the year						18,410	18,410	
					727,430	727,430	272,230	272,230

6.5 Glossary

. . . .

| Extended trial balance | An adaptation of a conventional trial balance, with extra columns showing adjustments and profit and loss and balance sheet items |

SELF-CHECK QUESTIONS

(This can be used as a revision test of Chapters 1–5.)

1 Management accounting is:
 a Used to make the business more cost-efficient
 b Required by the Companies Act
 c Used only by people outside the business
 d Used to prepare a trial balance

2 Double-entry bookkeeping means:
 a There are two doors leading into the accountant's office
 b Every transaction is entered twice on the debit side and twice on the credit side
 c Transactions are entered in two separate parts of the bookkeeping system
 d All work is duplicated with no real benefit

3 GAAP stands for:
 a Generally Available Accounting Practices
 b Generally Accepted Accounting Principles
 c Government Authorised Accounting Principles
 d Give Accountants A Present

4 Which of the following is a fundamental accounting concept?
 a Prepayments
 b Prudish
 c Gone Concern
 d Consistency

5 Current assets include:
 a Stock, debtors and prepayments
 b Stock, debtors and accruals
 c Stock, creditors and prepayments
 d Stock, creditors and accruals

6 Depreciation is provided because:
 a Most fixed assets tend to lose value over time
 b Money must be set aside to replace the assets
 c Every fixed asset loses value over time
 d The owners know exactly how much fixed assets lose in value over time

7 Long-term liabilities are those which:
 a Are due for repayment in less than one year
 b Are never repaid
 c Are due for repayment after more than one year
 d Will be repaid in one year's time

8 'Drawings' is shown on the balance sheet as:
 a An addition to the capital account
 b A deduction from the capital account
 c Part of current liabilities
 d Part of current assets

9 The accounting equation can be shown as:

  a Assets − Expenses = Liabilities + Capital + Income

  b Assets + Expenses = Liabilities − Capital + Income

  c Assets + Expenses = Liabilities + Capital − Income

  d Assets + Expenses = Liabilities + Capital + Income

10 Which of the following will result in a change in capital?

  a A fixed asset bought by the business for £10,000

  b A profit made by the organisation

  c A payment received from a debtor

  d A creditor paid by the business

11 A grocer buys a delivery van from Homer Motors for £9,000 by cheque. The entries to be made in the grocer's accounting system are:

  a Debit Delivery Van, Credit Bank

  b Debit Purchases, Credit Bank

  c Debit Delivery Van, Credit Homer Motors

  d Debit Bank, Credit Delivery Van

12 Another name for the impersonal ledger is:

  a Purchase Ledger

  b General Ledger

  c Sales Ledger

  d Cash Ledger

13 In a business's bank account as shown in its Cash Book, a debit balance means:

  a The business has paid out too many cheques

  b The business owes the bank some money

  c The business has an overdraft

  d The business has money in the bank

14 Debtors are:

  a Customers who owe money to the business

  b Customers who buy goods for cash

  c Suppliers who are owed money by the business

  d Suppliers who have been paid by the business

15 A jam factory pays £3 for a stapler for use in its office. How would this be shown in the financial summaries?

  a As a fixed asset in the balance sheet

  b As purchases in the profit and loss account

  c As stationery in the profit and loss account

  d As a current asset in the balance sheet

16 The imprest system is used to control which of the following?

  a The design of the company's advertising campaigns

  b Petty Cash expenditure

  c The rate of pay of employees

  d The amount of money the owner can take from the business

17 If a ledger account has debit entries totalling £450 and credit entries totalling £200, the balance on the account is:

  a Credit balance £250

  b Debit balance £250

  c Debit balance £650

  d Credit balance £650

18 During a month a business spends £195 on petty cash items and pays into petty cash a £5 note which the owner had borrowed previously. There was a cash float of £200 at the start of the month. Using the imprest system, how much will be paid into petty cash at the start of the next month?

   a £200

   b £10

   c £190

   d £390

19 An unpresented cheque is:

   a A cheque which has not been processed by a bank

   b A cheque which a customer forgot to pay to the business

   c A cheque without all the necessary details filled in

   d A duplicated cheque

20 A bank reconciliation:

   a Checks the completeness of the information in the cash book and bank statements

   b Is a statement of the maximum amount a bank is prepared to lend a business

   c Tells the business that the cash book is 100% accurate

   d Compares the bank balances of two separate businesses

21 A debit balance may appear on a purchases ledger account because:

   a A supplier has overpaid

   b A purchase invoice has been duplicated

   c A business may have returned goods to a supplier after paying for them

   d The business has paid the amount it owes a creditor

22 Relating to the closing stock for a financial period, which of the following is true?

   a The figure is shown only in the profit and loss account

   b The figure is shown only in the balance sheet

   c The figure is shown in both the profit and loss account and the balance sheet

   d The figure is shown as part of 'purchases' in the profit and loss account

23 A business started its year owing £4,000 for electricity. During the year it paid electricity bills totalling £24,000 but owed £5,000 by the end of the period. What will be the figure transferred to the profit and loss account for electricity?

   a £33,000

   b £15,000

   c £23,000

   d £25,000

24 A business installs a machine costing £40,000. The machine is expected to last for five years and have a residual value of £4,000. What is the machine's net book value at the end of 2 years' ownership?

   a £25,600

   b £7,200

   c £14,400

   d £21,600

25 A car is bought for £16,000. It is to be depreciated on a reducing balance basis using a rate of 40% p.a. What is the car's net book value at the end of 2 years' ownership?

   a £9,600

   b £5,760

   c £12,800

   d £3,200

26 For a pen factory, indirect costs could include:
   a The cost of gold to make the pens
   b The cost of heating the factory
   c The wages paid to the skilled workers making the pens
   d The cost of velvet-lined boxes in which each pen is packaged

27 Which of the following headings appears in a manufacturing account?
   a Cost of Sales
   b Gross Profit
   c Prime cost of production
   d Net Profit

28 A company has opening stock £6,900, closing stock £7,800, purchases
   £33,650, carriage inwards £700 and purchases returns £400. What is its cost
   of goods sold?
   a £31,650
   b £33,850
   c £33,050
   d £48,650

29 An appropriation account is *not* part of the profit and loss account for which
   type of business organisation?
   a Sole trader
   b Partnership
   c Limited company
   d PLC (Public Limited Company)

30 A business sells an asset on 1 January for £12,000. The asset was bought
   exactly 2 years previously for £24,000 and depreciation was charged over
   5 years on the straight line method, assuming no residual value. What is the
   profit or loss on disposal?
   a £7,200 loss
   b £2,400 loss
   c £12,000 loss
   d £12,000 profit

31 A company starts business on 1 January. In that month it buys 300 grecks at
   £40 each, then 200 at £50 each. On the last day of the month it sells 400
   grecks. If it uses FIFO to value stock, what is the stock value at 31 January?
   a £4,500
   b £4,000
   c £5,000
   d £5,500

32 A company selling designer watches bought 400 for £60 each. Normal selling
   price is £100 per watch, but a change in fashion has resulted in all the
   watches being saleable at only £30 each, after a different strap, costing £2
   each, has been fitted to them. How should the stock of watches be valued?
   a £11,200
   b £24,000
   c £39,200
   d £12,000

33 What is a doubtful debt?
   a A debt where there is some hope of getting paid
   b A debt where there is no hope of getting paid
   c A debt which is bad
   d A debt where the customer has queried an invoice

34 At the start of a year, a business has £3,000 on its provision for doubtful debts account. By the end of the year, doubtful debts have increased to £4,200. What entries would be shown in the financial summaries?
   a 'Expenses' include £7,200 and debtors are reduced by £7,200
   b 'Expenses' include £4,200 and debtors are reduced by £4,200
   c Profit is increased by £1,200 and debtors are reduced by £4,200
   d 'Expenses' include £1,200 and debtors are reduced by £4,200

35 If a bad debt is unexpectedly paid some years after it was written off, what would be the effect in the financial summaries for that year?
   a Increase profit and decrease debtors' balances
   b Increase profit and increase the bank account
   c Increase the debtors' balances shown under current assets
   d No effect

Further questions can be found on the accompanying website (www.booksites.net/black).

SELF-STUDY QUESTIONS

(Answers in Appendix 2)

Question 6.1

From the following trial balance and attached notes, prepare a profit and loss account for the year ended 30 September 2003 and a balance sheet as at that date.

Felicity Frankton
Trial Balance as at 30 September 2003

	Dr £	Cr £
Bad debts written off	500	
Bank balance	1,260	
Capital, 1 October 2002		15,940
Carriage inwards	320	
Carriage outwards	430	
Computers, at cost	3,610	
Creditors		13,600
Debtors	24,200	
Depreciation on computers, 1 October 2002		1,850
Depreciation on motor cars, 1 October 2002		7,600
Discount allowed	340	
Drawings	16,900	
Light and heat	2,200	
Motor cars, at cost	16,500	
Opening stock, 1 October 2002	16,520	
Proceeds of sale of motor car		1,500
Provision for doubtful debts, 1 October 2002		800
Purchases	32,410	
Rent and rates	3,200	
Sales		105,800
Sundry office expenses	10,200	
Wages and salaries	18,500	
	147,090	147,090

Notes:
1 Closing stock was valued at £14,560.
2 A car costing £7,900 on 1 October 2000 was sold during the year for £1,500. Depreciation to the date of sale was £6,000. No entries had been made relating to this sale, other than crediting the proceeds to a separate general ledger account.
3 £600 was owed for rent and rates at the end of the year, and £200 had been prepaid at the end of the year relating to sundry office expenses.
4 The provision for doubtful debts was to be adjusted to 5% of the closing debtors total.
5 Depreciation is charged as follows:
   Computer equipment: over 5 years on the straight line basis, assuming no residual values
   Motor cars: 60% p.a. on the reducing balance basis, with no depreciation being charged in the year of sale.

Question 6.2

From the following trial balance and attached notes, prepare a profit and loss account for the year ended 31 December 2003 and a balance sheet as at that date.

Patrick Cooper
Trial Balance as at 31 December 2003

	Dr	Cr
	£	£
Sales		289,512
Purchases	132,950	
Opening stock	5,620	
Discount allowed	200	
Bank interest	950	
Wages and salaries	39,540	
Drawings	22,000	
Administration expenses	55,500	
Capital		16,268
Debtors	6,300	
Creditors		5,210
Provision for doubtful debts		300
Bad debts written off	250	
Selling expenses	37,790	
Equipment at cost	14,000	
Depreciation on equipment at 1 January 2003		2,350
Bank overdraft		1,600
Cash in hand	140	
	315,240	315,240

Notes:
1 Closing stock was valued at £4,900.
2 There was an accrual of £300 for selling expenses and £150 of the administration expenses were prepaid.

3 An item of equipment bought for £600 on 1 January 2000 was sold for £100 on 1 January 2003. The proceeds are shown as part of 'Sales'. Equipment is depreciated at 20% p.a. on the straight line basis, with no residual values.

4 The provision for doubtful debts is to be increased to £550.

Further questions can be found on the accompanying website (www.booksites. net/black).

CASE STUDY
....

Marvin's second birthday

Marvin (see previous case studies) celebrated two years in business on 30 June 2002. At that date, his versatile assistant, Chiquita, produced the following trial balance:

	Dr	Cr
	£	£
Appearance fees as entertainer		45,200
Cost of magician's equipment	7,700	
Cost of 'saw the lady in half' prop	3,000	
Bad debt	200	
Purchases of novelties for resale	15,600	
Sales of novelties		35,900
Marvin's drawings	32,000	
Wages to assistant (Chiquita)	24,600	
Travel to performance venues	6,220	
Cleaning	1,320	
Loss on disposal of 'disappearing lady' apparatus	160	
Opening stock of novelties	2,400	
Opening capital, 1 July 2001		18,300
Creditors		480
Debtors	2,600	
Bank balance	5,160	
Depreciation on magician's equipment, 1 July 2001		1,080
	100,960	100,960

Notes:

1 At the very start of the year he closed down the manufacturing section, selling stock of raw materials and machinery at their book values. There is no need to prepare a manufacturing account.

2 Closing stock of bought-in novelties at 30 June 2002 was £2,500.

3 Marvin owed £250 for dry-cleaning at 30 June 2002, but had paid £600 on 1 April 2002 for a rail season ticket lasting 12 months.

4 Depreciation for the year on the magician's equipment was £1,300. The 'saw the lady in half' prop is depreciated over 4 years, assuming a residual value of 20% of cost price.

5 A provision for doubtful debts is to be created of 5% of the closing debtors total.

Prepare Marvin's profit and loss account for the year ended 30 June 2002 and a balance sheet as at that date.

(Answer in Appendix 3)

References

Look in your college library for introductory financial accounting textbooks (Library section 657). They will all contain questions requiring the preparation of financial summaries from a trial balance. Practise as many as possible.

CHAPTER 7

Accounting and funding of multi-owner organisations

Objectives

When you have read this chapter you will be able to:

➤ Identify the accounting requirements of sole traders, partnerships and limited companies
➤ Appreciate the different funding possibilities for various types of business organisation
➤ Distinguish between rights issues and bonus issues
➤ Understand the meaning of 'published accounts'
➤ Give a simple definition of a 'group' of companies

7.1 Introduction

In the preceding chapters, the main emphasis has been on the preparation and summarising of a sole trader's accounting information. Many businesses, including the largest in terms of sales and profitability, are not sole traders but are formed as partnerships or limited companies. Limited companies themselves can be either 'private' limited companies (Ltd) or public limited companies (plc's). Many limited companies are *subsidiary* companies, owned by another company, in what is known as a 'group' of companies. All these have differing accounting requirements, some more complex than others. In this chapter we shall be taking an overview of these, with the emphasis on limited company accounts. We shall also look at the sources of finance available for the different forms of business enterprise.

7.2 Sole traders

Sole traders, by definition, are businesses owned by one person. Advantages of operating as a sole trader are as follows.

➤ The owner has absolute control over the business.
➤ The business can be established without any legal formalities.
➤ Personal supervision by the owner may result in a better service to customers and clients.
➤ The owner does not have to reveal the financial results of the business to the general public.

However, there are also disadvantages, including the following.

➤ The owner has personal liability for all the debts of the business, without limit.
➤ Total control and personal supervision usually require long hours and very hard work.
➤ There is no co-owner with whom to share the problems and anxieties associated with running the business.
➤ If the owner is absent from the business due to sickness or other reasons, this may have a serious effect on the state of the business.
➤ Future prospects for expansion are restricted, as they depend on the owner's ability to raise finance.

Main sources of finance for a sole trader are:

➤ capital introduced by the owner,
➤ loans from friends and family,
➤ bank borrowings, through overdrafts or loans,
➤ profits ploughed back into the business.

DID YOU KNOW?

A survey[1] showed that at the start of 1996 there were 3.7 million businesses in the UK, of which:

➤ *2.5m had no employees*
➤ *1m had 1–9 employees*
➤ *166,000 had 10–49 employees*
➤ *26,000 had 50–249 employees*
➤ *7,000 had over 250 employees*

Although many people prefer independence and quite happily continue as sole traders, it is extremely difficult to expand a business without also increasing the number of people who own it. The main choice for sole traders wishing to convert to or form multi-ownership enterprises is between a partnership and a limited liability company.

7.3 Partnerships

A partnership is defined in the Partnership Act of 1890 as

'The relation which subsists between persons carrying on a business in common with a view of profit'.

Often partnerships are formed by professional people such as architects, accountants and solicitors. Whilst the minimum number of partners (fairly obviously) is two, the maximum is 20 (though there is no maximum in the case of professionals such as chartered accountants who are not allowed to form limited companies).

DID YOU KNOW?

The accounting firm PricewaterhouseCoopers has over 9,000 partners world-wide.

Advantages of partnership include the following.

➤ The problems and pleasures of running the business are shared.
➤ There is access to greater expertise and financial input.
➤ Losses as well as profits are shared.

---

[1] *SME Statistics for the UK* (1996), Sheffield: SME Statistics Unit

➤ Few legal formalities are involved, though a partnership agreement should be drawn up to avoid misunderstandings.

➤ The financial results do not have to be made public.

Disadvantages include the following.

➤ Personality clashes may threaten the business and ultimately break up the partnership.

➤ In the vast majority of partnerships, there is no restriction on the personal liability of partners for the debts of the business (occasionally a limited partnership may be formed, but at least one partner must have unlimited liability).

➤ Generally there is less access to funding for expansion than for a limited company.

Main sources of finance for a partnership are:

➤ capital introduced by the partners,

➤ loans from friends and family of partners,

➤ bank borrowings, through overdrafts or loans, secured either on the partnership's assets or on the personal assets of individual partners,

➤ profits ploughed back into the business.

7.3.1 Accounting requirements of partnerships

In most respects, including the day-to-day bookkeeping aspects, partnership accounting is identical with that of a sole trader. The only difference is that accounts must be opened showing the financial implications of the partnership agreement. These include details of:

➤ shares of profits and losses,

➤ capital introduced and withdrawn by each partner,

➤ drawings made by each partner,

➤ whether any partners are to receive a guaranteed salary (e.g. if only one partner works full-time for the partnership),

➤ interest charged on drawings (to discourage individual partners from drawing excessive amounts),

➤ interest allowed on capital balances (to reward those partners who have invested more than others).

Occasionally partners can't agree over vital matters such as how to split profits and losses. In such cases the Partnership Act of 1890 states that they should be shared equally.

7.3.2 Capital accounts and current accounts

These are the key accounts recording the details of each partner. Sometimes all relevant transactions are recorded in Capital accounts, which work in a similar way to a sole trader's capital account. In many partnerships Capital accounts record only 'fixed' agreed capital balances, with all other transactions recorded in 'current' accounts (not to be confused with bank current accounts).

7.3.3 Partnership appropriation accounts

When preparing a partnership's financial summaries, the profit and loss account will be produced in exactly the same way as that for a sole trader. The only additional information, an appropriation account, comes in a separate section after the net profit or loss has been determined, as the profit or loss has to be 'appropriated' between the partners according to their partnership agreement. If partners have also agreed to pay themselves salaries or charge interest on drawings or capital, this is also shown in this section.

ACTIVITY 7.1

Gilbert and Bufton are partners sharing profits and losses in the ratio 3:2. The net profit for the year ended 31 December 2000 was £60,000. As Gilbert worked full-time whilst Bufton worked part-time for the partnership, Gilbert was allowed a salary of £12,000 p.a. No interest was charged on drawings or credited on capital balances. Show the appropriation account section of the profit and loss account for the year.

Answer

	£	£
Net profit for the year		60,000
Appropriated as follows:		
Gilbert: salary		(12,000)
		48,000
Gilbert: share of profit (60% × £48,000)	28,800	
Bufton: share of profit (40% × £48,000)	19,200	
		48,000

PAUSE FOR THOUGHT

Gilbert's salary, unlike employees' salaries, is not shown as an 'expense' in arriving at the net profit figure. It is part of the way in which the partners have decided to share the profit. If interest on capital or drawings had been agreed, the amounts would be added (interest on drawings) or deducted (interest on capital) from the £48,000 sub-total prior to the calculation of the share of profits.

7.3.4 *Partnership balance sheet*

The 'top half' of the balance sheet, showing fixed and current assets and liabilities, is identical with that of a sole trader. However, the sole trader's capital account is replaced by details of partners' capital accounts (and current accounts if they are maintained).

ACTIVITY 7.2

Gilbert and Bufton (see Activity 7.1) started the year with capital balances of £25,900 and £15,750 respectively. During the year, Gilbert had drawings of £35,000 whilst Bufton drew £17,000. No current accounts were maintained for the partnership. Show the relevant extract from the partnership balance sheet as at 31 December 2000.

Answer

	£	£
(Assets less liabilities)		49,650
Gilbert's Capital Account		
Opening balance, 1 January 2000	25,900	
Add: Salary	12,000	
Share of profit	28,800	
	66,700	
Less: Drawings	(35,000)	
Closing balance, 31 December 2000		31,700
Bufton's Capital Account		
Opening balance, 1 January 2000	15,750	
Add: Share of profit	19,200	
	34,950	
Less: Drawings	(17,000)	
Closing balance, 31 December 2000		17,950
		49,650

PAUSE FOR THOUGHT *Any interest on capital or drawings would also have been adjusted within the capital accounts. Interest on capital is added, whilst interest on drawings is deducted.*

7.4 Limited companies

Although there are many advantages in running a business as a sole trader or a partnership, these can be outweighed by the fact that the owner or partners have personal responsibility for meeting all the debts of their business. Whilst this may be of little concern to the proprietors of healthy, profitable businesses, it can have a devastating effect on the fortunes of owners of failing or loss-making enterprises, as they must meet the claims of creditors from their personal assets if the business's assets are insufficient.

Another major disadvantage for the ambitious business owner is the restricted scope they have for raising funds for expansion. To overcome these, many businesses are organised as *limited companies*. Their main features are:

➤ They are separate legal entities, able to trade, own assets and owe liabilities (including tax on their profit) in their own right independently from their owners.

➤ Ownership is (with rare exceptions) divided into shares ('the share capital') which can be bought and sold.

➤ The owners (known as 'shareholders' or 'members') have limited liability for the debts of the company, so even if the company fails with considerable debts, their loss is restricted to the value of their part of the share capital.

➤ Management is in the hands of *directors*, who might own only a small part of the share capital. They are elected by the shareholders.

DID YOU KNOW?
The directors of Tesco plc, the UK's largest supermarket company, owned 6.9 million out of 6.7 billion shares issued by the company.

➤ Public limited companies (plc's) are allowed to sell their shares to the general public, which enables them to have access to massive funds for expansion. Public limited companies are the largest businesses in the country. Private limited companies (Ltd) cannot sell their shares to the public.

DID YOU KNOW?
In their last published balance sheet Tesco plc disclosed that it had raised over £1.9 billion from shareholders.

➤ Limited companies can raise money by issuing *debentures*, which are fixed interest loans usually secured on the company's assets, and by issuing convertible loan stock, which are loans which can be converted into shares at a later date. *Neither debentures nor loan stocks are part of a company's share capital.*

Limited companies do have a number of disadvantages when compared to other forms of business organisations:

➤ Lack of secrecy, as companies have to publish financial information, though large companies have to disclose more than small ones.
➤ Extra costs of complying with legislation, which includes the 1985 Companies Act. For large companies this requires the appointment of an *auditor* who is an independent qualified accountant responsible for reporting if the published financial information shows a 'true and fair view'.
➤ More formality – shareholders' meetings must be held, annual returns must be completed and sent to the government, etc.

7.4.1 Accounting requirements of limited companies

As with partnerships, the day-to-day bookkeeping will be identical with that of sole traders. Records are also needed of the following items which are specific to limited companies.

Expenses
➤ Payments to directors (also called remuneration or emoluments), which are classified as an expense of the company, and therefore included within the profit and loss account under that heading.
➤ Auditors' fees (though not all companies have auditors).
➤ Interest on debentures and loan stock.

Appropriations of profit
As with partnerships, the profit or loss needs to be 'appropriated'.

➤ A limited company is responsible for taxation on its own profits, so the first appropriation is to the government in the form of the corporation tax provision for the year.
➤ Rewards to the owners are in the form of *dividends* on their shares. These are usually expressed as 'pence per share' and might be paid once a year (a 'final' dividend) or more frequently ('interim' dividends and a final dividend).
➤ The last appropriation is to the company itself, as it can hold profits in the form of *reserves*. The main reserve is known simply as the Profit and Loss Account – it represents the profits retained in the company after all other appropriations have been made.

Balance sheet items

The total net assets section of a limited company's balance sheet looks very similar to any other balance sheet, though sometimes you might see a fixed asset called 'goodwill', which occurs when one business has taken over another business and paid a price greater than the value of the individual net assets acquired. Under 'Creditors due for payment within one year' (current liabilities), the following additional items are shown:

➤ Taxation, being the corporation tax due to the government at the balance sheet date.

➤ Proposed dividend, being the final dividend for the year which will be paid to shareholders once it has been approved at the company's Annual General Meeting (AGM). The AGM takes place some months after the date of the balance sheet.

'Creditors due for payment after more than one year' (long-term liabilities) may also include the following.

➤ Debentures, assuming that the loan has more than one year before it is due to be repaid. Otherwise it will be shown as a current liability.

It is the 'capital' side of a limited company's balance sheet which shows major differences compared with sole traders or partnerships. It is divided into two main sections:

➤ Share capital, which is the total share capital issued to shareholders. The vast majority of these shares are known as 'ordinary shares' or the *equity capital* of the company. Each share carries an equal right to vote at company meetings and to share in any dividends, so the more shares owned, the more votes and dividends a shareholder has. Shares have a *nominal value* (also called a *par* value), e.g. 25p or 5p. Sometimes dividends are expressed as a percentage of this nominal value. Each company has a maximum number of shares which it is allowed to issue (its *authorised* share capital), whilst the actual amount of share capital in the hands of shareholders is known as the *issued* or *called-up* share capital. Some companies, as well as having ordinary shares, issue *preference* shares, which carry a fixed rate of dividend and have priority over the ordinary shares in respect of the payment of their dividends and the repayment of capital in the event of the company's liquidation. These shares might be *redeemable*, which means that the company can refund the preference shareholders' capital (subject to certain rules to protect the overall capital of the company) after a specified timescale.

➤ Reserves, which are classified as either *capital reserves* or *revenue reserves*. The main revenue reserve is the profit and loss account, which represents all the retained ('unappropriated') profits of the company, not just for the current year but since the company formed. Revenue reserves are known as 'distributable' – they can be used for paying company dividends.

> **DID YOU KNOW?**
> Tesco plc had issued 6.7 billion ordinary shares of 5p nominal value at its last balance sheet date.

> **DID YOU KNOW?**
> Tesco plc's Profit and Loss Account stood at £2.4 billion at its last balance sheet date.

The main capital reserve is the *share premium account*, which is the amount *above the nominal value* paid into the company by shareholders.

For example, a company might sell its 25p nominal value shares for £2.75, in which case the 25p's go into the share capital section of the balance sheet, whilst the remaining £2.50's are shown under 'share premium account'.

Another capital reserve would arise if a company decided to *revalue* some of its fixed assets (specifically land and buildings). For example, if a plot of land bought several years ago for £30,000 is now worth £90,000, the company might wish to show this increase by adding £60,000 to the fixed asset value and creating an 'asset revaluation reserve' for the same amount. The £60,000 is known as an *unrealised* gain (unrealised meaning that the land has not been sold), and is not included in the profit and loss account. However, the overall result is that the asset value shown in the balance sheet is more realistic. It is important to note that capital reserves are 'non-distributable' – they cannot be used to pay a dividend.

ACTIVITY **7.3**

Smithdown plc's trial balance as at 31 May 2001 was as follows:

	Dr	Cr
	£	£
Advertising	3,400	
Bank overdraft		4,000
Carriage out	1,890	
Directors' remuneration	77,300	
Fixed assets (office equipment and showroom) – net book value as at 1 June 2000	248,720	
Interest	1,900	
Interim dividend, paid 10 January 2001	5,000	
Office expenses	10,930	
Office salaries	26,200	
Opening stock at 1 June 2000	23,500	
Profit and loss account as at 1 June 2000		245,000
Purchases	117,620	
Sales		345,000
Salesforce wages	36,640	
Share capital (25p nominal shares)		100,000
Share premium account		140,000
Trade creditors		86,200
Trade debtors	367,100	
	920,200	920,200

Notes:

1 Closing stock at 31 May 2001 was £27,900.
2 Depreciation for the year: office equipment £3,820, showroom £4,500.
3 There were neither accruals nor prepayments at the year-end.

4 Corporation tax amounting to £16,000 was to be provided for.

5 A final dividend of 2p per share was proposed.

Prepare the company's profit and loss account for the year ended 31 May 2001 and its balance sheet as at that date.

Answer

Smithdown plc

Profit and loss account for the year ended 31 May 2001

	£	£
Sales		345,000
Less **Cost of goods sold**		
Opening stock at 1 June 2000	23,500	
Add Purchases	117,620	
	141,120	
Less Closing stock at 31 May 2001	(27,900)	
		(113,220)
Gross profit		231,780
Less **Expenses**		
Directors' remuneration	77,300	
Salesforce wages	36,640	
Office salaries	26,200	
Advertising	3,400	
Interest	1,900	
Carriage out	1,890	
Depreciation on office equipment	3,820	
Depreciation on showroom	4,500	
Office expenses	10,930	
		(166,580)
Net profit for the year, before taxation		65,200
Less Provision for taxation		(16,000)
Net profit for the year, after taxation		49,200
Less Dividends:		
Interim (paid)	5,000	
Final (proposed)	8,000	
		(13,000)
Retained profit for the year		36,200

Smithdown plc

Balance sheet as at 31 May 2001

	£	£	£
Fixed assets			
(details would be shown)			240,400
Current assets			
Stock		27,900	
Trade debtors		367,100	
c/f		395,000	240,400

	b/f	395,000	340,400

Less **Creditors due for payment within one year**			
Trade creditors	86,200		
Taxation	16,000		
Proposed dividend	8,000		
Overdraft	4,000		
		(114,200)	
Net current assets			280,800
Total net assets			521,200
Capital and reserves			
Called-up share capital (25p shares)			100,000
Share premium account			140,000
Profit and loss account:			
Balance at 1 June 2000		245,000	
Retained profit for the year		36,200	
			281,200
			521,200

PAUSE FOR THOUGHT

Of the £65,200 net profit, £16,000 goes to the government, £13,000 to shareholders (the final dividend is calculated as 400,000 shares @ 2p each) and the balance of £36,200 is left within the company and added to the retained profits at the start of the year. Note that the word 'reserve' is not the same as 'cash'. Reserves are represented by many different types of net assets, one of which might or might not be a cash balance.

7.4.2 Rights issues and bonus issues

A company's share capital might change for a number of reasons, including, for a plc, a new share issue to the general public or, for a private limited company, new shares issued to family and friends. Two other reasons for a change are as follows.

➤ A *rights issue*, which is a further share issue to existing shareholders, in proportion to existing holdings (e.g., a '3 for 2' rights issue gives the holders of two existing shares the 'right' to buy a further three shares, so if you hold 6,000 shares you could buy a further 9,000 shares). A rights issue is often the easiest way for a company to raise more capital, and shares are usually offered at an attractive price to tempt investors. Obviously, an unsuccessful company may have difficulties in attracting more capital from their shareholders.

➤ A *bonus issue* is a *free* issue of shares to existing shareholders, again in proportion to their existing holdings, so a '1 for 4' bonus issue would mean that a shareholder with 1200 shares would be *given* a further 300. Bonus share issues (also called scrip or capitalisation issues) are a way of transferring reserves (revenue or capital) back to the shareholders, without the need for any cash payments to be made by the company. It is, on the face of it, a cosmetic exercise to rearrange a balance sheet where reserves have grown disproportionately in relation to the company's share capital. However, if a company uses its revenue reserves to make a bonus issue, it is thereby reducing the reserves available for dividend payments in the future (remember that only revenue reserves can be used for dividend payments). This may not be welcomed by all shareholders.

ACTIVITY **7.4**
••••••••••••••

The 'share capital and reserves' section of Smithdown plc's balance sheet at 31 May 2001 (see Activity 7.3) was as follows:

	£	£
Capital and reserves		
Called-up share capital (25p shares)		100,000
Share premium account		140,000
Profit and loss account:		
Balance at 1 June 2000	245,000	
Retained profit for the year	36,200	
		281,200
		521,200

Assume that on 1 June 2001 a rights issue on a '3 for 5' basis was made at 80p per share. All the existing shareholders decided to take up their shares, and paid for them in full by 30 June 2001. Six months later, the company made a bonus issue on a '2 for 1' basis, the issue being paid up equally from the share premium account and the profit and loss account. Show the revised 'share capital and reserves' section, firstly after the rights issue and secondly after the bonus issue. Ignore any trading profit which may have been made in the period.

Answer

a Balance sheet after the rights issue:

	£	£
Capital and reserves		
Called-up share capital (25p shares)[1]		160,000
Share premium account[2]		272,000
Profit and loss account:		
Balance at 1 June 2001		281,200
		713,200

Note that the balance sheet totals will agree, as £192,000 will be added to the bank balance under 'current assets' (240,000 shares issued at 80p = £192,000).

Notes:

1 Original 400,000 shares, plus 240,000 issued as '3 for 5' = 640,000 @ 25p nominal value = £160,000.
2 Original £140,000, plus share premium on rights issue (240,000 × [80p – 25p]) = £272,000.

b Balance sheet after the rights issue and the bonus issue:

	£	£
Capital and reserves		
Called-up share capital (25p shares)[1]		480,000
Share premium account[2]		112,000
Profit and loss account[3]		
Balance at 1 June 2001		121,200
		713,200

Notes:

1 '2 for 1' trebles the previous share capital (an extra 1,280,000 shares @ 25p each = £320,000).

2 Half of the bonus comes out of the share premium account (£272,000 – £160,000 = £112,000).

3 Half of the bonus comes out of the profit and loss account (£281,200 – £160,000 = £121,200).

PAUSE FOR THOUGHT   *Note that the bonus issue has no effect on the balance sheet total!*

7.5 Published accounts

Companies legislation requires that all companies must publish financial statements. For smaller companies, only a brief summary of their finances is required, but for the largest companies, including all plc's, an 'annual report' must be prepared (often at great expense) which is sent to all shareholders and Companies House, which is the UK government's 'storehouse' of company information. The public have a right of access to the information – see the web site http://www.companies-house.gov.uk/ for details.

Many plc's regard their annual report as an opportunity to show off the best of their company, in effect treating it as a public relations exercise. The glossy photographs of the company's products and exotic locations of major contracts can give some reports the style of a travel brochure. In recent years, companies have been allowed to save costs by producing two versions of their annual report:

➤ a summarised version, sent to all shareholders,
➤ a fully detailed version, sent to Companies House and only those shareholders specifically requesting it.

A key feature of published profit and loss accounts and balance sheets is that they have to follow specific *formats* of presentation as laid down in the Companies Act. These formats were devised to ensure a degree of uniformity across the European Community, as they apply to all member countries. Although there is a small amount of flexibility allowed (for example, a company can produce statements in either a 'vertical' or a 'horizontal' format), virtually all UK companies follow the 'vertical' style format. Companies also have to follow a regulatory framework laid down by the Accounting Standards Board, which issues *Financial Reporting Standards* which set out best practice to be adopted in specific accounting situations.

In practice, the production of 'published' accounts follows all the normal conventions, but the following should be noted.

➤ Profit and loss expenses are grouped into two main categories, 'selling and distribution' and 'administration expenses'.
➤ Interest charges are shown separately.
➤ The Companies Act requires that certain expenses, such as the audit fee and directors' remuneration, must be shown, usually as a note.

The detailed requirements of the Companies Act are outside the scope of this book, but Activity 7.5 shows how a simple set of published statements can be produced.

ACTIVITY **7.5**

Prepare the published version of Smithdown plc's profit and loss account as shown in the answer to Activity 7.3.

Answer

Smithdown plc
Published profit and loss account for the year ended 31 May 2001

	£	£
Sales		345,000
Less **Cost of goods sold**		(113,220)
Gross profit		231,780
Less **Expenses**		
Selling and distribution expenses[1]	46,430	
Administration expenses[2]	118,250	
		(164,680)
Operating profit for the year, before interest[3]		67,100
Interest		(1,900)
Operating profit for the year, before taxation		65,200
Less Provision for taxation		(16,000)
Operating profit for the year, after taxation		49,200
Less Dividends		(13,000)
Retained profit for the year		36,200

Notes:
1 Salesforce wages, carriage out, advertising, depreciation on showroom.
2 All other expenses except interest.
3 Note that the Companies Act format refers to 'operating' profit, not 'net' profit.

Various notes will be given, including a breakdown of the cost of sales figure, dividends and key items required to be disclosed under the Companies Act, such as directors' remuneration.

Note that the published balance sheet will be identical to that shown in the answer to Activity 7.3, but with notes giving a detailed breakdown of items such as fixed assets.

7.6 Groups of companies

Many companies are owned by other companies. This means that either all, or a majority, of the voting shares of the one company (the 'subsidiary' company) are held by the other company (the 'parent' company). This relationship is referred to as a 'group' of companies, and special accounting requirements exist to reflect the finances of the entire group, as well as the individual companies comprising the group. Specifically, a *consolidated* (or *'group'*) *profit and loss account* and a *consolidated* (or *'group'*) *balance sheet* must be prepared. The procedures relating to group accounting are outside the scope of this book, but you may come across the word 'consolidated' or 'group' when you look at the annual reports of public limited companies.

7.7 Glossary

AGM	Annual General Meeting, which must be held by a limited company for various official purposes including the approval of the accounts and the appointment of directors
Asset revaluation reserve	A capital reserve created when an asset (usually land or buildings) is revalued. It records an *unrealised* gain
Auditor	An independent qualified accountant who reports on whether published accounts show a true and fair view
Authorised share capital	The maximum share capital a limited company is allowed to issue
Bonus issue	Free shares given to existing shareholders to transfer part of a company's reserves to them without any cash changing hands
Called-up share capital	The actual value of shares issued by a limited company. Also known as issued share capital
Capital reserves	Reserves built up from shareholders' contributions (the share premium account) or through unrealised gains (asset revaluation reserve)
Consolidated accounts	The accounts of a group of companies
Convertible loan stock	Loans raised by a limited company which may be converted into shares of that company at a future date
Debentures	Loans raised by a limited company, usually secured on the company's assets
Directors	The officers who manage a limited company
Dividend	The reward on capital which shareholders receive from a limited company
Equity capital	The ordinary shares of a limited company

Group of companies	A situation where one company (the parent company) owns one or more other companies (subsidiaries)
Issued share capital	Another term for called-up share capital
Limited company	A business organisation whose owners have limited liability for the debts of their business
Limited liability	The restriction on liability of shareholders for the debts of their company to the amount of the capital which they have invested in the company
Liquidation	The end of a company's existence, whereby all its assets are sold and its liabilities paid, any surplus capital being returned to shareholders
Ltd	Abbreviation denoting a private limited company
Members	Another word for shareholders
Nominal value	The 'face value' of a share, e.g. £1 or 25p. Also called par value
Ordinary shares	The most common form of shares issued by limited companies. Each share carries equal voting and dividend rights. Also known as the equity capital
Par value	Another term meaning nominal value
Partnership	The relation which subsists between persons carrying on a business with a view of profit
Partnership appropriation account	Part of the profit and loss account of a partnership, showing how profits or losses are apportioned between partners according to their partnership agreement
Partnership capital Account	The record of the capital of individual partners
Partnership current account	The record of individual partners' financial dealings with the partnership, other than their capital balances
plc	Abbreviation denoting a public limited company
Preference shares	A class of shares carrying a fixed rate of dividend and giving the holders preference over equity shareholders regarding payment of dividends and repayment of capital in the event of the company's liquidation
Private limited company	A limited company which is prohibited from selling its shares to the public
Public limited company	A company which is allowed to sell its shares to the general public
Published accounts	The annual financial report of a limited company, produced in accordance with the Companies Act and other relevant rules and regulations laid down by the accounting profession or the Stock Exchange

Reserves	Funds set aside within a limited company, created from profits or paid in by shareholders. They are not the same as 'cash'
Retained profits	The profits left over after all appropriations (tax, dividends,etc.) have been made
Revenue reserves	Reserves built up from retained profits via the profit and loss account of a limited company. They can be used to pay dividends
Rights issue	The right given to existing shareholders to buy more shares
Share premium account	The capital reserve built up from amounts paid by shareholders for their shares, in excess of the nominal value of those shares
Shareholders	The owners of a limited company
Sole trader	A business owned by one person
Unrealised gain	A surplus arising after the revaluation of an asset such as land, where the asset itself is not sold. It is treated as a capital reserve

SELF-CHECK QUESTIONS

1 plc stands for:
 a Private limited company
 b Public liability company
 c Public limited company
 d Public limited corporation
2 Which of the following is a disadvantage of trading as a partnership?
 a Access to other people's expertise and finance
 b Sharing of losses
 c Privacy of financial results
 d Partners usually have unlimited liability for partnership debts
3 Share capital is:
 a The way in which capital is divided at the end of each year
 b The way in which partners decide to divide profits and losses
 c Another name for London's stock exchange
 d The way in which the ownership of a limited company is divided
4 Payments to directors would be shown in the financial statements as:
 a An expense in the profit and loss account
 b An appropriation of profit
 c A current asset
 d Part of share capital
5 Another name for 'current liabilities' in a company balance sheet is:
 a Creditors due for payment within six months
 b Creditors due for payment within one year
 c Creditors who are overdue
 d Creditors due for payment after more than one year

6 **A debenture is:**

   a **Another name for 'share capital'**

   b **A loan usually secured on a company's assets**

   c **A loan convertible into shares at some future time**

   d **The person who manages a company on behalf of the shareholders**

7 **If a new company has issued 200,000 ordinary shares of 20p nominal value at a price of £2, what will be the entries in the Share Capital and Share Premium accounts?**

   a **Share Capital £40,000, Share Premium £360,000**

   b **Share Capital £40,000, Share Premium £400,000**

   c **Share Capital £400,000, Share Premium £360,000**

   d **Share Capital £400,000, Share Premium £40,000**

8 **What is a major difference between a revenue reserve and a capital reserve?**

   a **Capital reserves can be used to pay a dividend but revenue reserves cannot**

   b **Capital reserves can be used to pay company bills, but revenue reserves cannot**

   c **Capital reserves cannot be used to pay a dividend but revenue reserves can**

   d **Capital reserves all come from the profit and loss account, revenue reserves all come from the shareholders**

9 **If a '5 for 3' rights issue is made at £1.90 per share, how much would a shareholder who owns 15,000 shares pay to the company to buy all the shares he is entitled to?**

   a **£28,500**

   b **£17,100**

   c **£47,500**

   d **£5,700**

10 **If a '3 for 2' bonus issue is made to a shareholder who originally paid £2 per share for 10,000 shares, how much would the shareholder pay for the bonus shares if the current market value is £4 per share?**

   a **£30,000**

   b **£60,000**

   c **£45,000**

   d **Nothing – the shares are free**

Further questions can be found on the accompanying website (www.booksites.net/black).

SELF-STUDY QUESTIONS

(Answers in Appendix 2)

Question 7.1

'A partnership is just a collection of sole traders'. Discuss this statement.

Question 7.2

Disraeli and Gladstone are partners, sharing profits and losses in the ratio 2:1. They have agreed that Disraeli should receive a salary of £9,000 and that interest on both partners' opening capital of 5% p.a. should be allowed. Disraeli's opening capital was £20,000, whilst Gladstone's was £15,000. During the year ended 31 December 2000, Disraeli had drawings of £18,000 and Gladstone drew £14,000. Net profit for the year was £40,000. No partnership current accounts were maintained, and no interest was charged on drawings.

Show the relevant extracts from the partnership profit and loss account for the year (appropriation section) and its balance sheet at the year-end.

Question 7.3

'After the ruinous departure of Mr Lane my father had taken into partnership another man, who had been a member of Lane and Newby's since its inception. Unfortunately, although the new partner was morally blameless, he was far less competent than his predecessor and the business suffered even more. Eventually death had removed him too and my father was forced to turn the business into a Limited Company.

'It seems probable that no one ever succeeded in explaining to my father what the formation of a Limited Liability Company entailed. I think he believed that it was a polite fiction that divested him of the onus of liability and at the same time allowed him to be a partnership without a partner' (from *Something Wholesale, My Life and Times in the Rag Trade* by Eric Newby)

a Using the information in the above extract, identify two problems associated with partnerships.
b To what extent is the author correct in asserting that a limited liability company is 'a polite fiction that divested him of the onus of liability and at the same time allowed him to be a partnership without a partner'?
c Write a brief report (200 words maximum) explaining to the author's father the main advantages and disadvantages of forming a limited liability company.

Question 7.4

'The biggest confidence trick of all time has nothing to do with social-security fraud, insider dealing or any of the exotic forms of computer-based racketeering beloved of magazine and television journalists short of a good story. Two little words sum up the swindle of the century – limited liability.

'This cunning wheeze, dreamed up more than a century ago, is a bigger rip-off than the enclosure movement, colonisation and industrialisation rolled into one. It allows all the benefits of so-called risk-taking to flow to the owners of capital whilst passing off on to the community at large all the costs.

'When a giant concern fails, a chain reaction can bankrupt smaller and smaller units down the economic ladder right to the individual worker. Worse, the liquidation of capital value inevitably pushes up insurance and borrowing costs for everybody else. The innocent pay, the guilty – sorry, the "entrepreneurs" – walk free. No such protection is available to the hapless ex-employee of the aforementioned failed giant concern.' (Dan Atkinson, *The Guardian*, 1 September 1997)

The author has taken an extreme view on the nature of limited liability, yet what he describes as a 'confidence trick', society appears to accept. To what extent do you think he is justified in his comments?

Question 7.5

From the following trial balance of Morse Ltd, prepare a detailed profit and loss account for the year ended 31 December 2000:

	Dr	Cr
	£	£
Directors' remuneration	59,200	
Wages of salesforce	65,230	
Office salaries	34,900	
Advertising and website charges	15,300	
Interest	2,502	
Carriage out	632	
Office expenses	33,897	
Sales		462,600
Opening stock at 1 January 2000	14,900	
Purchases	140,800	
Share capital (50p nominal shares)		25,000
Share premium account		15,000
Bad debts written off	750	
Profit and loss account as at 1 January 2000		12,600
Delivery vehicles, cost as at 1 January 2000	143,600	
Depreciation of delivery vehicles at 1 January 2000		27,800
Trade debtors	64,100	
Trade creditors		32,711
Debenture (repayable in 2012)		10,000
Provision for doubtful debts		1,600
Bank balance	11,500	
	587,311	587,311

Notes:
1 Closing stock at 31 December 2000 was £17,650.
2 Depreciation on delivery vehicles is chargeable at 30% on the reducing balance basis.
3 £800 was owing for office expenses and £160 had been prepaid for website charges at 31 December 2000.
4 The provision for doubtful debts was to be decreased by £600.
5 Taxation amounting to £24,000 is to be provided for.
6 The company is proposing a dividend of 10p per share.

Question 7.6
A limited company's share capital and reserves in its balance sheet were as follows:

	£	£
Capital and reserves		
Called-up share capital (£1 shares)		100,000
Share premium account	75,000	
Asset revaluation reserve	140,000	
Profit and loss account	330,000	
		545,000
		645,000

a To what extent is it true to say that reserves equal cash?
b Explain the difference between a revenue reserve and a capital reserve and give one example of each from the above balance sheet.

c What is a share premium? If the company had only ever made one issue of shares, what price was each share sold for?

d Explain why an asset revaluation reserve is created. What other balance sheet item, not listed above, would have been affected when this reserve was created?

e Explain a way in which the company could return reserves to shareholders without paying cash to them.

f If the company, immediately after extracting the above balance sheet, made a rights issue on a '3 for 2' basis at £2.40 per share, what effect would that have on the balance sheet, assuming that all shareholders took up their rights?

Further questions can be found on the accompanying website (www.booksites. net/black).

CASE STUDY

Marvin and Chiquita make Machiq, but Esmeralda makes trouble

Marvin and Chiquita (see previous case studies) have been working very successfully together, so on 1 July 2002, the start of Marvin's third year in business, they decided to form a partnership, to be called Machiq & Co., sharing profits or losses in the ratio Marvin 3/5 and Chiquita 2/5. All of Marvin's assets and liabilities are transferred to the partnership at their book values on 30 June 2002. This totals £17,570, which is credited to Marvin's capital account. Chiquita pays in a cheque for £10,000 as her capital. No payment was required for the 'goodwill' built up by Marvin in the previous two years.

They agree that no interest should be charged on their drawings or credited on their capital balances. No salaries are to be paid to either partner. During a successful year together the partnership earned a net profit of £58,800. Marvin had drawings of £32,850 and Chiquita drew £18,520.

a Show the relevant extracts from the partnership profit and loss account for the year ended 30 June 2003 (appropriation section) and its balance sheet at that date. Assume that no partnership current accounts are opened.

On 30 June 2003, the partners received the following letter from Esmeralda, Marvin's former assistant:

'Dear Marvin
My seven brothers and sisters and I have consulted legal advice and are going to sue you for £10 million as compensation for wrongful dismissal when you sacked us two years ago. We would have written sooner but it has taken us this long to recover from the shock of losing our jobs.
Hope you are keeping well.
Esmeralda'

Marvin thinks (incorrectly!) that the only protection from this claim is to immediately form a limited company, so Machiq & Co. became Machiq Limited with effect from 1 July 2003. The company took over all the assets and liabilities of Machiq & Co. at their book values, and had a share capital of 14,000 ordinary shares of £1 each. The shares, which were issued at a premium, were allocated to Marvin and Chiquita in the same proportions as their closing capital balances in the partnership. During the year ended 30 June 2004, Machiq Limited made a net profit before taxation of £92,000. Taxation was to be provided on this amount at 20%, and a dividend of

£2.25 per share was declared. Nothing further was heard from Esmeralda or her family during the year, although there were rumours that she had rejoined her former employer, Kaboosh Limited.

b Show Machiq Limited's profit and loss account (appropriation section only) for the year ended 30 June 2004, and the 'Capital and Reserves' section of the balance sheet as at that date.

(Answers in Appendix 3)

References

The official web site for Companies House:
http://www.companies-house.gov.uk/
Take a complete break from accounting, and learn a few magic tricks at:
http://www.montysmagic.com/

Incomplete records and club accounts

8.1 Introduction

This chapter focuses on two separate areas, incomplete records and club accounts.

- ➤ *Incomplete records* shows how the reliability of an organisation's accounting statements is undermined because less than a full double-entry system is in operation.
- ➤ *Club accounts* sets out the special accounting needs of societies and associations, whose main activities are neither trading nor profit-making, but the provision of, for example, social, sporting or cultural activities for their members. Many such organisations have excellent financial systems in place, but occasionally a lack of accounting expertise amongst members may result in only very basic financial statements being prepared.

8.2 What are 'incomplete records'?

An organisation which does not use a full double-entry system is described as having 'incomplete records'. There are varying levels of incompleteness, ranging from a total absence of written records through to a practical invoice-based system which provides details of debtors, creditors and cash balances but little else.

There might be various reasons why a full accounting system is not maintained, including:

- ➤ A calamity has happened such as a fire, or a virus has wiped out computer records.
- ➤ A deliberate attempt has been made to evade taxation by keeping no written records. All transactions are made in cash.

> Lack of expertise has restricted the records kept to a list of invoices issued and received and bank statements. Some of the documents may be missing, and a professional accountant is employed to prepare annual financial summaries.

ACTIVITY **8.1**

Rodney is a second-hand car dealer. The only record he keeps is a list of purchases and sales of cars, which is written in pencil on the wall above his telephone. On hearing of a visit by the tax authorities, he hastily arranges for his office to be repainted to conceal the information.

What problems may result from Rodney's actions?

Answer

Your answer should include:

> The taxation authorities are likely to take a dim view of the events and make an estimated punitive assessment of taxation owing.
> Rodney has no control over expenses and is unable to compare one period with another.
> It is difficult to deal with queries from customers or suppliers relating to car values.
> No continual record is made of assets, liabilities and owner's capital.
> Rodney may not know how much profit or loss has been made.
> The cost of employing an accountant to unravel the financial puzzle may outweigh any perceived savings.

Note that limited companies (see Chapter 7) are required by legislation to keep proper accounting records and it is the duty of the company's directors to ensure that an adequate system is in place.

DID YOU KNOW?

If businesses have a turnover (total sales) which exceeds a set limit (approximately £50,000 p.a.) they have to register for Value Added Tax in the UK. This means that they have to keep accurate records of sales and purchases and may be subject to periodic inspection visits from HM Customs and Excise officials.

8.3 Statement of affairs

Where no written records have been maintained, the first step towards establishing the financial position is to create a 'statement of affairs' at the start of the period. This is effectively an opening balance sheet showing all the assets and liabilities of the business, though some detective work may be necessary to establish with any accuracy what assets and liabilities the owner had at that date. Using the accounting equation (see Chapter 1), the net assets total equals the owner's capital balance. A similar statement is prepared at the close of the period, and the closing capital is compared with the opening. After adjusting for owner's drawings and any capital introduced or withdrawn during the period, the difference between the two capital figures equals the profit or loss for the period.

ACTIVITY **8.2**
··············

Rodney (see Activity 8.1) asks an accountant, Cuthbert, to calculate his profit or loss for the year ended 31 December 2000. Cuthbert interviews Rodney and establishes the following facts:

➤ The premises are rented.
➤ At the start of the year, Rodney owned cars for resale which had cost £15,000, a car which he kept for business use worth £8,000, an office desk and chair which were worth £300, and he had a cash balance of £4,000 which he kept in his back pocket. He owed £3,000 to a car auction company and £600 for newspaper advertisements.
➤ At the end of the year, Rodney had cars for resale which had cost £18,000, the car which he kept for business use was now worth £6,000, the office desk and chair were worth £200 and he had a cash balance of £1,000. He was owed £2,000 by a customer and had a creditor of £500 for one car.
➤ During the year he withdrew £12,000 for personal use. He won £5,000 on a lottery, which he paid in to the business.

By drawing up Statements of Affairs at the start and end of 2000, calculate Rodney's profit or loss for the year.

Answer

(A columnar presentation has been used to avoid the need to repeat information. It would be perfectly acceptable to draw up two separate Statements at the start and end of the year.)

Rodney's Statement of Affairs at the start and end of 2000

	1 January 2000		31 December 2000	
	£	£	£	£
Fixed assets				
Motor vehicle	8,000		6,000	
Fixtures	300		200	
		8,300		6,200
Current assets				
Stock	15,000		18,000	
Debtors	–		2,000	
Cash	4,000		1,000	
	19,000		21,000	
Less **Current liabilities**				
Creditors	(3,600)		(500)	
Net current assets		15,400		20,500
Total net assets		23,700		26,700
Capital		23,700		26,700

Calculation of the trading result for the year ended 31 December 2000

	£
Opening capital (see opening Statement of Affairs)	23,700
Add Cash introduced	5,000
	28,700
Less Drawings	(12,000)
Adjusted capital balance	16,700
Closing capital (see closing Statement of Affairs)	26,700
Increase in net worth (i.e. profit)	10,000

PAUSE FOR THOUGHT

Did you wonder why you were told that Rodney's premises were rented?
We knew that Rodney had 'his office repainted' (Activity 8.1), so we needed to know whether or not he owned the premises. If he had owned them, a value would have been required for the Statement of Affairs.

8.4 Use of control accounts to deduce information

Statements of affairs will be used only when an organisation's records are minimal. If sufficient information is available there is no reason why full financial statements should not be prepared even if a full double-entry system is lacking. Minimum information required is:

➤ Debtors and creditors at the start and end of the period
➤ Accruals and prepayments at the start and end of the period
➤ Details of cash paid and received
➤ Fixed and current asset valuations and details of liabilities other than creditors (e.g. loans).

ACTIVITY 8.3

For the trading account, the key is the preparation of control accounts, using balancing figures to give the total sales and purchases figures. On the advice of Cuthbert, Rodney (see Activities 8.1 and 8.2) turns over a new leaf in the year ended 31 December 2001, and keeps some written records of cash payments and receipts during the year. He also gives the following information:

➤ Opening balances, 1 January 2001 (from Activity 2's 31 December 2000 figures): Fixed assets £6,200 (Motor vehicle £6,000, Fixtures £200), Current assets £21,000 (Stock £18,000, Debtors £2,000, Cash £1,000), Trade creditors £500
➤ Closing balances, 31 December 2001: Fixed assets £5,100 (Motor vehicle £5,000, Fixtures £100), Current assets £19,000 (Stock £14,000, Debtors £3,000, Cash £2,000), Trade creditors £4,000
➤ Cash paid for cars for resale £45,020, for office expenses £7,000
➤ Cash received from customers for car sales £84,000
➤ Discount allowed for prompt payment by a customer £250
➤ Discount received for prompt payment for a car £80
➤ Bad debt written off £850
➤ Drawings for the year £30,980
➤ There were neither accruals nor prepayments at the start or end of the year.

Prepare financial statements for Rodney for the year ended 31 December 2001.

Answer

(The starting point is to create an opening Statement of Affairs. We did this in Activity 8.2.) The next step is to produce control accounts (see Chapter 3), as follows:

Sales Control Account

	£		£
Opening debtors	2,000	Cash received	84,000
Sales (balancing figure)	86,100	Discounts allowed	250
		Bad debt written off	850
		Closing debtors	3,000
	88,100		88,100

Purchases Control Account

	£		£
Cash paid for cars for resale	45,020	Opening creditors	500
Discount received	80	Purchases (balancing figure)	48,600
Closing creditors	4,000		
	49,100		49,100

The profit and loss account and balance sheet can then be prepared:

Rodney's Profit and loss account for the year ended 31 December 2001

	£	£
Sales		86,100
Less Cost of goods sold		
Opening stock	18,000	
Purchases	48,600	
	66,600	
Less Closing stock	(14,000)	
		(52,600)
Gross profit		33,500
Add Discounts received		80
		33,580
Less Expenses		
Office expenses	7,000	
Bad debt written off	850	
Discounts allowed	250	
Depreciation (6,000 + 200) – (5,000 + 100)	1,100	
		(9,200)
Net profit		24,380

Balance sheet as at 31 December 2001

	£	£
Fixed assets		
Motor vehicle	5,000	
Fixtures	100	
		5,100
Current assets		
Stock	14,000	
Debtors	3,000	
Cash	2,000	
c/f	19,000	5,100

	b/f	19,000	5,100
Less **Current liabilities**			
Creditors		(4,000)	
Net current assets			15,000
Total net assets			20,100
Capital			
Opening balance, 1 January 2000		26,700	
Add Net profit		24,380	
		51,080	
Less Drawings		(30,980)	
Closing balance, 31 December 2001			20,100

8.5 Club accounts
••••••••••••••••••••••••

Groups of individuals often form clubs or associations to pursue common aims and interests. For example, you might be a member of a golf club, music society or students' union society. All of these are known as 'not-for-profit' organisations as their principal aims relate to the provision of services or activities for members rather than the generation of a profit for owners. We shall use the word 'club' when referring to all of these 'not-for-profit' organisations.

DID YOU KNOW?
Charities are 'not-for-profit' organisations and are subject to special accounting rules contained within the Charities Act 1993. These are outside the scope of this book.

Although most clubs will have a member who acts as a treasurer, it often happens that the individual appointed will have few or no accounting skills. Often their main role is to act as a cashier, taking responsibility for collecting and banking money and paying bills as they fall due. The only record kept might be a basic cash book. Because of this, periodic financial statements may be in the form of a simple summary of the cash book, known as a Receipts and Payments Account.

PAUSE FOR THOUGHT *The author was once treasurer of a Students' Union and had to present a financial report at its Annual General Meeting. Knowing the level of interest that students traditionally have in accountancy matters, he produced overhead slides of the financial statements and deliberately projected them on to a screen so out of focus that they were illegible. He then asked if anyone wanted to ask any questions on the accounts. Nobody did!*

8.5.1 Receipts and Payments Account

If only very simple club accounts can be prepared, then a Receipts and Payments Account represents the bare minimum which is acceptable as a financial statement. It summarises cash and bank transactions for a period, but *fails* to show:

➤ the club's assets (other than any bought during the period and the cash and bank balances),
➤ the club's liabilities,

➤ how the club's income compared with its expenditure,
➤ depreciation,
➤ the accumulated total of the club's wealth.

ACTIVITY **8.4**
....

Rodney (see previous activities) is treasurer of the Used Car Dealers' Cultural Association (UCDCA), which organises social events for car dealers. During the year ended 31 December 2002, the club's bank statements showed the following information:

UCDCA in account with Grimley's Bank plc 2002		DR £	CR £	BAL £
Jan 1	Opening balance			800CR
Jan 31	Subscriptions		1,200	2,000CR
Feb 1	Visit to Glyndebourne Opera: Cheque for coach travel	400		1,600CR
Feb 1	Opera tickets bought	600		1,000CR
Feb 16	Sales of opera tickets to members		1,350	2,350CR
May 1	Byte plc: Computer to keep club records	2,000		350CR
May 9	Honorarium to club secretary	100		250CR
Oct 12	Visit to British Museum: Cheque for coach travel	150		100CR
Oct 18	Tickets for British Museum coach trip sold to members		280	380CR
Dec 20	Bar sales: Christmas party		900	1280CR
Dec 22	The Temperance Brewery plc	650		630CR

DID YOU KNOW?
An honorarium is a 'gift' of cash given to a club official in recognition of the time he or she spends on club administration.

Prepare a Receipts and Payments Account for the year ending 31 December 2002.

Answer

**The Used Car Dealers' Cultural Association
Receipts and Payments Account
for the year ended 31 December 2002**

	£	£
Opening bank balance, 1 January 2002		800
Add **Receipts:**		
Subscriptions	1,200	
Ticket sales: Glyndebourne Opera visit	1,350	
British Museum visit	280	
Bar sales (Christmas party)	900	
		3,730
	c/f	4,530

		b/f	4,530
Less Payments:			
Coach travel: Glyndebourne Opera visit	400		
British Museum visit	150		
Opera tickets purchased	600		
Computer	2,000		
Honorarium to club secretary	100		
Drinks from brewery	650		
			(3,900)
Closing bank balance, 31 December 2002			630

8.5.2 Income and Expenditure Account

The Receipts and Payments Account is an imperfect reporting tool, as although it gives members a summarised view of the cash and bank transactions for the period it does not follow the accruals concept nor any other accounting convention. As a result, the club's financial position cannot be ascertained, which may result in mismanagement of its affairs. Assets might be sold without members' knowledge or debts amassed without proper financial provision being made to meet them.

Although a Receipts and Payments Account might be sufficient where there is only a handful of members and very few financial complications, more sophisticated control must be exercised in other circumstances. This is achieved by producing an Income and Expenditure Account and Balance Sheet which conform to all normal accounting principles. Within these statements there are a number of features which tend to be unique to clubs:

➤ For 'not-for-profit' organisations, the words 'profit' and 'loss' are often replaced by 'surplus' and 'deficit'.

➤ Income often comes from ad hoc activities such as social events, raffles, jumble sales and bar sales. Where possible, income from such activities is matched to the relevant expenditure. For example, a 'bar account' can be included (the equivalent of a trading account) to let members see the bar's surplus or deficit for the period.

➤ The accruals concept (see Chapter 1) must be applied to membership subscriptions.

➤ The balance sheet does not show a capital balance. The equivalent item is termed an 'accumulated fund' which increases or decreases by the surpluses or deficits for the period. Any donations made to the club will also increase the fund. There is no equivalent to 'owner's drawings'.

ACTIVITY 8.5

Rodney (see Activity 8.4) has decided that he should produce an Income and Expenditure Account for the UCDCA for the year ended 31 December 2002. He obtains the following further information:

➤ Assets at 1 January 2002 (in addition to the bank balance) were a photocopier valued at £500 and bar stock which had cost £600. Membership subscriptions owing for 2001 totalled £120.

➤ Liabilities at 1 January 2002 were: Creditors: Temperance Brewery plc £400 and Photocopier Repairs Limited £180. Prepaid membership subscriptions for 2002 paid in 2001 totalled £90.

➤ In January 2002, all the bar stock owned at the start of the year was sold at a club party. The cash takings of £1,050 were used to pay the two creditors, who each allowed 10% cash discount. The balance of cash was used to buy stationery for the club.

➤ At the end of the year, in addition to the bank balance, there was a stock of stationery valued at £100, and subscriptions owing for 2002 totalled £180. £70 subscriptions by members for 2003 had been paid in advance. Closing bar stock was valued at £500 and it was estimated that both the photocopier and computer had depreciated by 25%. An advertisement placed in a local newspaper at a cost of £120 to recruit new members was owing.

Prepare the Income and Expenditure Account for the year ended 31 December 2002 and a Balance Sheet as at that date.

Answer

The Used Car Dealers' Cultural Association
Income and Expenditure Account
for the year ended 31 December 2002

	£	£
Income		
Bar Account:		
Sales of drinks (1,050 + 900)		1,950
Less Cost of drinks sold		
Opening stock	600	
Purchases	650	
	1,250	
Less Closing stock	(500)	
		(750)
Surplus on bar		1,200
Other income:		
Membership subscriptions (see Working 1)		1,280
Surplus on visit to Glyndebourne Opera [1,350 – (400 + 600)]		350
Surplus on visit to British Museum (280 – 150)		130
Discount received [10% × (400 + 180)]		58
Total income		3,018
***Less* Expenditure**		
Honorarium to club secretary	100	
Stationery (see Working 2)	428	
Advertisement	120	
Depreciation: computer (25% × £2,000)	500	
Depreciation: photocopier (25% × £500)	125	
		(1,273)
Surplus of income over expenditure		1,745

Balance sheet as at 31 December 2002

	£	£	£
Fixed assets			
Computer		2,000	
Less depreciation		(500)	
			1,500
Photocopier		500	
Less depreciation		(125)	
			375
			1,875
Current assets			
Bar stock		500	
Stationery stock		100	
Subscriptions owing		180	
Bank		630	
		1,410	
***Less* Current liabilities**			
Creditors	120		
Subscriptions paid in advance	70		
		(190)	
Net current assets			1,220
Total net assets			3,095
Accumulated fund			
Opening balance, 1 January 2002 (see Working 3)		1,350	
Add Surplus of income over expenditure		1,745	
Closing balance, 31 December 2002			3,095

PAUSE FOR THOUGHT *All the usual accounting conventions have been followed in preparing the Income and Expenditure Account and Balance Sheet. Only some of the terminology used may be unfamiliar to you. If you are a member of a club or association, obtain a copy of its last annual report and see the extent to which the financial statements follow 'best practice'.*

Workings

1

Subscriptions (2002)

	£		£
Opening unpaid subscriptions re 2001	120	Opening subscriptions paid in advance re 2002	90
Income and expenditure account (balancing figure)	1,280	Subscriptions received, as per bank account	1,200
Closing subscriptions paid in advance re 2003	70	Closing unpaid subscriptions re 2002	180
	1,470		1,470

2 Stationery

	£	£
Bar stock sold for cash, January		1,050
Less payments to creditors:		
Temperance Brewery plc	400	
Photocopier Repairs Limited	180	
	580	
Less 10% cash discount	(58)	
		(522)
Stationery bought		528
Less Closing stock of stationery		(100)
Expense for the year		428

This working is needed because we need to calculate how much cash was used from the bar's takings to buy stationery. £528 was paid for stationery, but of this, £100 was still in stock, leaving £428 as the stationery used in the year.

3 Accumulated fund at start of 2002

	£	£
Assets		
Photocopier		500
Bar stock		600
Subscriptions owing		120
Bank balance		800
		2,020
Less **Liabilities**		
Subscriptions paid in advance	90	
Creditors (400 + 180)	580	
		(670)
Net assets		1,350

8.6 Glossary

Accumulated fund	Shown in the balance sheet of a not-for-profit organisation, it represents the net worth (assets – liabilities) of the organisation at the start or end of the financial period. It is broadly equivalent to 'capital'
Balancing figure	A figure inserted into an account to make each side have the same total
Control accounts	Accounts which summarise information, particularly purchases and sales, to either confirm the accuracy of underlying ledger accounts or calculate required totals as 'balancing figures' where records are incomplete
Honorarium	A gift given by a not-for-profit organisation to an office holder in that organisation in recognition of services rendered

Income and Expenditure Account	The equivalent of a trading and profit and loss account produced for a not-for-profit organisation
Incomplete records	Any method of recording the financial transactions of an organisation which does not use a full double-entry system
Not-for-profit organisation	An organisation which does not exist for the creation of profit. It may be a club or association which exists to provide a service or activities for its members
Receipts and Payments Account	A simple financial statement created by summarising cash and bank records for a period
Statement of Affairs	Where records are incomplete, this is effectively a balance sheet prepared to show all the assets and liabilities of the business at the start and/or end of a financial period

SELF-CHECK QUESTIONS

1 Accounting records are referred to as 'incomplete' when
   a A supplier has forgotten to send an invoice to a business
   b A business has paid only some of its creditors
   c Less than a full double-entry system is in operation
   d A trial balance fails to balance

2 If a trader keeps poor accounting records, a consequence might be
   a Higher accountants' fees
   b Lower accountants' fees
   c Lower tax to pay
   d Easier to deal with customers' queries

3 A business has Opening creditors £22,000, Cheques paid to suppliers £39,000, Discount received £400 and Closing creditors £16,000. What is the Purchases' figure for the period?
   a £33,400
   b £45,400
   c £32,600
   d £1,400

4 A 'not-for-profit' organisation is
   a A business that always makes a loss
   b A business that has a moral objection to profit-making
   c An organisation that provides services or activities for its members
   d An inefficient organisation

5 A Receipts and Payments Account is
   a A copy of an organisation's bank statements
   b Another name for a balance sheet
   c Another name for an Income and Expenditure Account
   d A summary of cash and bank transactions

6 Limited companies should not have incomplete records because:
   a The law requires companies to keep proper accounting records
   b Directors must be qualified accountants
   c Limited companies are wealthy enough to employ accountants
   d All limited companies are registered for Value Added Tax

7 **An accumulated fund of an organisation is the same as:**
   a The bank balance of the organisation
   b The profit of the organisation
   c The net worth of the organisation
   d The assets of the organisation

8 **From the following information, what figure for 'subscriptions' would be shown in a club's income and expenditure account for the year 2002?**
   ➤   Balances at 1 January 2001: Owing re 2001 £190, Prepaid re 2002 £170
   ➤   Balances at 31 December 2001: Owing re 2002 £220, Prepaid re 2003 £60
   ➤   Subscriptions received during 2002: £3,260
   a £3,440
   b £3,080
   c £3,120
   d £3,400

9 **An honorarium is:**
   a A room in the clubhouse where sporting trophies are displayed
   b A payment made to a club official in recognition of services to the club
   c A payment made by a club member for a life membership
   d A payment made to a club member on being made an honorary member of the club

10 **A subscription paid in advance by a member for the following year would be shown in the club's financial summaries for the current year as:**
   a A current asset in the balance sheet
   b A current liability in the balance sheet
   c Subscriptions in the income and expenditure account
   d A fixed asset in the balance sheet

Further questions can be found on the accompanying website (www.booksites. net/black).

SELF-STUDY QUESTIONS

(Answers in Appendix 2)

Question 8.1

Delia Trelawney runs a music shop, known as 'Soul Trading'. She doesn't have a full bookkeeping system, but has given you the following information relating to the year ended 31 May 2003:

(i)   Summarised bank account information:

	£		£
Cash banked	35,500	Opening balance b/f	1,740
		Rent and rates	1,500
		Sundry expenses	603
		Telephone and electricity	871
		Shop fittings	6,402
		Paid to suppliers	10,854
		Drawings	6,670
		Advertising	520
		Closing balance c/f	6,340
	35,500		35,500

(ii)   All sales were for cash.
(iii)   Trade creditors at 31 May 2002 were £2,105, and at 31 May 2003 were £6,320.

(iv) The gross profit for the year was 55% of sales.

(v) Closing stock was valued at £3,045.

(vi) A van with a book value of £3,480 on 31 May 2002 was sold for £3,000 on 1 June 2002. This was paid into the business bank account. No replacement van was purchased.

(vii) All takings from customers were banked with the exception of £720 which was used by Delia to pay for a holiday, and 50 weeks' wages at £120 per week paid to a shop assistant.

(viii) £140 was owing to the telephone company at the start of the year, and £203 was owing to the telephone company at the end of the year.

(ix) Shop fittings owned at 31 May 2002 had cost £7,900 and had been depreciated for a full two years at 30% on the reducing balance basis. A full year's depreciation is charged in the year of purchase, regardless of the purchase date.

a Prepare a profit and loss account for the year ended 31 May 2003, and a balance sheet as at that date.

b Delia needs advice on how she can improve her system for keeping track of her creditors. Currently she keeps all invoices in a box, and pays bills only when she gets a phone call from suppliers demanding payment. Suggest two ways in which she can keep better control over her creditors' invoices.

Question 8.2

Tilly Snowdon has operated a shop selling specialist mountaineering equipment for several years, but has never maintained full bookkeeping records. An analysis of her bank records for the year ended 31 December 2002 was as follows:

	£		£
Opening balance	2,800	Purchase of goods	66,200
Cash banked	86,900	New shop fittings	3,000
Closing balance	6,670	Rent and rates	4,600
		Light and heat	3,900
		New van (balance of purchase price)	4,000
		Van running expenses	1,400
		Wages to shop assistants	9,070
		Advertising	840
		Insurance	560
		Sundry expenses	2,800
	96,370		96,370

Details of Tilly's assets and liabilities at the start and end of the year are:

	1 January 2002	31 December 2002
	£	£
Debtors	600	850
Creditors	2,400	3,300
Insurance prepaid	80	120
Advertising accrued	140	120
Stocks at cost	16,800	23,700
Van (net book value)	2,400	?
Shop fittings (cost)	1,500	?
Depreciation on shop fittings	450	?

Notes:

1 Tilly had banked all takings, with the exception of personal drawings of £200 per week for 50 weeks, and £500 which she had used to pay for a holiday.
2 Closing debtors included an amount of £100 which had been outstanding for over six months. It has now been decided to write it off as a bad debt.
3 The van owned on 1 January 2002 was traded in for £2,000 on a part exchange deal to purchase a new one.
4 Depreciation policy is to provide a full year's depreciation in the year of purchase but none in the year of sale. Depreciation rates are 25% p.a. straight line on vans and 30% p.a. reducing balance on shop fittings. No shop fittings had been sold during the year.

Prepare a profit and loss account for Tilly Snowdon for the year ended 31 December 2002 and a balance sheet as that date.

Question 8.3

The treasurer of the Razmatazz Sports and Social Club prepared the following Receipts and Payments Account for the year ended 31 December 2003:

	£	£
Opening bank balance, 1 January 2003		1,470
Add Receipts		
Subscriptions re 2002	620	
re 2003	14,080	
Competition fees	2,590	
Proceeds from sale of van (1 January 2003)	1,000	
Sales of dance tickets	1,778	
		20,068
		21,538
Less Payments		
Wages	8,450	
Printing and advertising	2,070	
Repairs to sports equipment	800	
Competition prizes	2,200	
Dance expenses	2,060	
Purchase of new van (1 January 2003)	6,300	
Motor expenses	1,200	
Sundry expenses	1,180	
		(24,260)
Bank overdraft at 31 December 2003		(2,722)

It was felt by many members that this information was inadequate to give a full picture of the club's financial situation, and the treasurer subsequently produced the following additional information:

1 The assets and liabilities at the start and end of 2003 were:

	1 January £	31 December £
Subscriptions due from members	1,440	1,620
Subscriptions received in advance	–	720
Stock of competition prizes	850	450
Value of computer (cost £2,000)	1,600	1,400
Value of sports equipment (cost £8,000)	6,200	5,400
Van	(see below)	(see below)

2 The van sold during the year had originally cost £4,000 in 2001 and had been depreciated at 25% p.a. on the reducing balance method for exactly two years up to the date of sale. The new van is to be depreciated on the same basis as the previous one.

Prepare an income and expenditure account for the year ended 31 December 2003 and a balance sheet as at that date.

Question 8.4

The treasurer of the Vim and Vigour Sports and Social Club presented the following Receipts and Payments Account for the year ended 31 December 2001:

	£	£
Opening bank balance, 1 January 2001		2,400
Add Receipts		
Subscriptions re 2000	1,800	
re 2001	25,200	
Competition fees	3,150	
Proceeds from sale of sports equipment	2,100	
Sales of dance tickets	2,460	
		34,710
		37,110
Less Payments		
Refund of subscription (re 2000) overpaid	60	
Wages of sports staff	29,700	
Printing and advertising	2,250	
Repairs to sports equipment	1,500	
Competition prizes	1,800	
Dance expenses	1,350	
Sports equipment purchased	10,800	
Sundry expenses	2,460	
		(49,920)
Bank overdraft at 31 December 2001		(12,810)

At the club AGM, several members criticised the treasurer for failing to provide full financial information. As a result, an accountant was appointed to present an income and expenditure account and balance sheet to a special meeting of members.

The accountant compiled the following additional information.

(1) The assets and liabilities at the start and end of 2001 were:

	1 January	*31 December*
	£	£
Subscriptions due from members	1,800	1,560
Subscriptions received in advance	840	–
Stock of competition prizes	1,050	600
Value of photocopier (cost £6,000)	4,200	3,600
Sports equipment (depreciated value)	12,000	15,000
Sports equipment (cost)	45,000	25,800

(ii) Sports equipment with a net book value of £6,000 on 1 January 2001 was sold during the year. The equipment had been owned for exactly four years prior to its sale, and had been depreciated on the straight line basis with an estimated life of five years.

(iii) Subscription rates are being increased from 1 January 2002 to £120 per annum compared to the existing level of £80 per annum.

a Prepare an income and expenditure account for the year ended 31 December 2001 and a balance sheet as at that date.

b Calculate the cash due to be received from subscriptions during 2002, on the assumptions that 20% of the existing membership resign during the year without paying their subscriptions and 40 new members are recruited. Assume that all members will have paid their subscriptions by the year-end.

Further questions can be found on the accompanying website (www.booksites. net/black).

CASE STUDY

The treasurer of the Abracadabra Club does a vanishing trick

After a busy day, Marvin and Chiquita (see previous case studies) liked nothing better than to relax at the Abracadabra Club, where magicians meet to discuss the tricks of their trade over a drink. The honorary treasurer, Milton Bezzler, was due to present the club's financial statements for the year ended 31 December 2003 at the Annual General Meeting of the club, to be held on 1 January 2004. On the night before the AGM, the club's chairman received a postcard from Argentina with the following message:

'I've vanished with the club's funds – how about that for a magic trick! Good-bye for ever, Milton'

Chiquita was immediately asked by the club's committee to investigate how much Milton had stolen. She set to work, and found the following copy of the club's balance sheet at 31 December 2002:

	£	£
Fixed asset		
Computer (bought 1 January 2001), at net book value		1,000
Current assets		
Stock of drinks	200	
Debtors (100 Club subscriptions)	360	
Balance at bank:		
General account	2,099	
'100 Club' account	711	
	3,370	
Less **Current liabilities**		
Creditor (100 Club prizes owed)	(2,000)	
Net current assets		1,370
Total net assets		2,370
Accumulated fund		
Balance brought forward, 1 January 2002		3,652
Less Excess of expenditure over income for 2002		(1,282)
		2,370

Chiquita was able to prepare a summary of the club's bank statements for the year ended 31 December 2003 as follows. (Note that she had not had sufficient time to calculate the 100 Club receipts.)

Receipts	£
100 Club subscriptions	?
Dance ticket sales	1,267
Drinks sold at dance	265
Bank interest	120
Computer (sale proceeds)	700

Payments	£
100 Club prizes (re 2002)	2,000
100 Club prizes (re 2003)	2,000
Dance band's fees	866
New computer	1,000
Drinks purchased	165
Sundries	87

Notes:

1 The '100 Club' is a money-raising venture, with the aim of recruiting 100 members who pay a subscription of £90 per annum in return for the chance of winning a cash prize. A prize draw is held once a year. All except one of the subscriptions owing at 31 December 2002 was paid during the year, the unpaid subscription being regarded as a bad debt. The club recruited exactly 100 members during the year, 95 of whom had paid their subscriptions by the year-end. No other membership fees are payable by members of the Abracadabra Club.

2 There was a stock of drinks at the year-end of £175.

3 There was a creditor for drinks at the year-end, totalling £28.

4 Computers are depreciated at 20% per annum on the straight line method, with a full year's depreciation charged in the year of purchase but none in the year of sale.

5 There were 'nil' balances in both bank accounts on 31 December 2003. Milton Bezzler had total authority to sign cheques. There were no cash transactions.

a Calculate how much Milton Bezzler appears to have stolen from the club.

b Prepare an Income and Expenditure Account for the year ended 31 December 2003 in as much detail as possible from the above information, showing separately any profit or loss on drinks sales. Show the theft as an 'exceptional expense'.

c Prepare a Balance Sheet as at 31 December 2003.

d Explain one advantage and one disadvantage of presenting a simple Receipts and Payments Account, rather than an Income and Expenditure Account and Balance Sheet.

e How could clubs minimise the risk of a treasurer misappropriating funds?

(Answers in Appendix 3)

References

. . . .

Internet pages:

Receipts and Payments Account of the Astronomical Society of Edinburgh:
http://www.roe.ac.uk/asewww/publications/reports/1998.html
(later years than 1998 may be available: when you access the page, scroll down
until you reach the Financial Report)

Can you find if the society bought any fixed assets during the year?

Income and Expenditure Account and Balance Sheet of the Ethiopiaid organisation (a limited company, but its financial statements follow the broad
principles set out in this chapter):
http://www.reed.co.uk/ethiopiaid/accounts/accounts.htm

See if you can find out how much income they raised in the year.

CHAPTER 9

Cash flow: past and future

Objectives

When you have read this chapter you will be able to:

➤ Understand the relative importance of cash and profit

➤ Be able to prepare a simple cash flow statement based on past transactions

➤ Be aware of the relevant Financial Reporting Standard relating to Cash Flow Statements

➤ Appreciate the necessity of forecasting future cash flows

➤ Understand the overall nature and purpose of business planning

9.1 Introduction

'Cash is the lifeblood of a business. If it dwindles the business will die. But it is also a very difficult figure to fiddle.'

This is how Professor Sir David Tweedie, Chairman of the Accounting Standards Board, introduced the very first Financial Reporting Standard, *FRS 1: Cash Flow Statements*, in 1991. In our study of accounting so far, cash (by which we mean a business's cash in hand plus its bank balances, less any bank overdrafts) has perhaps taken a back seat when compared to profits: after all, accounting concepts require us to adjust cash for debtors, creditors, accruals, prepayments, unsold stock and provisions when preparing the profit and loss account. Even within the balance sheet, cash and bank balances are just two items appearing within the list of current assets, with no special prominence.

If cash really is the 'lifeblood of the business', it would make sense to give this asset a statement of its own, which is in fact what we do by preparing a Cash Flow Statement, which summarises the cash inflows and outflows over the past financial period. In this chapter we shall also be looking at the crystal-ball gazing aspect of accounting known as 'cash flow forecasting', where we attempt to anticipate the trend of *future* cash flows.

One of the many enigmas of accounting is that it is quite possible for profitable businesses to fail through poor cash management. After all, a creditor owed £20,000 is not going to be impressed by being told that, although the business made a profit of £100,000, the bank overdraft limit has been reached and no further cheques can be paid out.

The part of David Tweedie's comment referring to cash being 'a very difficult figure to fiddle' relates to the widely held (though inaccurate) perception that, whilst the existence (or non-existence) of cash and bank balances can be proved with certainty, 'profit' can be adjusted up or down ('fiddled') in accordance with a business's requirements, unrelated to the underlying financial transactions. The vast majority of information contained within the financial summaries is based on objective, verifiable data. However, there is scope for subjectivity as well, in such areas as the amount of depreciation to be charged, how stock should be valued, and whether a provision for doubtful debts is needed. The publication of Accounting Standards has narrowed considerably the areas of individuality available to accountants and their scope for 'creative accounting'. Remember also that many limited companies must appoint independent auditors who report on whether or not the accounts show a 'true and fair view' of the business.

9.2 Cash versus profit

If a business has sufficient cash to draw upon to meet its liabilities as they fall due, it is said to have good *liquidity*. It can also be referred to as being *solvent*. This would also apply if it could quickly change assets into cash if the need arose. Such 'liquid' assets would include investments such as shares which could be sold on a stock market, and bank deposit accounts where relatively short notice could be given to gain access to the money. Surprisingly enough, it is also possible for a business to be too liquid: if it has excessive cash then it is not reinvesting it. Rather than hoarding cash it should be buying new fixed assets, taking over other businesses or using the cash to fund research and development projects. In this way the business can expand and become more profitable. The ideal business is profitable and liquid, and in the next chapter we will look at ways of analysing both these aspects of a company's performance.

PAUSE FOR THOUGHT *Can you ever have too much cash? Apparently the combined wealth of the 200 richest men in the USA exceeds the total wealth of China, and the wealthiest, Bill Gates, had a fortune estimated at $100.9bn on 1 March 2000. Not all of it was in cash, though!*

9.3 The Cash Flow Statement

Just as there is a set way of presenting the profit and loss account and balance sheet, there is a format to follow for the Cash Flow Statement. Although the statement is nothing more than a summary of cash and bank transactions over a financial period, the information is made more meaningful by grouping the transactions into key headings. These key headings are set out in the Financial Reporting Standard (FRS 1) mentioned earlier, though at this stage in your studies it is sufficient to understand a slightly summarised version of the format.

FRS 1 in fact exempts small companies[1] from preparing a Cash Flow Statement, though a separate Financial Reporting Standard for Smaller Enterprises issued in 1998 states that smaller businesses are '... encouraged, but not required, to provide a cash flow statement'.

---

[1] Small, as defined by the Companies Act, 1985

All public limited companies have to present a Cash Flow Statement as part of their published annual report, and it is regarded as a 'primary statement' of equal importance to the profit and loss account and balance sheet. For example, Tesco plc's cash flow statement (in an 'abridged' version) for 1999 (with 1998's figures given for comparison) was as follows:

Tesco plc
Cash Flow Statement for the year ended 27 February

	1999 £m	1998 £m
Net cash inflow from operating activities	1,321	1,156
Net interest paid	(129)	(94)
Tax	(237)	(238)
Net capital expenditure	(1,005)	(723)
Changes in financing	739	344
Dividends	(238)	(214)
Business acquisitions/disposals	(255)	(359)
Increase/(decrease) in cash for the period	196	(128)

The structure of the 1999 statement can be explained as follows:

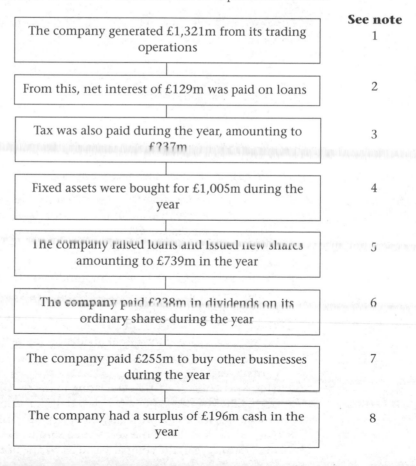

	See note
The company generated £1,321m from its trading operations	1
From this, net interest of £129m was paid on loans	2
Tax was also paid during the year, amounting to £237m	3
Fixed assets were bought for £1,005m during the year	4
The company raised loans and issued new shares amounting to £739m in the year	5
The company paid £238m in dividends on its ordinary shares during the year	6
The company paid £255m to buy other businesses during the year	7
The company had a surplus of £196m cash in the year	8

Notes:

1 This is not the same as the profit for the year! To arrive at the figure, the profit has to be adjusted as follows:

> ➤ Add back any provisions deducted in arriving at the profit (particularly depreciation). This is because depreciation (and also profits or losses on the sale of fixed assets), whilst included in the profit and loss account, has no effect on cash flow.

> ➤ Adjust for changing stock, debtors and creditors values, as follows:

Increases in cash flow requiring amounts to be added back to profit:

Change	Reason
Decrease in stock	Less cash tied up in stock
Decrease in debtors	More customers have paid their bills
Increase in creditors	We owe more (i.e. we have held on to our cash)

Decreases in cash flow requiring amounts to be deducted from profit:

Change	Reason
Increase in stock	More cash tied up in stock
Increase in debtors	Fewer customers have paid their bills
Decrease in creditors	We have paid more to our creditors

For Tesco in 1999, the 'net cash inflow from operating activities' figure was arrived at as follows:

£m	
Operating profit	934
Depreciation and amortisation	406
Increase in stock	(56)
Increase in debtors	(12)
Increase in trade creditors	81
Decrease in other creditors	(32)
Net cash inflow from operating activities	1,321

2 This is a net figure, representing interest paid less any interest received.

3 This is the tax actually *paid* in the year (probably on the previous year's profits), not the tax *provided* on the profits for the current year.

4 Again, this is a net figure, so any proceeds of sale of fixed assets would be deducted from the cost of assets bought.

5 'Financing' refers to the long-term funding of the business from sources such as loans and share capital. It is also a net figure, so any loans repaid would be deducted from the cash received from loans and share issues.

6 These are the ordinary share dividends actually *paid* in the year, so would not include the *provision* for a final dividend. In practice it would represent the previous year's final dividend, plus any interim dividends paid during the current year.

7 This represents the cash flow relating to the purchase or sale of businesses during the year (e.g. after a takeover bid). It is another net figure, so if it sold any businesses (e.g. a subsidiary company) for cash this would be deducted.

8 The company finished the year with a surplus of £196m cash. Note that in the previous year, the company had a *decrease* of £128m in the year.

The balance sheets of Copperfield plc as at 31 May 2001 and 31 May 2002 are as follows.

	2002			2001		
	£000	£000	£000	£000	£000	£000
Fixed assets (net book value)			54,000			47,000
Current assets:						
Stock		14,000			11,000	
Debtors		19,100			17,400	
		33,100			28,400	
Less						
Creditors due for payment within one year:						
Creditors	14,200			15,500		
Taxation	14,000			13,000		
Proposed dividends	16,000			8,500		
Bank overdraft	3,600			2,400		
		(47,800)			(39,400)	
Net current liabilities			(14,700)			(11,000)
Total net assets			39,300			36,000
Capital and reserves						
Ordinary shares of 5p each			21,000			10,000
Share premium account			7,500			17,500
Profit and loss account			10,800			8,500
			39,300			36,000

The summarised profit and loss accounts for the two years ended 31 May 2002 are as follows:

	2002	2001
	£000	£000
Gross profit	153,340	132,200
Less Interest paid	(10,000)	(10,000)
	143,340	122,200
Less Expenses	(105,640)	(94,900)
	37,700	27,300
Profit/(Loss) on sale of fixed assets	(1,400)	2,800
Profit before taxation	36,300	30,100
Less taxation	(14,000)	(13,000)
Profit after tax	22,300	17,100
Less Dividends, paid and proposed	(20,000)	(11,500)
Retained earnings for the year	2,300	5,600
Retained earnings b/f	8,500	2,900
Retained earnings c/f	10,800	8,500

Notes:

1 A bonus issue was made during the year to 31 May 2002 by utilising £10,000 from the share premium account.

2 A summary of the company's fixed assets account in the general ledger for the year ended 31 May 2002 is shown below:

		£000			£000
1/6/01	Cost brought forward	87,000	31/5/02	To Disposals Account	12,000
31/5/02	Additions	14,000	31/5/02	Cost carried forward	89,000
		101,000			101,000

The assets which were sold realised £2,400,000, which represented a loss on disposal of £1,400,000 when compared with their book value.

Produce a Cash Flow Statement for the year ended 31 May 2002.

Answer

Step 1

Using the 'Tesco' cash flow statement as our guide, we can start by calculating the net cash flow from operating activities. The major problem is that we are not given the depreciation total for the year, but have to calculate it. The clues we need are within the balance sheet and the fixed assets account given in the note. We can re-create the depreciation account, as follows:

Depreciation Account

	£000		£000
Disposal of assets[1]	8,200	Balance b/f (87,000 − 47,000)	40,000
Balance c/f (89,000 − 54,000)	35,000	Depreciation for the year (balancing figure)	3,200
	43,200		43,200

[1] The assets were sold for £2.4m at a loss of £1.4m, so the net book value at the time of sale must have been £3.8m. If the cost of the assets sold (as shown in the fixed assets account) was £12m, the depreciation on the assets sold must have been £12m − £3.8m = £8.2m.

Step 2

Having calculated the depreciation for the year, we can proceed to calculate the net cash from operating activities. Because we show interest separately in the cash flow statement, we must start with the operating profit before interest:

	£000
Operating profit (36,300 + 10,000)	46,300
Depreciation (see Step 1)	3,200
Loss on sale of fixed assets	1,400
Increase in stock (14,000 − 11,000)	(3,000)
Increase in debtors (19,100 − 17,400)	(1,700)
Decrease in creditors (15,500 − 14,200)	(1,300)
Net cash inflow from operating activities	44,900

Step 3

We've done the hardest part, so we can now set out the Cash Flow Statement as follows, starting with the net cash inflow from operating activities as calculated in Step 2:

Copperfield plc
Cash Flow Statement for the year ended 31 May 2002

	£000
Net cash inflow from operating activities	44,900
Interest paid[1]	(10,000)
Tax[2]	(13,000)
Net capital expenditure[3]	(11,600)
Changes in financing[4]	1,000
Dividends[5]	(12,500)
Business acquisitions/disposals	–
Decrease in cash for the period	(1,200)

Notes:

1 As there was no interest received, the word 'Net' can be omitted.

2 The amount *paid* in the year (i.e. the previous year's provision).

3 This can be analysed as follows:

Purchase of fixed assets	(14,000)
Receipts from sales of fixed assets	2,400

4 There was a bonus issue during the year. This is a *free* issue of shares so therefore does not involve a cash flow. The amount was £10,000 so the remaining part of the £11,000 difference between opening and closing share capital amounts must be a result of a new share issue.

5 This represents the dividends actually paid in the year: the liability in the opening balance sheet (£8,500) plus the part of the dividends shown in this year's profit and loss account which must have been paid during the year, as they are not shown as a liability at the end of the year (£20,000 − £16,000 = £4,000).

Step 4

We can prove the closing figure in the Cash Flow Statement by preparing a simple reconciliation of the opening and closing cash balances (i.e. bank overdraft in this case):

	£000
Opening bank overdraft, 1 June 2001	2,400
Closing bank overdraft, 31 May 2002	3,600
Increase in overdraft (i.e. decrease in cash for the period)	(1,200)

9.4 Cash flow forecasts
....

Whereas cash flow statements are based on historic (past) events, a cash flow forecast is essentially a practical exercise where a business is looking ahead to assess not only future income and expenditure but also the level of funding required for a defined period.

Key areas to consider include:

> the period of the forecast (3, 6, 12 months, etc.),
> the degree of analysis required (weekly, monthly, quarterly, etc.),
> the timing of sales revenues,
> the relative proportions of cash and credit sales,
> potential changes in the level of overheads and the timing of their payment,
> the effect of seasonal changes in income and expenditure.

The forecast is usually shown in a specific format, as in Figure 9.1.

There is no universally agreed way of presenting a cash flow forecast, but the advantage of the layout shown is that columns are provided for the business owner to insert not only the forecast results, but also the *actual* month's results when they are known. This provides an important means of financial control, as variances between forecast and actual can be investigated and appropriate action taken. No forecast is likely to be wholly accurate; it is the best estimate based on information available at the time of preparation. Some information may be wholly accurate, for example the amount of loan repayments due, or expenditure where the price has been agreed in advance. Other information, such as levels of sales income, might be based on a previous year's sales figures with adjustments made for inflation, relative decline or increase in trading, etc.

ACTIVITY **9.2**
• • • • • • • • • • • •

Look carefully at the cash flow forecast in Figure 9.1, then answer the following questions:

1   What is the overall forecast change in the bank balance in the three months?
2   What action does the business need to take in March to avoid a major problem?
3   What forecast bank balance would start April's forecast?
4   Explain the meaning of 'capital injected' and 'capital expenditure'.

Answer

1   The balance is forecast to decline from £1,650 (positive balance) on 1 January to an overdraft of £6,940 at the end of March, an overall cash outflow of £8,590.
2   The overdraft limit is only £6,000 but this will be exceeded if the forecast proves accurate. The business must either renegotiate a higher overdraft facility, decrease expenditure or increase income.
3   An overdraft of £6,940.
4   Capital injected means that cash from the owner(s) is forecast to be paid in during January. Capital expenditure means that fixed assets are forecast to be purchased in February.

figure 9.1

Cash flow forecast

Cash flow forecast from 1 January 2004 to 31 March 2004

Period – Monthly	Jan-04 Forecast	Jan-04 Actual	Feb-04 Forecast	Feb-04 Actual	Mar-04 Forecast	Mar-04 Actual
(£s)						
Receipts						
Sales – cash	2,350		1,450		3,410	
Sales – debtors	1,620		1,200		2,330	
Capital injected	6,000		–			
Other receipts	–		–		1,000	
A: Total Receipts	9,970		2,650		6,740	
Payments						
Purchases – cash	1,520		800		1,200	
Purchases – creditors	680		750		800	
Wages and salaries	2,210		2,210		2,420	
Rent, rates	300		300		320	
Light, heat, power	250		250		250	
Insurance	300		–		120	
Transport, packaging	140		60		250	
Maintenance	–		–		400	
Advertising	390		120		220	
Postage/stationery and telephone	220		200		220	
Professional fees	300		–		–	
Bank/finance charges & interest	350		300		400	
Drawings/fees	1,500		1,500		1,500	
Sundry expenses	400		400		400	
Loan repayments	500		500		500	
Capital expenditure	–		2,500		–	
B: Total Payments	9,060		9,890		9,000	
C: Net Cash Flow (A – B)	910		(7,240)		(2,260)	
D: Opening Bank Balance	1,650		2,560		(4,680)	
E: Closing Bank Balance (D –/– C)	2,560		(4,680)		(6,940)	
Note: Agreed Overdraft Facility	6,000		6,000		6,000	

9.5 Cash flow forecasts and business planning

A cash flow forecast is often presented as part of a business plan. A business plan can have many different uses, one of which is to present a detailed appraisal of the business to a bank when applying for finance. However, it must not be seen as just a document to show the bank manager and then file away. A regularly updated business plan is an invaluable management tool, allowing performance to be monitored against targets ('forecast' compared with 'actual'), and provides direction for management and staff.

Business plans are usually written for one or more of the following reasons:

➤ To raise finance, by informing potential lenders or investors about the business
➤ To identify the business's strengths and weaknesses
➤ To identify opportunities for expansion and threats to the business's survival
➤ To set realistic and achievable targets
➤ To plan the future direction of the business

The content of the business plan will vary depending upon what the business is aiming to achieve. Many business plans are highly complex documents, as the very survival of the business depends upon them. Every business plan should include the following as key components:

➤ Title page
➤ Contents page
➤ An executive summary (key points at a glance)
➤ Business background (brief history of the business, key personnel)
➤ Legal set-up – sole trader/partnership/limited company?
➤ Summary of financial background of the business and its present financial state
➤ Short/medium/long-term plans for the business
➤ Mission statement ('why the business exists')
➤ Products and/or services
➤ Overview of each product/service
➤ Marketing strategies
➤ Organisation chart
➤ Forecast cash flows
➤ Forecast profit and loss account
➤ Forecast balance sheet
➤ Statement of how much funds are required, their intended purpose and their projected impact on the profitability of the business
➤ Potential rewards for investors

Note that a forecast profit and loss account and balance sheet would be included in addition to the cash flow forecast. This will enable the reader of the plan to assess the anticipated profitability of the business (vital to a future investor) as well as its viability as shown by the change in its net asset position and liquidity as disclosed in the forecast balance sheet.

9.6 Glossary

Business plan	A document drawn up by a business for a number of different purposes, including planning, fund-raising and setting targets. A cash flow forecast is a key component of a business plan
Cash flow	The inflows and outflows of cash through a business over a particular period
Cash flow forecast	Predictions of cash inflows and outflows over a future period
Cash flow statement	A summary of cash and bank transactions over a defined past period. When published it must be set out in a format prescribed by the relevant Financial Reporting Standard
Financial Reporting Standards (FRSs)	Regulations which are expected to be followed by companies and accountants in order to comply with best practice. FRS 1 is the Standard which applies to the presentation of cash flow statements
Insolvent	A business or individual with more liabilities than assets and without the means to pay debts as they fall due
Liquidity	The ability of a business to access enough cash (including bank balances) to pay debts as they fall due
Primary statement	A financial summary of importance. Primary statements include the profit and loss account, the balance sheet and the cash flow statement
Solvency	The ability of a business to pay its debts as they fall due. The opposite is *insolvency*

SELF-CHECK QUESTIONS

1 Cash has been described as:
   a The lifebuoy of the business
   b The lifeboat of the business
   c The lifeline of the business
   d The lifeblood of the business

2 The definition of cash as used in Cash Flow Statements includes:
   a Only cash balances
   b Only bank balances
   c Bank balances and bank overdrafts
   d Cash in hand plus bank balances less bank overdrafts

3 How can a profitable business fail?
   a Because it can't pay its bills
   b Because it has more current liabilities than current assets
   c Because it has a bank overdraft
   d Because it has too much cash

4 FRS 1 states that:
   a All companies must prepare a Cash Flow Statement
   b All small companies must prepare a Cash Flow Statement
   c All small companies must prepare a Cash Flow Forecast
   d Small companies are exempt from preparing a Cash Flow Statement

5 The heading in a Cash Flow Statement 'Changes in Financing' means:
   a The cash outflow due to loan interest payments being made
   b The cash flow from share and loan issues and repayments
   c Cash dividends paid to shareholders
   d The change in the level of bank balances in the period

6 If 'Taxation' is shown on the Cash Flow Statement, it is likely to be:
   a The taxation paid this year on the current year's profit
   b The taxation payable next year on this year's profit
   c The taxation paid this year on last year's profit
   d The taxation provided on this year's profit

7 Depreciation is added back to profit when arriving at the cash flow from operating activities because:
   a Depreciation is only an estimated amount
   b Depreciation does not affect profit
   c Depreciation does not result in a flow of cash
   d Depreciation affects only the balance sheet, not the profit and loss account

8 If net profit before taxation and interest was £95,000, depreciation for the year was £17,000, stock has decreased during the year by £7,000, debtors have increased by £11,000 and creditors have decreased by £4,000, what is the overall cash flow from operating activities?
   a £104,000
   b £112,000
   c £98,000
   d £134,000

9 A business plan is often prepared:
   a To comply with FRS 1
   b To show customers where the head office is situated
   c To set targets for the business
   d To be filed away in a drawer

10 Which of the following are all Primary Statements?
   a The profit and loss account, balance sheet and cash flow statement
   b The profit and loss account, balance sheet and cash flow forecast
   c The profit and loss account, business plan and cash flow statement
   d The profit and loss account, balance sheet and financial reporting statement

Further questions can be found on the accompanying website (www.booksites.net/black).

SELF-STUDY QUESTIONS

(Answers in Appendix 2)

Question 9.1

From the following information, calculate the missing figure in each column.

(£s)	A	B	C	D
Net cash flow from operating activities	14,800	?	21,400	48,660
Net interest paid	(5,800)	(2,900)	(6,000)	(2,950)
Tax	(7,200)	(4,500)	(7,100)	(24,880)
Net capital expenditure	17,300	(2,970)	?	(6,520)
Changes in financing	800	(1,800)	14,680	(17,490)
Dividends	(9,820)	(4,200)	(3,300)	?
Increase/(Decrease) in cash for the period	?	6,200	11,750	(9,450)

Question 9.2

From the following information, calculate the cash flow from operating activities for each column. Put brackets around figures where appropriate.

(£s)	A	B	C	D
Net profit before interest	36,620	29,937		20,060
Net loss before interest			22,660	
Depreciation	12,000	16,000	24,000	15,000
Increase in stock	9,650			14,850
Decrease in stock		5,840	5,622	
Increase in debtors			2,240	12,795
Decrease in debtors	7,980	6,722		
Increase in creditors	3,380		9,713	
Decrease in creditors		6,840		11,629
Cash flow from operating activities	?	?	?	?

Question 9.3

The balance sheets of Dombey plc as at 31 May 2000 and 31 May 2001 are as follows:

	31 May 2001		31 May 2000	
	£000	£000	£000	£000
Fixed assets (net book value)		43,000		32,000
Current assets:				
Stock	19,000		18,000	
Debtors	9,000		7,500	
Bank	–		4,800	
	28,000		30,300	
Less **Creditors due for payment within one year:**				
Creditors	6,100		9,900	
Taxation	5,000		4,000	
Proposed dividends	3,000		2,000	
Bank overdraft	2,700		–	
	(16,800)		(15,900)	
Net current assets		11,200		14,400
Total net assets		54,200		46,400
Share capital and reserves				
Ordinary shares of 25p each		24,000		33,000
Share Premium Account		300		200
Retained earnings		29,900		13,200
		54,200		46,400

The summarised profit and loss accounts for the two years ended 31 May 2001 are as follows:

	2001 £000	2000 £000
Gross profit	46,100	38,900
Less Expenses (including £1.2m interest)	(18,200)	(22,100)
	27,900	16,800
Less Loss on sale of fixed assets	(3,200)	—
Operating profit	24,700	16,800
Less Taxation	(5,000)	(4,000)
Operating profit after tax	19,700	12,800
Less Dividends	(3,000)	(2,000)
Retained profits	16,700	10,800
Retained profits b/f	13,200	2,400
Retained profits c/f	29,900	13,200

Notes:

A summary of the company's Fixed Assets Account in the General Ledger for the year ended 31 May 2001 is shown below (all figures in £000s):

		£000			£000
1 Jun 2000	Cost brought forward	76,000	31 May 2001	To Disposals Account	8,000
31 May 2001	Additions	22,000	31 May 2001	Cost carried forward	90,000
		98,000			98,000

The assets which were sold realised £1,800,000, which represented a loss on disposal of £3,200,000 when compared with their book value.

Produce a Cash Flow Statement for the year ended 31 May 2001, and reconcile the cash increase or decrease for the year as shown on the statement with the change in the bank balance shown in the balance sheets.

Question 9.4

The following information relates to The Marshes Gallery, which has been set up by Clara Pilbeam to help rural craftsmen to sell their products to the tourist trade. Clara is submitting a business plan to Midlays Bank plc. She has found what she thinks are ideal premises, a disused colliery building in South Wales. She has saved £4,000 as initial capital, which she would pay in to the Gallery's bank account on 1 July 2002, which will be the effective starting date of the enterprise. Forecast information for the six months to 31 December 2002 is as follows:

➤ The landlord requires a deposit of £3,000, and rent of £1,000 per month, payable quarterly in arrears. The deposit will be paid on 1 July 2002, the first quarter's rent on 2 October 2002, the second quarter on 3 January 2003.

➤ Income will be generated from commissions on works of art sold through the gallery. The average commission taken by the gallery will be 40%, and sales of artworks (in £s) are forecast as follows:

July	August	September	October	November	December
8,000	4,000	7,000	12,000	18,000	24,000

➤ All sales are for cash, and are banked immediately without deduction. Amounts due to artists are paid one month after the relevant sales are made.
➤ The Gallery will receive a 'one-off' grant of £5,000 from the Welsh Tourist Board in August.
➤ The cost of redecorating the building will be £7,000, payable in two instalments: £4,000 in August, the balance in September.
➤ General overheads (including any bank interest payable) are expected to be £2,000 per month, payable one month in arrears.
➤ Wages to assistants will be £750 per month and are payable at the end of the month.
➤ Clara Pilbeam will draw £600 per month until December, when she will draw £900.
➤ Various items of equipment will be purchased for £3,000 in July, payable two months later. Depreciation for the six months will be £150.
➤ Initial advertising will cost £500, payable in August.

Prepare a cash flow forecast for The Marshes Gallery for the six months to 31 December 2002. Comment on the forecast, and state whether you think that the project appears feasible.

Further questions can be found on the accompanying website (www.booksites. net/black).

CASE STUDY

There's the profit, but where's the cash?

Machiq Limited (see previous case studies) was formed on 1 July 2003 and has been making increasing profits. By 30 June 2005 it reported the following sum- marised profit and loss accounts and balance sheets:

Machiq Limited
Profit and loss accounts for the year ended 30 June

	2005	2004
	£	£
Gross profit	176,400	133,260
Less Expenses (includes interest of £1,800 p.a.)	(60,400)	(41,260)
Net profit for the year, before taxation	116,000	92,000
Less Provision for taxation	(26,950)	(18,400)
Net profit for the year, after taxation	89,050	73,600
Less Dividends	(32,000)	(31,500)
Retained profit for the year	57,050	42,100
Retained profit brought forward	42,100	–
Retained profit carried forward	99,150	42,100

Balance sheets as at 30 June

	2005 £	2005 £	2004 £	2004 £
Fixed assets (net book value)		165,980		74,040
Current assets:				
Stock	32,650		17,370	
Debtors	30,950		39,560	
Bank	–		6,240	
	63,600		63,170	
Less **Creditors due for payment**				
within one year:				
Creditors	14,080		10,210	
Taxation	26,950		18,400	
Proposed dividends	32,000		31,500	
Bank overdraft	2,400		–	
	(75,430)		(60,110)	
Net current assets/(liabilities)		(11,830)		3,060
Total net assets		154,150		77,100
Capital and reserves				
Called-up share capital (5p shares)		24,000		14,000
Share premium account		31,000		21,000
Profit and loss account:				
Retained profit for the year		99,150		42,100
		154,150		77,100

The changes in the share capital and share premium account were due to a sale of shares to Trixie Richardson, who had recently left Kazam Limited after 10 years' service as chief accountant. Trixie was appointed managing director of Machiq Limited on 10 April 2005. During the year ended 30 June 2005, Machiq Limited bought two Braganza Rapido motor cars for £48,500 each for Marvin's and Chiquita's use. No assets were sold in the year. Trixie is concerned that, whilst the company seems to be profitable, its cash flow appears to be poor.

a Prepare a Cash Flow Statement for the year ended 30 June 2005, and reconcile the cash increase or decrease for the year as shown on the statement with the change in the bank balance shown in the balance sheets.
b Do you agree with Trixie's opinion of the cash flow? What have been the key cash inflows and outflows in the year?

The three shareholders of Machiq Limited, Chiquita, Marvin and Trixie, decide to draw up a cash flow forecast for the six months ended 31 December 2005. They have an agreed bank overdraft limit of £6,000. They prepare the following predictions:

Income: Sales will be £30,000 each month, except November which will be £40,000. Half the sales will be on credit, with debtors paying one month after the sale; the rest will be for cash. Debtors owing at 30 June 2005 will pay in July 2005.
Expenditure: Purchases and all expenses other than wages and salaries will be a constant £35,000 per month, payable one month after purchase. Wages and

salaries amounting to £6,000 per month will be paid at the end of the same month, but a bonus of an extra £8,000 will be paid in December. Creditors owing at 30 June 2005 will be paid in July. Assume that neither the taxation nor the proposed dividend will be paid during the period.

c Prepare the Cash Flow Forecast for the six months ending 31 December 2005. Will Machiq Limited have to renegotiate its bank overdraft limit?

(Answers in Appendix 3)

References
••••••••••••••

J. Sainsbury plc's cash flow statement (which can be downloaded as an Excel spreadsheet file):
http://www.j-sainsbury.co.uk/finres/1999_final/a_accoun/cash_flow.html
(This has the Cash Flow Statement from the 1999 Annual Report – later years may be available as they are published)

A web page which calculates Bill Gates' wealth on a daily basis:
http://www.webho.com/WealthClock

CHAPTER 10

Making sense of
financial statements

Objectives

When you have read this chapter you will be able to:

➤ Be aware of the need for plc's to publish information
➤ Undertake preliminary research prior to analysing company accounts
➤ Appreciate the key components of an annual report, including the statement of total recognised gains and losses
➤ Distinguish between, and compute, a vertical and horizontal analysis of financial information and make a simple interpretation of the data revealed by the analysis
➤ Prepare ratios within five main groupings and analyse the data revealed
➤ Understand concerns regarding the validity of accounting information

10.1 Introduction

The published financial information of Tesco plc, as referred to in the previous chapter, comes in two versions:

➤ The Annual Review and Summary Financial Statement, intended for users who do not require fully comprehensive financial information but need only the key highlights of the company's performance. The most recently published statement contained 28 pages. Summarised versions of the profit and loss account, balance sheet, cash flow statement and various other items of financial data appeared on seven of these pages, the rest being devoted to general information about the company, with many full-colour photographs of stores, products, customers and employees

➤ The Annual Report and Financial Statements, which gives all the information required to be published by the Companies Act, Accounting and Financial Reporting Standards and the Stock Exchange. This contained 40 pages, including not only the Primary Financial Statements but also 16 pages of detailed notes to the accounts.

Tesco has approximately 200,000 shareholders (of whom 70,000 are also employees)[1] and the production of glossy, full-colour reports with tempting photographs of foodstuffs and smiling shop assistants is used partly as a public relations exercise to keep shareholders loyal and maintain confidence in the

[1] Source: Tesco plc's Investor Relations Department, September 1999

company. Smaller companies might have very few shareholders and so the annual accounts, whilst still containing the Primary Statements, will tend to be matter-of-fact documents without any frills. The Companies Act gives various exemptions for such companies, so even though information has to be published, it would not be nearly as comprehensive as that required for a plc.

As neither sole traders nor partnerships are required to publish accounts, their financial summaries will in practice be seen by only a handful of people: the owner or partners, the accountant who produced the accounts, the taxation authorities and possibly a bank manager. Any wider distribution is entirely at the discretion of the owner(s).

10.2 Data for analysis

The purpose of this chapter is to *make sense* of the information contained in the financial summaries – to analyse, interpret and come to a conclusion. To illustrate the analytical process, we shall use the financial statements of a fictitious company, Madison plc, for the years 2000 and 2001 as set out below.

Madison plc
(published) Profit and Loss Account for the years ended
31 December 2001 and 2000

	2001	2000
	£000	£000
Turnover	6,590	4,350
Less Cost of sales	(4,220)	(2,820)
Gross profit	2,370	1,530
Less Expenses:		
Administrative	(380)	(300)
Selling and distribution	(320)	(170)
Net profit before interest	1,670	1,060
Less Interest payable	(60)	(70)
Net profit before taxation	1,610	990
Less Taxation	(450)	(270)
Profit after taxation	1,160	720
Less Dividends, paid and proposed	(360)	(120)
Retained earnings for the year	800	600
Retained earnings b/f	1,600	1,000
Retained earnings c/f	2,400	1,600

Madison plc
Balance sheets as at 31 December 2001 and 2000

	2001 £000	2001 £000	2001 £000	2000 £000	2000 £000	2000 £000
Fixed assets (net book value)			6,200			5,320
Current assets:						
Stock		2,200			680	
Debtors		550			500	
Bank balance		250			200	
		3,000			1,380	
Less **Creditors due for payment within one year:**						
Trade creditors	390			210		
Taxation	450			270		
Proposed dividends	360			120		
		(1,200)			(600)	
Net current assets			1,800			780
			8,000			6,100
Less **Creditors due for payment after more than one year:**						
Debentures			(1,000)			(1,500)
Total net assets			7,000			4,600
Capital and reserves						
Ordinary shares of £1 each			3,100			2,500
Share premium account			1,500			500
Profit and loss account			2,400			1,600
			7,000			4,600

Additional information:

Stock at 1 January 2000 = £640,000

Stock market prices: end 2001 = 561p, end 2000 = 547p

There were no 'cash' sales or purchases during either year

figure 10.1

Madison plc

Cash Flow Statement for the years ended 31 December 2001 and 2000

	2001	2000
	£000	£000
Net cash inflow from operating activities	665	810
Interest paid	(65)	(60)
Tax	(270)	(170)
Net capital expenditure	(1,260)	(320)
Changes in financing	1,100	–
Dividends	(120)	(90)
Business acquisitions/disposals	–	(160)
Increase in cash for the period	50	10

10.3 The first stage: preliminary research

There are many reasons for analysing financial statements, including:

➤ Investment – you may be an existing shareholder or considering investing in a business.

➤ Curiosity – you may have used a business's products or services and wish to find out more about what they do.

➤ Commercial reasons – you trade with the business or are considering trading with it.

➤ Lending decisions – banks and other financial institutions need to know if a business is capable of repaying loans or is in a sound position if loans are being requested.

➤ Self-interest – you may want to find out more about the company that employs you. For example, is it likely to continue trading and keep you as an employee?

➤ Business rivalry – how well or badly is a competitor doing compared with your business?

> Taxation – the taxation authorities may need to be satisfied that the accounts appear complete and trustworthy

> Environmental factors – local communities and pressure groups may wish to find out more about local companies, including their employment and ecological attitudes.

> Economic analysis – business trends can be ascertained by analysing company results.

Those wishing to make the analysis may already know a great deal about the company, as shareholders, as workers or by virtue of publicly available information such as newspaper comment. The key background information which is needed prior to starting a detailed numerical analysis of the financial statements includes:

> Type of trade – what do they do?
> Competitors – who do they compete against? What share of the market do they have?
> Geographical spread – where do they sell their goods and services and which countries do they buy from?
> Management – who are they and how well qualified are they?
> Quality of products – how reliable are the products they sell?

Much of this information can be gleaned from the 'non-financial' parts of the annual report, by accessing data via the Internet or in libraries, or even by visual inspection of products, stores, advertisements, etc. All this preliminary research is useful in placing the business in an appropriate context prior to making any detailed financial calculations.

The full annual reports of plc's will contain several sections in addition to the financial summaries, the key ones being as follows.

> *Operating and financial review*, which contains a commentary on the results of the period, a review of the group's needs and resources and an assessment of their shareholders' return on their investment in the company.

> *Directors' report*, which contains various items of statutory information such as the principal activities of the company, the names of the directors and auditors, a brief summary of the company's financial results and how many shares the directors own.

> *Auditors' report*, which is a statement from an independent qualified accountant (or firm of accountants) as to whether or not the accounts show a true and fair view of the state of the company's affairs and its profit or loss and cash flows.

> *Statement of total recognised gains and losses*, which is a primary statement like the profit and loss account, balance sheet and cash flow statement. It summarises *all* the gains and losses which appear in the financial summaries. This means that it will show not only the profit for the period as revealed by the profit and loss account, but also profits shown only within the balance sheet such as revaluation gains on land and buildings credited to an Asset Revaluation Reserve (see page 128).

> *Statement of Accounting Policies*, which sets out the principles adopted by the company when dealing with various items included within the summaries,

such as how stocks are valued, what depreciation methods have been followed, etc.

➤ *Notes to the financial statements*, which set out detailed explanations of figures contained within the financial statements to comply with the requirements of the Companies Acts, Accounting and Financial Reporting Standards and the Stock Exchange.

Having obtained a good general impression of the scope and nature of the business, the analyst should then read through the annual report, making a note of any unusual or interesting items such as changes in accounting policies, businesses acquired in the year, etc. By looking at the 'bottom lines' of the three main financial summaries, an immediate impression can be gained of the business's progress in the year. For Madison plc, this shows:

Profit and loss account:	Retained profit for the year has increased from £600,000 to £800,000, with total retained earnings rising from £1.6m to £2.4m.
Balance sheet:	Total net assets/total capital employed has risen from £4.6m to £7m in the year.
Cash flow statement:	Cash has increased by £50,000, compared to an increase of only £10,000 in the previous year.

By all three measures the company appears to have performed well.

ACTIVITY **10.1**
....

Obtain a copy of an annual report of a plc and identify the sections listed above. Read through the auditors' report to see if the accounts show a 'true and fair view', and try to find out how many shares the Chief Executive owns and how much he or she was paid as a director. Look at the bottom lines of the three main financial statements (use 'group' figures where there is a choice). How do you think the company performed in the year?

Answer

Obviously the answer depends on which company's report you are looking at, but as an illustration, Tesco plc's latest annual report at the time of writing showed a true and fair view according to the auditors, PricewaterhouseCoopers. The company's Chief Executive, Mr T. P. Leahy, owned 1.2m shares and was paid £901,000 for the year. The company's financial summaries showed solid progress:

Profit and loss account:	Retained profit for the year increased from £277m to £329m.
Balance sheet:	Total net assets/total capital employed rose from £3,903m to £4,377m in the year.
Cash flow statement:	Cash increased by £196m, compared to a decrease of £128m in the previous year.

PAUSE FOR THOUGHT

Tesco plc had 6.7bn shares in issue, so Mr Leahy owned under 0.02% of the company, and his pay was 0.3% of the retained profits.

10.1 The second stage: horizontal and vertical analysis

Having gathered the background information, the next stage is to start the numerical analysis of the financial statements. Advanced mathematics is not required, but you should understand percentage and ratio calculations. Refresh your memory with the next activity.

ACTIVITY **10.2**

Calculate the following:

(i)   6,815 as a percentage of 27,260
(ii)   3,720 as a percentage of 1,200
(iii) The increase from 3,120 to 11,232 as a percentage of the former figure
(iv) The decrease from 16,040 to 12,832 as a percentage of the former figure
(v)   The ratio of 5,541 compared with 18,470
(vi) The ratio of 46,000 compared with 11,500

Answer

		Calculation
(i)	25%	$\dfrac{6,815}{27,260} \times 100 = 25\%$
(ii)	310%	$\dfrac{3,720}{1,200} \times 100 = 310\%$
(iii)	increase of 260%	$11,232 - 3,120 = 8,112$
		$\dfrac{8,112}{3,120} \times 100 = 260\%$
(iv)	decrease of 20%	$16,040 - 12,832 = 3,208$
		$\dfrac{3,208}{16,040} \times 100 = 20\%$
(v)	0.3:1	$\dfrac{5,541}{18,470} = 0.3$
(vi)	4:1	$\dfrac{46,000}{11,500} = 4$

Horizontal and vertical analysis is a simple means of comparing the relative size of individual components within the summaries. Horizontal analysis achieves this by calculating the percentage change from the preceding year to the current year, whilst vertical analysis expresses each profit and loss account item as a percentage of the sales total, each balance sheet item as a percentage of the total net assets, and cash flow statement items as a percentage of the net cash flow from operating activities.

Using the Madison plc statements, the analysis will be as follows (figures have been rounded to the nearest whole number):

Madison plc
(published) Profit and Loss Account for the years ended
31 December 2001 and 2000

	2001	2000	'Horizontal' analysis	'Vertical' analysis 2001	2000
	£000	£000	% change	%	%
Turnover	6,590	4,350	+ 51	100	100
Less Cost of sales	(4,220)	(2,820)	+ 50	(64)	(65)
Gross profit	2,370	1,530	+ 55	36	35
Less Expenses:					
Administrative	(380)	(300)	+ 27	(6)	(7)
Selling and distribution	(320)	(170)	+ 88	(5)	(4)
Net profit before interest	1,670	1,060	+ 58	25	24
Less Interest payable	(60)	(70)	– 14	(1)	(1)
Net profit before taxation	1,610	990	+ 63	24	23
Less Taxation	(450)	(270)	+ 67	(7)	(6)
Profit after taxation	1,160	720	+ 61	17	17
Less Dividends, paid and proposed	(360)	(120)	+ 200	(5)	(3)
Retained earnings for the year	800	600	+ 33	12	14
Retained earnings b/f	1,600	1,000	+ 60		
Retained earnings c/f	2,400	1,600	+50		

Note that each percentage in the 'horizontal' column is calculated using the following formula:

$$\frac{2001 \text{ amount} - 2000 \text{ amount}}{2000 \text{ amount}} \times 100$$

The figures in the 'vertical' columns are calculated as a percentage of the sales figure. The quickest way of doing this is to multiply each figure by the formula (entered as a constant on your calculator):

$$\frac{100}{\text{Sales figure}}$$

The balance sheet and cash flow statement can be analysed in a similar way:

Madison plc
Balance sheets as at 31 December 2001 and 2000

	2001	2000	'Horizontal' analysis	'Vertical' analysis 2001	2000
	£000	£000	% change	%	%
Fixed assets	6,200	5,320	+ 17	88	116
Current assets:					
Stock	2,200	680	+ 223	31	15
Debtors	550	500	+ 10	8	11
Bank balance	250	200	+ 25	4	4
c/f	3,000	1,380	+ 117	43	30

	c/f 3,000	1,980	+ 117	43	30
Creditors due for payment within one year:					
Trade creditors	390	210	+ 86	6	5
Taxation	450	270	+ 67	6	6
Proposed dividends	360	120	+ 200	5	2
	(1,200)	(600)	+100	(17)	(13)
Net current assets	1,800	780	+ 131	26	17
	8,000	6,100	+ 31	114	133
Creditors due for payment after more than one year:					
Debentures	(1,000)	(1,500)	− 33	(14)	(33)
Total net assets	7,000	4,600	+ 52	100	100
Capital and reserves					
Ordinary shares of £1	3,100	2,500	+ 24	44	54
Share premium account	1,500	500	+ 200	22	11
Profit and loss account	2,400	1,600	+ 50	34	35
	7,000	4,600	+ 52	100	100

Note that each figure in the vertical analysis is expressed as a percentage of the balance sheet total.

Madison plc
Cash Flow Statement for the years ended 31 December 2001 and 2000

	2001	2000	'Horizontal' analysis	'Vertical' analysis 2001	2000
	£000	£000	% change	%	%
Net cash inflow from operating activities	665	810	− 18	100	100
Interest paid	(65)	(60)	+ 8	(10)	(7)
Tax	(270)	(170)	+ 59	(41)	(21)
Net capital expenditure	(1,260)	(320)	+ 294	(189)	(40)
Changes in financing	1,100	–	n/a	165	–
Dividends	(120)	(90)	+ 33	(18)	(11)
Business acquisitions/disposals	–	(160)	n/a	–	(20)
Increase in cash for the period	50	10	+ 400	7	1

Note that each figure in the vertical analysis is expressed as a percentage of the net cash flow from operating activities.

10.4.1 Interpreting the analysis

It is obvious that the company has expanded in 2001. The horizontal analysis shows within the profit and loss account how much the increase has been, and the noteworthy changes have been the size of dividends (increased by 200%), the seemingly disproportionate increase in selling and distribution expenses when compared with administration expenses (88% increase compared with 27%) and the reduction in interest (−14%) which has resulted from a part repayment of the debenture as disclosed by the balance sheet.

The vertical analysis reveals that the decline in administrative expenses as a percentage of sales (from 7% to 6%) has been offset by a similar increase in selling and distribution expenses. Other amounts have remained fairly constant, apart from the near doubling in dividend levels as a percentage of sales. Retained earnings as a percentage of sales has declined from 14% to 12% as a result of the increased dividends.

The balance sheet's horizontal analysis reveals the first worrying statistic about the company – the fact that stock levels have increased by 223% in the year, even though total net assets have increased by 'only' 52%. The 200% increase in the share premium account shows that the shares issued in the year were sold at an amount considerably in excess of their nominal value. The vertical analysis of the balance sheet again highlights the increasing amount of stock held by the company at the end of 2001 and the more generous dividend policy.

The horizontal analysis of the cash flow statement again shows some areas of concern. Net cash inflow from operating activities has declined by 18%, with massive increases in net capital expenditure (fixed asset purchases less sales). Overall there was a healthy 400% rise in the amount by which cash had increased. The vertical analysis for 2001 shows that the cash outflow on capital expenditure was almost matched by financing changes (new shares being issued less debentures repaid).

10.5 The third stage: ratio analysis

Having established the percentage movements between the two years, and assessed the relative strengths of the component parts of the financial statements, the next step is to calculate specific percentages and ratios to reveal further aspects of the business's performance. The following table represents the more common ones which are calculated, divided into five groups.

Group	Name of ratio	Formula
Profitability	ROCE (Return on Capital Employed)	$\dfrac{\text{Net profit before interest and tax}}{\text{Share capital + Reserves + Long-term loans}} \times 100$
	Gross Margin (or Gross Profit Margin)	$\dfrac{\text{Gross profit}}{\text{Sales}} \times 100$
	Mark-up	$\dfrac{\text{Gross profit}}{\text{Cost of goods sold}} \times 100$
	Net Margin (or Net Profit Margin)	$\dfrac{\text{Net profit before interest and tax}}{\text{Turnover}} \times 100$

Group	Name of ratio	Formula
Efficiency	Fixed assets turnover	$\dfrac{\text{Total sales}}{\text{Fixed assets at net book value}}$
	Stock turn	$\dfrac{\text{Average stock}}{\text{Cost of sales}} \times 365$
	Debtors' collection period	$\dfrac{\text{Trade debtors}}{\text{Credit sales}} \times 365$
	Creditors' payment period	$\dfrac{\text{Trade creditors}}{\text{Credit purchases}} \times 365$
Short-term solvency and liquidity	Current ratio (or 'working capital' ratio)	Current assets:Current liabilities
	Acid test (or 'Quick assets' test)	(Current assets – Stock):Current liabilities
Long-term solvency and liquidity	Gearing	$\dfrac{\text{Preference shares (if any)} + \text{Long-term loans}}{\text{Share capital} + \text{Reserves} + \text{Long-term loans}} \times 100$ (note that there are other ways of calculating gearing: see p. 194)
	Interest cover	$\dfrac{\text{Profit before interest}}{\text{Interest payable}}$
Investment ratios	eps (earnings per share)	$\dfrac{\text{Profit available for ordinary dividend}}{\text{Number of equity shares issued}}$
	p/e (price/earnings)	$\dfrac{\text{Market price}}{\text{Earnings per share}}$
	Dividend cover	$\dfrac{\text{Profit available to pay dividend}}{\text{Dividends paid and proposed}}$
	Dividend yield	$\dfrac{\text{Dividend per share}}{\text{Market price per share}} \times 100$

Using the data from Madison plc's financial summaries, the ratios are explained in Sections 10.5.1–10.5.5.

10.5.1 Profitability group of ratios

	Madison plc	
Name of ratio	2001	2000
ROCE (Return on Capital Employed)	$\dfrac{1,670}{7,000 + 1,000} \times 100 = 20.87\%$	$\dfrac{1,060}{4,600 + 1,500} \times 100 = 17.38\%$
Gross Margin (or Gross Profit Margin)	$\dfrac{2,370}{6,590} \times 100 = 35.96\%$	$\dfrac{1,530}{4,350} \times 100 = 35.17\%$
Mark-up	$\dfrac{2,370}{4,220} \times 100 = 56.16\%$	$\dfrac{1,530}{2,820} \times 100 = 54.26\%$
Net Margin (or Net Profit Margin)	$\dfrac{1,670}{6,590} \times 100 = 25.34\%$	$\dfrac{1,060}{4,350} \times 100 = 24.37\%$

➤ *Return on Capital Employed* (ROCE) is a fundamental measure of business performance as it compares the profit before interest and tax with the total capital used to generate that profit. Notice that we have used year-end figures for capital rather than average figures for the year, though it is permissible to use the average. A viable business should generate a considerably higher return than that available by investing in a bank or other similar interest-bearing deposits. In the case of Madison plc, the return has increased marginally during the year, and is significantly higher than bank deposit rates. However, for a full assessment to be made (and this applies to all the ratios which we have calculated), we would also need to know comparative figures for other businesses operating in the same business sector. For example, if Madison plc was an engineering company and other engineering business were generating only 15% ROCE, we could assume that Madison was doing relatively better than its competitors. If competitors were reporting ROCE of 27%, we might consider Madison plc as under-performing. What is certain is that we cannot make any meaningful statement about *any* ratio without having some comparable figure (previous year, competitor's results, etc.) to use as a yardstick.

➤ *Gross Margin* shows the proportion of sales revenue which resulted in a gross profit to the company. It is affected by various factors, including changing price levels and different products being sold ('sales mix'). The margin might be reduced by aggressive companies wanting to expand their share of the market, or increased if there is reduced competition. Inaccurate stock valuations or the theft of goods may also affect the ratio. In the case of Madison plc, there has been a slight upward movement in the year, resulting in £35.96 of gross profit out of every £100 sales (previous year: £35.17 per £100).

➤ *Mark-up* indicates the pricing policy of the business, as it shows the percentage addition to cost price to arrive at the selling price. In 2001, every £100 of goods bought by Madison plc was sold for £156.10 (previous year: £154.20).

ACTIVITY **10.3**

The higher the gross margin, the higher will be the mark-up percentage. For example, a gross margin of 50% results in a mark-up of 100%, whilst a gross margin of 25% means a mark-up of 33.3%.

If a business has a gross margin of 20%, what would be the mark-up?

Answer

The mark-up is 25%.

(Sales = 100, Cost of sales = 80, GP = 20, therefore mark-up is $\frac{20}{80} \times 100$)

➤ *Net Margin* shows the proportion of sales which resulted in a profit after all overheads (other than interest) had been deducted. In 2001, £25.34 out of every £100 sales resulted in net profit, an increase on the previous year's £24.37. Net profit can be improved by reducing overheads, but a balance has to be achieved between cutting expenses and maintaining business efficiency.

ACTIVITY **10.4**
....

Calculate and comment upon the four profitability ratios for the large UK supermarket groups Tesco plc and Sainsbury plc, from the following information:

(£m)	Tesco plc		Sainsbury plc	
	This year	Previous year	This year	Previous year
Sales	17,158	16,452	16,433	14,500
Gross profit	1,308	1,235	1,317	1,183
Share capital and reserves	4,377	3,903	4,689	4,165
Long-term loans	1,230	812	804	949
Net profit	932	834	943	769

Answer

(%)	Tesco plc		Sainsbury plc	
Name of ratio	This year	Previous year	This year	Previous year
ROCE	16.62	17.69	17.17	15.04
Gross Margin	7.62	7.51	8.01	8.16
Mark-up	8.25	8.12	8.71	8.88
Net Margin	5.43	5.07	5.74	5.30

Comment: Tesco's ROCE slipped slightly in the year whereas Sainsbury's increased. However, Tesco's gross margin (and mark-up) increased whilst Sainsbury's declined, perhaps indicating that Tesco's prices were edging up towards those of Sainsbury, with Sainsbury cost-cutting to maintain their market share. Net margins for both companies improved in the year, with Sainsbury's higher than Tesco's in both years. Note how supermarket groups are under such intense competitive pressure that their gross margins are only slightly higher than their net margins.

10.5.2 Efficiency group of ratios

	Madison plc	
Name of ratio	2001	2000
Fixed assets turnover	$\frac{6,590}{6,200} = 1.06$ times	$\frac{4,350}{5,320} = 0.82$ times
Stock turn	$\frac{(2,200 + 680)/2}{4,220} \times 365 = 124.5$ days	$\frac{(680 + 640)/2}{2,820} \times 365 = 85.4$ days
Debtors' collection period	$\frac{550}{6,590} \times 365 = 30.5$ days	$\frac{500}{4,350} \times 365 = 42$ days
Creditors' payment period	$\frac{390}{5,740*} \times 365 = 24.8$ days	$\frac{210}{2,860*} \times 365 = 26.8$ days
	*Purchases = Cost of sales plus closing stock, less opening stock (4,220 + 2,220 – 680)	*(2,820 + 680 – 640)

➤ *Fixed assets turnover* indicates that 2001 was a more efficient year than 2000 in that every £1 of fixed assets generated £1.06 of sales in 2001, but only 82p in the previous year.

➤ *Stock turn* shows the effect of the massively increased stock at the end of 2001 as it indicates that, on average, stock took 124.5 days to sell in 2001 but 'only' 85.4 days in 2000. This is a significant increase and one which should cause concern to the company management. There may however be a rational explanation, such as a deliberate increase in the stock at the end of 2001 to coincide with a major sales campaign at the start of 2002.

➤ *Debtors' collection period* shows an improved time period for collecting outstanding debts, down from 42 days to just over 30 days. This could be because more resources have been applied to credit control, or prompt-payment discounts have been offered. Efficient businesses collect their debts quickly, as illustrated by Figure 10.2.

figure 10.2
Debt collection practice: good and bad

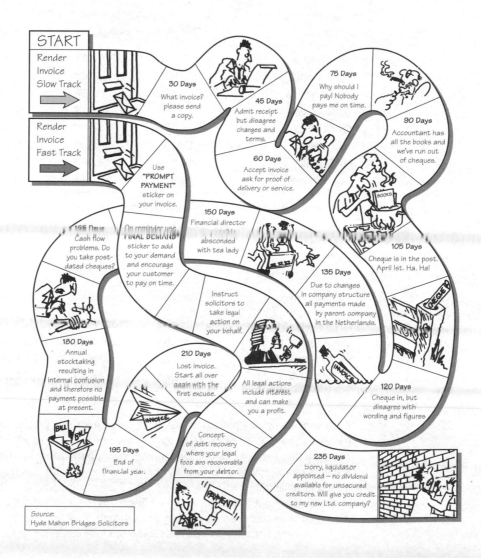

A survey (UK Ltd, KPMG, 1997) showed that the average number of debtors' days was 42 in the UK, bills being paid quickest in Scotland and the west of England (40 days), with the Midlands at 43 and the north-east and south-east lagging behind on 44.

➤ *Creditors' payment period* shows that the company paid its creditors slightly faster in 2001 than in 2000. This may have resulted from being offered discounts for prompt payment. It is good practice not to pay creditors *too* quickly, as it is a form of interest-free credit to the business. However, great care must be taken not to alienate suppliers by delaying payment beyond a reasonable time.

ACTIVITY **10.5**

Calculate and comment upon the four efficiency ratios for Tesco plc and Sainsbury plc, from the following information:

(£m)	Tesco plc		Sainsbury plc	
	This year	Previous year	This year	Previous year
Fixed assets	7,105	6,311	6,409	6,133
Stock (ave)	625	567	793	743
Trade debtors	100	96	54	50
Trade creditors	1,100	972	1,084	902
Credit sales[1]	1,200	1,132	650	600
Total sales	17,158	16,452	16,433	14,500
Purchases	14,599	14,083	15,195	13,288
Cost of sales	15,850	15,217	15,095	13,289

[1] Estimated – the vast majority of the companies' sales are cash sales

Answer

(%)	Tesco plc		Sainsbury plc	
Name of ratio	This year	Previous year	This year	Previous year
Fixed assets turnover	2.41 times	2.61 times	2.56 times	2.36 times
Stock turn	14.4 days	13.6 days	19.17 days	20.41 days
Debtors collection	30.42 days	30.95 days	30.32 days	30.42 days
Creditors payment	27.5 days	25.19 days	26.04 days	24.78 days

Comment: Sainsbury generated £2.56 of sales from every £1 of fixed assets (previous year £2.36) whereas Tesco declined from £2.61 to £2.41. One explanation could be that Tesco expanded by opening new supermarkets, with a time delay before sales were being generated from these new assets. Sainsbury increased the speed at which stock was sold (every 19.17 days compared with 20.41 days in the previous year), but it was no match for Tesco, which, despite a slow-down, still managed to sell its average stock every 14.4 days. Debtors' collection periods were fairly constant, but both companies took more interest-free credit off their suppliers.

10.5.3 Short-term solvency and liquidity group of ratios

Name of ratio	Madison plc	
	2001	2000
Current ratio (or 'working capital' ratio)	3,000:1,200 = 2.5:1	1,380:600 = 2.3:1
Acid test (or 'Quick assets' test)	800*:1,200 = 0.67:1	700*:600 = 1.17:1
	*(3,000 – 2,200)	*(1,380 – 680)

➤ The ideal *current ratio* is often quoted as 2:1 (i.e. twice as many current assets as current liabilities), but it depends upon the type of business. For Madison plc the ratios for both years appear healthy, with current assets strong compared with current liabilities. Contrast this position with the current ratios of the supermarket groups which you will calculate in the next activity. Note that it is possible to have a current ratio which is too strong, for the following reasons:
   — too much stock may be held, resulting in high costs for storage and security, plus interest on overdrafts and loans used to pay for it;
   — inadequate control of debtors may result in uncollected debts;
   — too much cash may mean that fixed assets are not being replaced or investment opportunities are not being considered.

➤ The *acid test* is the crucial measure of whether a business seems able to meet its debts as they fall due. 'Quick' assets are those which can be converted quickly into cash as the need arises, and it is normal to exclude stock and work-in-progress from the ratio. The 'ideal' ratio is often quoted as 1:1 (£1 of 'quick' assets to every £1 of current liabilities), but look at the supermarkets' calculations below to see how viable businesses can survive on much lower ratios. In the case of Madison plc, the exclusion of the high closing stock in 2001 results in a dramatic decline in the acid test ratio, which would be of concern to the company's directors.

ACTIVITY 10.6

Calculate and comment upon the two short-term solvency and liquidity ratios for Tesco plc and Sainsbury plc, from the following information:

(£m)	Tesco plc		Sainsbury plc	
	This year	Previous year	This year	Previous year
Current assets[1]	1,146	942	1,834	1,256
Stock (ave)	625	567	793	743
Creditors[1] < 1 year	3,075	2,713	2,880	2,499

[1] excluding Sainsbury's Bank

Answer

(£m)	Tesco plc		Sainsbury plc	
	This year	Previous year	This year	Previous year
Current ratio	0.37:1	0.35:1	0.64:1	0.50:1
Acid test	0.17:1	0.14:1	0.36:1	0.21:1

Comment: It is apparent that neither company came anywhere near the 'ideal' ratios of 2:1 and 1:1. Put in simple terms, in the current year Tesco had only 17p of quickly realisable assets to meet each £1 of current liabilities! The massive cash inflows of the companies should ensure enough day-to-day liquidity to meet creditors as they fall due. However, there may come a point when any company is threatened with liquidation if it cannot ensure that suppliers are paid on time. Both companies have very poor acid test ratios, and would be looking to improve these in future years.

10.5.4 Long-term solvency and liquidity group of ratios

	Madison plc	
Name of ratio	2001	2000
Gearing	$\dfrac{1,000}{7,000 + 1,000} \times 100 = 12.5\%$	$\dfrac{1,500}{4,600 + 1,500} \times 100 = 24.6\%$
Interest cover	$\dfrac{1,670}{60} = 27.8$ times	$\dfrac{1,060}{70} = 15.14$ times

➤ *Gearing* reflects the relationship between a company's equity capital (ordinary shares and reserves) and its other forms of long-term funding (preference shares, debentures, etc.). A company may exist solely on its equity (i.e. have no gearing), but to expand it may have to issue preference shares carrying a fixed dividend rate, or borrow money on which interest must be paid. Management strategy may be to run a high-geared company, making use of a high proportion of borrowed funds to expand. This has its risks, as many companies have gone into liquidation due to borrowing money and then finding that insufficient profits are generated to repay the loans and interest. However, the rewards for ordinary shareholders can be much greater in a successful high-geared company than in its low-geared equivalent, as the increased profits, less the interest or fixed dividend payments, result in higher dividend payments. Figure 10.3 explains the advantages and disadvantages of different gearing levels.

There are a number of different ways to calculate gearing levels. In the example of Madison plc, the gearing percentage can never be greater than 100% as the loans are added to the divisor in the formula. Another way of calculating gearing would be to omit the loans from the divisor, in which case the gearing could be over 100% if borrowings were greater than the

figure 10.3
Gearing levels

	Advantages		Disadvantages	
	Company	*Shareholders*	*Company*	*Shareholders*
High gearing	Prospect of high profit using borrowed money to expand	Potential of high dividends	High interest burden	Risk of no dividends and company failure if profits can't cover high interest burden
Low gearing (or no gearing)	More profit available (as less interest), less risk of liquidation	Safety of dividends	Company reliant on internal funding, less scope to expand	Relatively low dividends, less scope for increases

equity and reserves. (For Madison, the revised gearing calculation would become $(1,000/7,000) \times 100 = 14.3\%$ in 2001 and $(1,500/4,600) \times 100 = 32.6\%$ in 2000.) As long as the calculations are consistently made, either formula can be used. Madison's gearing has halved in 2001 as a result of the stronger balance sheet and the part repayment of the loan in the year.

➤ *Interest cover* indicates the relative safety of the interest payments by comparing the interest with the profit available to make the payments. Madison has nearly 28 times the interest payments available, which appears very safe and will give assurance to lenders that there would have to be a very dramatic decline in profit before their interest payments were threatened.

ACTIVITY **10.7**

Calculate and comment upon the two long-term solvency and liquidity ratios for Tesco plc and Sainsbury plc, from the following information:

(£m)	Tesco plc		Sainsbury plc	
	This year	*Previous year*	*This year*	*Previous year*
Profit before interest	932	834	943	769
Interest payable	90	74	55	78
Capital and reserves	4,377	3,903	4,689	4,165
Long-term debt	1,230	812	804	949

Answer

(£m)	Tesco plc		Sainsbury plc	
	This year	*Previous year*	*This year*	*Previous year*
Gearing	21.94%	17.22%	14.64%	18.56%
Interest cover	10.36 times	11.27 times	17.15 times	9.86 times

Comment: Tesco's gearing has increased and its interest cover has decreased in the current year, the reverse of Sainsbury's position. In Activity 10.5 we saw how Tesco's fixed assets total had increased by nearly £800m, compared with an increase for Sainsbury's of 'only' £276m. Tesco has been borrowing to expand, hence the increased gearing and poorer interest cover.

10.5.5 Investment group of ratios

Name of ratio	Madison plc 2001	2000
eps (earnings per share)	$\dfrac{£1,160,000}{3,100,000 \text{ shares}} = 37.4\text{p}$	$\dfrac{£720,000}{2,500,000 \text{ shares}} = 28.8\text{p}$
p/e (price/earnings)	$\dfrac{561\text{p}}{37.4\text{p}} = 15 \text{ times}$	$\dfrac{547\text{p}}{28.8\text{p}} = 19 \text{ times}$
Dividend cover	$\dfrac{1,160}{360} = 3.2 \text{ times}$	$\dfrac{720}{120} = 6 \text{ times}$
Dividend yield	$\dfrac{11.6\text{p*}}{561\text{p}} \times 100 = 2.07\%$	$\dfrac{4.8\text{p*}}{547\text{p}} \times 100 = 0.88\%$
	*Dividends/No. of shares £360,000/3,100,000	*Dividends/No. of shares £120,000/2,500,000

➤ *Earnings per share* (eps) and the *price/earnings* (p/e) ratio are important indicators of a company's performance. The eps is always shown at the foot of a plc's profit and loss account, its calculation being the subject of a Financial Reporting Standard.[2] The p/e ratio, where the market price per share is expressed as a multiple of the eps, is the clearest indication of how the stock market rates a particular company. The higher the multiple, the greater the expectation of future profits, with investors having pushed up the market price in anticipation. A low p/e ratio results from losses or poor profits, with a depressed share price. Although Madison's eps has increased (resulting from the 61% increase in after-tax profits but only a 24% increase in share capital), the stock market appears unimpressed as the p/e ratio has slumped from 19 times to 15 times in the year. If the stock market sentiment had remained as positive in 2001 as it had been in 2000, the share price would have been 711p (19 × 37.4p) instead of 561p.

➤ *Dividend cover* is similar to interest cover, in that it indicates the relative safety of the dividends for the year by comparing them with the profit available to make the payments. The increased dividends in 2001 have resulted in a halving of the cover, with available profit just over three times the dividend.

➤ *Dividend yield* measures the actual rate of return obtained by investing in an ordinary share at the current market price. Someone buying a Madison share at £5.61 would obtain a yield of 2.07%, which is a significant increase on that of the previous year.

[2] FRS 14, *Earnings per share*, Accounting Standards Board, London

ACTIVITY **10.8**

Calculate and comment upon the four investment ratios for Tesco plc and Sainsbury plc, from the following information:

	Tesco plc		Sainsbury plc	
	This year	Previous year	This year	Previous year
Earnings (£m)	606	532	598	469
Dividends (£m)	277	255	294	264
No. of shares (m)	6,627	6,553	1,918	1,902
Market price (p)	177	172	385	467

Answer

	Tesco plc		Sainsbury plc	
	This year	Previous year	This year	Previous year
eps (p)	9.14	8.12	31.12	24.66
p/e (times)	19.37	21.18	12.37	18.94
Dividend cover (times)	2.19	2.09	2.03	1.78
Dividend yield (%)	2.36	2.26	3.98	2.97

Comment: The raw eps figures cannot be used for comparison between the companies as they have different numbers of shares in issue. However, the p/e ratio shows how Tesco is much more highly rated by the Stock Exchange than Sainsbury, with future profit expectations pushing up the share price. Dividend cover is broadly similar for the two companies, but the decline in Sainsbury's share price has increased the yield considerably in the current year.

10.6 The validity of the financial statements

In the analysis of company reports, it has been assumed that the information is accurate and reliable and provides a suitable basis for study. Whist it is true that the published financial statements of a plc will be audited and so, with very rare exceptions, show a 'true and fair view' according to an independent firm of qualified accountants, many objective observers have questioned the validity of financial statements for various reasons, including the following.

➤ Financial summaries are drawn up under the *historic cost convention*, whereby items are included at their purchase price at the time of acquisition, and *no account is taken of inflation* on the replacement price of assets such as stock or machinery. This problem is more acute when inflation rates are high, and attempts at introducing alternative inflation-adjusted accounting methods were tried in the 1970s and 1980s when UK inflation peaked at over 25% p.a. No method was felt reliable enough to replace the traditional historic cost convention, though it was felt acceptable to allow revaluations of certain assets (notably land and buildings) where market values had changed significantly when compared to book values. The use of asset revaluation reserves to record such changes was explained in Chapter 7.

➤ The rules and regulations of accounting allow flexibility, so that companies faced with the same accounting problem may come to differing solutions. This flexibility is seen by some as a strength of UK accounting procedures where the requirements of specific companies allow individual accounting treatments to be adopted where appropriate. An example is depreciation, where the judgement of the length of a time period over which assets should be depreciated is left to the discretion of the directors. In some countries, *governments* decree the time period for depreciating different types of asset. The issuing of Accounting and Financial Reporting Standards has greatly reduced the scope for 'creative accounting', but unscrupulous directors will always try and find a loophole.

➤ Information is based on past events, but it is argued that meaningful decisions can be taken only on the basis of forecasts of future performance. Unfortunately, the future is rather harder to verify than the past, so historical documents tend to be seen as a more reliable guide to future prospects than future predictions, however well researched. The ideal is perhaps a balance between the two, with a company's forecasts being published alongside the conventional historical information. However, companies are naturally reluctant to divulge information which may be of use to competitors, so the forecast information may be so vague and generalised as to be of little use to anybody.

10.7 Glossary

Acid test	The comparison between the 'quick' assets and the current liabilities (creditors due for payment within one year)
Current ratio	The comparison between current assets and current liabilities (creditors due for payment within one year)
Dividend cover	The ability of a company to meet its dividends, measured by expressing the profit available for dividends as a multiple of the dividends paid and proposed
Earnings	Profit available to meet equity dividends
Earnings per share (eps)	Earnings divided by the number of ordinary shares issued. Eps is always measured in pence and forms part of the p/e ratio
Gearing	The relationship between a company's equity capital (ordinary shares) and its other forms of long-term funding (preference shares, debentures, etc.)
Historic cost convention	The traditional accounting convention which values assets at their purchase price at the time of acquisition with no allowance made for subsequent inflation

Horizontal analysis	Comparison of values within financial statements by calculation of percentage changes between one year and the next
Interest cover	The ability of a company to meet its interest commitments, measured by expressing the profit before interest as a multiple of the interest paid and payable
Margin	Profit as a percentage of sales
P/e ratio	*see* 'Price/earnings ratio'
Price/earnings ratio	Market price as a multiple of the latest earnings per share. Used as a relative measure of stock market performance
Quick assets	Assets which can be turned quickly into cash. Usually the current assets, other than stock
Statement of total recognised gains and losses	A primary statement summarising all gains and losses recorded within the financial statements, whether within the profit and loss account or the balance sheet
Vertical analysis	Analysis of the relative weighting of components within financial statements by expressing them as a percentage of a key component in that statement
Yield	The percentage return obtained from an investment

SELF-CHECK QUESTIONS

1 Which of the following requires limited companies to publish financial information?
   a The Companies Act 1985
   b The Corporation Act 1992
   c European Union Directive 421B, 1994
   d The Partnership Act 1890

2 Which of the following, found within an annual report, is a primary statement?
   a Auditors' report
   b Operating and financial review
   c Statement of accounting policies
   d Statement of total recognised gains and losses

3 Horizontal analysis is:
   a The calculation of the relative weighting of components within a financial statement in a particular financial period
   b The comparison of the current year's figures with the previous year's figures
   c The comparison of one company's results with another company
   d The comparison of the profit and loss account with the balance sheet

4 ROCE means:
   a Return On Current Expenses
   b Reserves Of Capital Equity
   c Return On Capital Employed
   d Ratio Of Capital Employed

5 If total net assets are £45,600, current liabilities £12,700, stock £3,900 and fixed assets £29,000, what is the Quick Assets Ratio?
   a 2:1
   b 2.3:1
   c 1.5:1
   d 1.75:1

6 Four companies have the following P/E ratios: A 17, B 24, C12, D 8. Which of the following statements about the companies is incorrect?

a B's share price must be twice that of C

b A's share price is 17 times its earnings

c D has the lowest share price relative to its earnings per share

d B has the Stock Market's greatest expectations for future profit growth

7 A company starts its year with stock of £2m and ends with £3m. If it had an overall cost of sales of £12.5m, what was its stock turn in days?

a 85 days

b 1,825 days

c 73 days

d 7.3 days

8 Low gearing means:

a A company depends largely on long-term loans

b A company has few, if any, long-term loans

c A company cannot pay a dividend

d A company has high interest payments

9 An advantage to a company of high gearing is:

a The company can rely on internal funding for expansion

b High interest payments

c Lower risk of liquidation

d Prospect of high profits from using borrowed money for expansion

10 One of the criticisms of accounting information has been:

a The information is always incorrect

b Accountants never follow rules and regulations

c Inflation is not normally reflected within the financial statements

d Companies should report the future instead of the past

Further questions can be found on the accompanying website (www.booksites. net/black).

SELF-STUDY QUESTIONS

(Answers in Appendix 2)

Question 10.1

Obtain an annual report of a trading company (see Reference to this chapter). Produce a vertical and horizontal analysis of the company's profit and loss account, balance sheet and cash flow statement for the current and previous years, and identify the main areas of change disclosed by the analysis.

Question 10.2

The management of Ercall Limited pays particular attention to the ratios and percentages which they calculate from their annual accounts. For the year ended 31 December 2000, they have calculated the following figures, which they are comparing with those of another company, Roden Limited, shown alongside:

	Ercall Ltd	Roden Ltd
Gross profit margin	60%	5%
Net profit margin	20%	2%
Debtors' collection period	30 days	5 days
Current ratio	2:1	0.4:1
Gearing percentage	20%	70%

One of the two companies is a manufacturing company, the other is a food retailer, with an expanding number of stores.

a Which of the two companies is the food retailer? Give two reasons for your choice.

b Assuming that the total cost of sales of Ercall Ltd was £200,000 in 2000, the closing cash and bank balances were £11,004 and the average stock for 2000 was £40,000, calculate:
   ➤ the total of Ercall Limited's debtors at 31 December 2000, assuming all sales were on credit terms;
   ➤ the total of Ercall Limited's current liabilities at 31 December 2000.

c Assuming you were an ordinary shareholder of Roden Limited, what is the significance *to you* of the company's gearing percentage?

Question 10.3

The balance sheets of Rodington Ltd and Rowton Ltd at 31 May 2001 were as follows:

	Rodington	Rowton
	£000	£000
Fixed assets	125	204
Current assets:		
Stock	85	120
Debtors	26	18
Bank balance	12	39
	123	177
Less Creditors due for payment within one year	(135)	(168)
Net Current Assets (Liabilities)	(12)	9
	113	213
Less Creditors due for payment after more than one year		
6% Debentures	–	(100)
Total net assets	113	113
Capital and reserves		
Ordinary shares of £1	50	100
Reserves	63	13
	113	113

Notes:

1 The profits of Rodington Limited are expected to continue at £40,000 per annum. The profits of Rowton Limited have averaged £40,000 before debenture interest.

2 Balance sheets at 31 May 2000 for both companies showed broadly similar figures to those for 2001.

a From the balance sheets as at 31 May 2001, calculate the following ratios for both companies, and give a brief explanation of their significance:
   ➤ Gearing ratio
   ➤ Current ratio

> ➤ Acid test ratio
> ➤ Return on capital employed

b Assume that you had been asked for advice by a cautious potential investor who has £20,000 available. Explain which of the two companies appears to represent the better choice of investment on the basis of the evidence provided.

c If the audit report on Rodington's accounts had stated that the business was not a going concern, how would that affect your views on the company, and in particular the advice given to the potential investor in (b) above?

Question 10.4

Uffington Limited was formed on 1 January 2000. The company's unpublished profit and loss account for 2000 and its balance sheet as at 31 December 2000 are as follows:

Uffington Limited
Profit and Loss Account for the year ended 31 December 2000

	£	£
Sales		670,000
Less Cost of goods sold		
Purchases	570,000	
Less Closing stock	(90,000)	480,000
Gross profit		190,000
Administration expenses	(117,350)	
Distribution expenses	(21,600)	(138,950)
Operating profit before interest		51,050
Interest payable		(5,600)
Profit for the year		45,450
Less Taxation		(5,450)
Profit after taxation		40,000
Proposed dividend		(15,000)
Retained profit for the year		25,000

Balance Sheet as at 31 December 2000

	Cost	Depreciation	Net
	£	£	£
Fixed assets:			
Freehold land	160,000	–	160,000
Fixtures	30,000	21,000	9,000
Motor vehicles	56,000	39,200	16,800
	246,000	60,200	185,800
Current assets:			
Stock		90,000	
Debtors		43,650	
Prepayments		600	
Bank		24,200	
	c/f	158,450	185,800

	b/f	158,450	185,800
Less **Creditors due for payment within one year:**			
Trade creditors	48,000		
Accruals	10,800		
Proposed dividend	15,000		
Taxation	5,450		
		(79,250)	
Net current assets			79,200
			265,000
Less **Creditors due for payment after more than one year:**			
7% Debentures			(80,000)
Total net assets			185,000
Share capital and reserves			
Ordinary shares of £1 each			100,000
Share Premium Account			60,000
Reserves			25,000
			185,000

The company is about to embark on an expansion programme which will require at least £6m for the purchase of new businesses and to support investment in increased stock levels. The chairman of the company has called for an analysis of the 2000 figures before approaching possible sources of funding.

a Comment on the performance of Uffington Limited for the year ended 31 December 2000 and of its financial position at that date. Support your comments with eight relevant accounting ratios.

b Suggest, and comment on the suitability of, three alternative ways for the company to raise £6m.

Further questions can be found on the accompanying website (www.booksites. net/black).

CASE STUDY
. . . .

Esmeralda springs a surprise

On 3 July 2005, Marvin, the founder of Machiq Limited (see previous case studies), was sorting through the morning's correspondence. After reading one particular letter, he immediately summoned his fellow directors, Chiquita and Trixie, to an emergency meeting. He passed the letter round and awaited their comments. The letter read as follows:

'Dear Marvin

I have not written to you since 30 June 2003, in which I demanded compensation for the cruel way you sacked me and my family book in 2001. However, I realised that you would not pay me the £10m I demanded, so I devoted my energies to building a rival business. I rejoined my old employer, Kaboosh Limited, and worked so hard that I was appointed managing director. When my close friend and company chairman, Cardew Kaboosh, died two months ago, he left all his shares to me, so I now own 95% of the company. My company's performance has been so impressive that I now want to take over your company. I am enclosing a copy of the most recent profit and loss account and balance sheet of Kaboosh Limited for information.

Yours sincerely,
Esmeralda'

After reading the letter, it was agreed that Trixie would analyse the financial summaries of Kaboosh Limited and compare them with those of Machiq Limited. She compiled the following summary:

Profit and loss accounts for the year ended 30 June 2005

	Machiq	Kaboosh
	£	£
Sales	705,600	1,102,500
Less Cost of sales	(529,200)	(661,500)
Gross profit	176,400	441,000
Less Expenses	(58,600)	(175,000)
Net profit for the year before interest	117,800	266,000
Less Interest	(1,800)	(12,000)
Net profit for the year, before taxation	116,000	254,000
Less Provision for taxation	(26,950)	(47,000)
Net profit for the year, after taxation	89,050	207,000
Less Dividends	(32,000)	(55,000)
Retained profit for the year	57,050	152,000
Retained profit brought forward	42,100	645,000
Retained profit carried forward	99,150	797,000

Balance sheets as at 30 June 2005

	Machiq Limited		Kaboosh Limited	
	£	£	£	£
Fixed assets (net book value)		165,980		950,000
Current assets:				
Stock	32,650		251,300	
Debtors	30,950		142,500	
Bank	–		36,200	
	63,600		430,000	
Less **Creditors due for payment within one year:**				
Creditors	14,080		108,000	
Taxation	26,950		47,000	
Proposed dividends	32,000		55,000	
Bank overdraft	2,400		–	
	(75,430)		(210,000)	
Net current assets/(liabilities)		(11,830)		220,000
		154,150		1,170,000
Creditors due for payment after more than one year:				
6% Debentures		–		(200,000)
Total net assets		154,150		970,000
Capital and reserves				
Called-up share capital (5p shares)		24,000		100,000
Share Premium Account		31,000		73,000
Profit and Loss Account:				
Retained profit for the year		99,150		797,000
		154,150		970,000

Additional information:

Stock figures represent average values.

P/e ratios for companies in the manufacturing sector average 15 times earnings.

There were no cash sales or purchases during the year for either company.

a Analyse each company's results into the following five groups of ratios, and comment on the relative performance of each company:

➤ Profitability

➤ Efficiency

➤ Short-term solvency and liquidity

➤ Long-term solvency and liquidity

➤ Investment ratios

b Advise the directors of Machiq Limited as to whether they should agree to the company being taken over by Kaboosh Limited. State four additional items of information which they might need before they come to a final decision.

(Answers in Appendix 3)

Reference

••••••••••••••

To obtain annual reports (free of charge to UK addresses):

http://www.icbinc.com/cgi-bin/ft.pl

CHAPTER 11

An introduction to management accounting

Objectives

When you have read this chapter you will be able to:

➤ Understand the role of management accounting
➤ Appreciate the nature of costs
➤ Distinguish between direct and indirect costs
➤ Distinguish between variable and fixed costs
➤ Prepare and comment upon a simple absorption costing statement
➤ Prepare and comment upon a simple marginal costing statement
➤ Understand the importance of contribution within marginal costing
➤ Prepare and comment upon a simple break-even chart

11.1 Introduction

The majority of the information contained in this book so far has been concerned with *financial* accounting, which is the branch of accounting which records and summarises financial transactions to satisfy the information needs of the various user groups such as investors, lenders, creditors and employees. It is sometimes referred to as meeting the *external* accounting needs of the organisation. Another major branch of accounting is *management accounting*, which is sometimes referred to as meeting the *internal* accounting needs of the organisation, as it is designed to help managers with decision making and planning. As such it often involves estimates and forecasts, and is not subject to the same regulatory framework (including Accounting Standards and Companies Acts) as financial accounting. This chapter gives an introduction to management accounting. If you wish to progress in the subject, there are many specialist textbooks (for an example, see References), and there is probably a specialised module of study available in your college or university. There is also a professional body based in the UK, the Chartered Institute of Management Accountants (CIMA), which sets its own professional examinations. CIMA has defined management accounting as:

'An integral part of management concerned with identifying, presenting and interpreting information used for:

➤ formulating strategy
➤ planning and controlling activities
➤ decision taking
➤ optimising the use of resources
➤ disclosure to shareholders and others external to the entity
➤ disclosure to employees
➤ safeguarding assets.

The above involves participation in management to ensure that there is effective:

> formulation of plans to meet objectives (strategic planning)
> formulation of short-term operation plans (budget/profit planning)
> acquisition and use of finance (financial management) and recording of transactions (financial accounting and cost accounting)
> communication of financial and operational information
> corrective action to bring plans and results into line (financial control)
> reviewing and reporting on systems and operations (internal audit, management audit)'[1]

The CIMA definition is deliberately all-embracing, and there are some obvious infringements on what financial accountants might see as their 'territory'. It reinforces the notion that there are overlaps between financial and management accounting, particularly in the recording, interpreting and communicating aspects.

There is an important sub-branch of management accounting, called *Cost Accounting*, which is defined by CIMA as:

'the establishment of budgets, standard costs and actual costs of operations, processes, activities or products; and the analysis of variances, profitability or social use of funds'.

As this chapter is just a brief introduction to management accounting, we shall be concentrating on the nature of costs and their use in a number of key techniques.

11.2 The nature of costs
···································

As we saw when we prepared a manufacturing account in Chapter 4, costs can be broken down into a number of separate elements, as follows:

> *Direct costs*, which can be readily identified with the items being produced. For example, in a bakery, the cost of flour, salt and yeast plus the wages paid to the bakery workers are direct costs. Another name for direct costs is *prime costs*.
> *Indirect costs* are all other expenses which cannot be directly associated with the items being produced. For the bakery these could include the wages paid to the security guards, the cleaners' wages and depreciation of the ovens.

Costs can also be broken down between those costs which are *variable* and those which are *fixed*:

> *Variable costs*, which change with the level of production (also known as 'sensitive' costs). For example, more flour would be used if more loaves are produced.
> *Fixed costs*, which remain constant, regardless of the level of production (also known as 'insensitive' costs). For example, the rent of the bakery would have to be paid whether 1,000 loaves were produced or 10,000.

[1] CIMA (1999) *Management Accounting: Official Terminology*, London

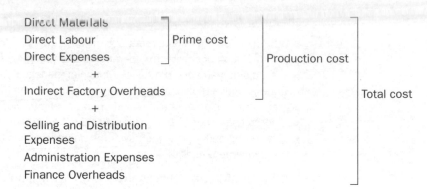

figure 11.1
The elements of cost

Note that some costs maybe regarded as semi-variable (or semi-fixed), in which case the total must be divided between the two categories. For example, part of the bakery's telephone bill is a standing quarterly charge which is fixed, whilst the remainder, representing the call costs, would be variable.

The distinction between the various types of cost are of great importance in understanding a number of management accounting techniques, in particular *absorption costing*, *marginal costing* and *break-even analysis*.

11.3 Absorption costing

Absorption costing is a technique whereby *all* factory indirect costs are allocated or apportioned to (i.e. 'absorbed by') various product lines (or 'units of production/service') to establish the comparative profitability of each product. The difference between fixed and variable costs is ignored, with all production costs being charged to the specific unit of product on a predetermined (and fairly arbitrary) basis. For example, in a bakery producing cakes and loaves as distinct product lines, the factory rent could be apportioned on the basis of the number of square metres occupied respectively by the cake ovens and the bread ovens. Sometimes, non-production costs are also allocated between products, particularly where selling prices are based on a mark-up on the total cost of a product.

ACTIVITY **11.1**

Acme Shirts Limited has produced the following analysis of its product range:

	Formal £000	Sports £000	Casual £000	Total £000
	Shirt range			
Sales (*A*)	340	200	300	840
Direct materials	60	50	70	180
Direct labour	40	50	48	138
Variable overheads	80	60	40	180
Other factory costs (apportioned)	60	70	68	198
Total factory cost (*B*)	(240)	(230)	(226)	(696)
Gross profit/(loss) (*A – B*)	100	(30)	74	144
Non-production overheads				(80)
Net profit				64

Note: 'Non-production overheads' include £10,000 which are variable non-production costs of which 40% relates to the Formal division, 20% to the Sports division and 40% to the Casual division.

The managing director has reviewed the information and believes that the Sports range should be discontinued since it appears to be making a loss. Do you agree with this course of action, and what would be its effect if implemented?

Answer

The allocation of all costs to products has resulted in a gross loss of £30,000 on the Sports shirt range, so it would appear that, by closing the division, the business's net profit would increase from £64,000 to £94,000. However, this ignores the fact that some of the factory costs apportioned to the Sports division will remain even if the division is closed. This aspect is explored in Activity 11.2 below, so we will defer a decision until that activity is completed.

11.4 Marginal costing

The distinction between variable and fixed costs is used in this technique, whereby only *variable* (or 'marginal') costs are charged to specific product units, with the difference between sales revenue (*S*) and variable costs (*C*) being known as the *contribution*:

$$S - V = C$$

PAUSE FOR THOUGHT

The 'contribution' is the amount which each product unit contributes to meeting the fixed costs of the organisation as a whole. Even divisions shown as making losses under absorption costing may be making a positive contribution towards fixed costs.

The fixed costs (*F*) of a period are deducted from the total contribution to establish the net profit (*P*):

$$C - F = P$$

Continuing the example of a bakery, assume it had the following costs in 2000:

	£
Rent and rates	26,000
Wages of bread bakers	20,000
Wages of cake bakers	4,000
Office workers' salaries	6,000
Cost of flour and other raw materials (80% for bread)	48,000
Telephone bills (including £500 standing charge)	5,500
Light and heat (30% fixed)	10,000
Other variable production expenses (75% for bread)	12,000

Sales in the period were £145,000, which represented 200,000 loaves sold at 60p each and 100,000 cakes sold for 25p each. Telephone, rent and rates, and light and heat are apportioned on the basis of Bread 75%, Cakes 25%.

Using *absorption costing techniques*, the information could be analysed as follows:

	Bread	Cakes	Total
Units sold	200,000	100,000	300,000
	£	£	£
Sales (*A*)	120,000	25,000	145,000
Direct materials	38,400	9,600	48,000
Direct labour	20,000	4,000	24,000
Variable production overheads	9,000	3,000	12,000
Other factory costs (apportioned):			
Phone	4,125	1,375	5,500
Light and heat	7,500	2,500	10,000
Rent and rates	19,500	6,500	26,000
Total factory cost (*B*)	(98,525)	(26,975)	(125,500)
Gross profit/(loss) (*A* – *B*)	21,475	(1,975)	19,500
Non-production overheads			
Office salaries			(6,000)
Net profit			13,500

This would seem to indicate that the company should consider closing the loss-making cake division. However, if the same data is redrawn using marginal costing techniques, a very different picture emerges:

		Bread	Cakes	Total
Units sold		200,000	100,000	300,000
		£	£	£
Sales (*A*)		120,000	25,000	145,000
Less Variable costs:				
Direct materials		38,400	9,600	48,000
Direct labour		20,000	4,000	24,000
Variable production overheads		9,000	3,000	12,000
Telephone (variable part only)		3,750	1,250	5,000
Light and heat (variable part only)		5,250	1,750	7,000
Total variable costs (*B*)		(76,400)	(19,600)	(96,000)
Contribution (*A* – *B*) = (*C*)		43,600	5,400	49,000
Less Fixed costs:				
Office salaries	6,000			
Rent and rates	26,000			
Light and heat	3,000			
Phone	500			
Total fixed costs (*D*)				(35,500)
Net profit (*C* – *D*)				13,500

The division of costs between variable and fixed shows that the cakes division made a *positive* contribution of £5,400 towards meeting the overall fixed costs of £35,500. Closing the cakes division on the basis of the 'loss' as shown in the absorption cost technique shown earlier would result in £5,400 less profit for the business as a whole in the next period, as *all* the fixed costs of £35,000 would have to be met by the bread division.

ACTIVITY **11.2**
·················

Look back at the Acme Shirts Limited problem in Activity 11.1. What conclusion can be drawn if marginal costing techniques are used?

Answer

If the results for the period are redrawn using marginal costing techniques, the Sports division is shown as making a positive contribution of £38,000 towards meeting the fixed costs of the whole business, as shown below:

		Shirt range			
		Formal	Sports	Casual	Total
		£000	£000	£000	£000
Sales (A)		340	200	300	840
Less Variable costs					
Direct materials		60	50	70	180
Direct labour		40	50	48	138
Other variable overheads		80	60	40	180
Variable non-production		4	2	4	10
Total variable costs (B)		(184)	(162)	(162)	(508)
Contribution (A − B) = (C)		156	38	138	332
Less fixed costs					
Other factory costs	198				
Non-production overheads	70				
Total fixed costs (D)					(268)
Net profit (C − D)					64

The conclusion must be that the Sports division should *not* be closed.

11.5 Absorption and marginal costing compared
···

Although the previous section would indicate that absorption costing, when contrasted with marginal costing, can lead to poor management decisions, there are advantages and disadvantages to both methods:

	Absorption costing	Marginal costing
Advantages	Indicates total costs of products and services (useful where pricing is on a 'cost plus' basis)	'Contribution per unit' useful for management purposes, including break-even analysis (see Section 11.6)
	Identifies profitability of different products and services	No arbitrary apportionment of costs
	Fits in well with financial accounting summaries showing gross and net profit	Identification of product units making a positive contribution is a better guide than an arbitrary overall profit calculation
Disadvantages	Potentially misleading guide to profitability of product units and could lead to closure of units making a positive contribution to meeting fixed costs	Might be difficult to determine variable/fixed costs: many costs are semi-variable
	Arbitrary allocation of fixed costs to product units in many cases	Doesn't accord with financial accounting split of gross/net profit

11.6 Break-even analysis

In marginal costing, the breakdown of costs into variable and fixed, together with the calculation of a contribution, enables management to answer a number of important questions, such as:

➤ How many units do I need to sell to 'break even' (i.e. reach the point at which sales revenue equals total costs)?
➤ If I sold a specified number of units, would I make a profit or a loss?
➤ How many units do I need to sell to achieve a specified profit target?
➤ Should special orders be accepted?

The key is to calculate a 'contribution per unit' and then use this with the other given data to answer such questions. It is also possible to construct a 'break-even chart' which enables you to read off profit/loss levels at different points of activity.

ACTIVITY **11.3**

Quill Limited, a company manufacturing quality fountain pens, operates from a small building in Newport, with fixed costs, including rent and rates, totalling £30,000 p.a.
  During 2004 it expects to produce 4,000 pens, which retail at £50 each. Total costs (including fixed costs) at this level of production would be £150,000.

1 Calculate the number of pens the company must sell in order to break even (i.e. make neither a profit nor a loss).
2 Calculate the company's likely profit or loss if it manages to sell only 3,200 pens.
3 How many pens would it have to sell to make a profit of £40,000?
4 The company is considering an additional special order from a local company, Global Gherkins plc, for 7,000 pens engraved with that company's logo. They are prepared to pay only £35 for each pen. The cost of engraving each pen is estimated at £2. No additional machinery or buildings would be needed to fulfil the order. Should Quill Limited accept the order?
5 Show the information (without the special order from Global Gherkins plc) in the form of a break-even chart. Read off the profit or loss at a sales level of 1,000 pens.

Answer

Preliminary calculation of the contribution per unit:

	£
Sales price per unit	50
Less variable costs per unit, (£150,000 – £30,000)/4,000	30
Contribution per unit	20

1 To break even, they must sell as many pens as are needed for the total contribution to exactly equal fixed costs. Fixed costs are £30,000 and the contribution per unit is £20, therefore the break-even point is £30,000/£20 = **1,500 pens**.
2 If only 3,200 pens are sold, total contribution = 3,200 × £20 = £64,000. Fixed costs are £30,000, therefore the profit will be £64,000 – £30,000 = **£34,000**.

3 To make a profit of £40,000, the total contribution (Profit + Fixed costs) would need to be £40,000 + £30,000 = £70,000. As the contribution per unit is £20, the number of pens which need to be sold is £70,000/£20 = **3,500**.

4 The decision whether or not to accept the additional special order is based on whether the order will make a positive contribution. The contribution per unit will be as follows:

	£
Sales price per unit	35
Less variable costs per unit (£30 + £2)	32
Contribution per unit	3

As the order is for 6,000 pens, the additional positive contribution will be 6,000 × £3 = **£18,000**, therefore they should accept the order.

5

figure 11.2
Break-even chart

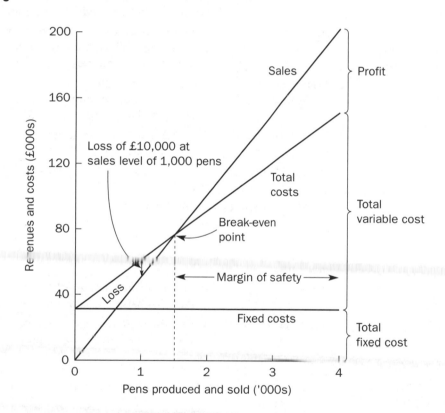

Note: The *margin of safety* indicates the number of units between the break-even point (1,500 pens) and the maximum output (4,000 pens). This informs management how much leeway they have if costs rise and the break-even point starts to 'travel' to the right along the total cost line. Obviously, if the break-even point is reached only on or after the 4,000 pen output line, no profit will be made unless the management takes action either to reduce costs, increase output or increase the selling price.

11.7 Glossary

Absorption costing	A management accounting technique where costs are allocated or apportioned to various product lines to establish the profitability or overall cost of each product
Break-even point	The point at which a business's revenue exactly meets its costs
Contribution	The difference between sales revenue and variable costs
Direct costs	Costs which can be readily identified with the particular units or type of product, such as raw materials and manufacturing wages
Fixed costs	Costs which remain constant, regardless of the level of production, e.g. the factory insurance might remain constant whether production is high or low
Indirect costs	Expenses which cannot be directly associated with the items being produced, such as supervisors' wages, the factory canteen, and rent and rates
Management accounting	The internal accounting needs of an organisation, involving planning, forecasting and budgeting for decision-making purposes
Margin of safety	The difference between a business's break-even point and its maximum production
Marginal cost	The extra cost that would result from producing one extra unit
Marginal costing	A management accounting technique where costs are divided between variable and fixed, and a contribution is established by deducting the variable costs from the sales revenue
Semi-variable costs	Costs where part is variable and part is fixed, e.g. a service contract for vans may consist of a fixed annual charge, plus a variable charge based on mileage
Variable costs	Costs which change with the level of production, e.g. a nail factory uses more iron if more nails are produced

SELF-CHECK QUESTIONS

1 In a company manufacturing paint, which of the following would not be a direct cost?
   a The cost of paint tins
   b The cost of dyes to colour the paint
   c The cost of advertising the paint
   d The cost of chemicals used to make the paint

2 Another name for direct costs is:
   a Prime costs
   b Fixed costs
   c Absorbed costs
   d Overhead costs

3 A feature of absorption costing is that:
   a The distinction between fixed and variable costs is ignored
   b A contribution is established
   c Only direct costs of production are considered
   d Loss-making divisions are closed

4 Which of the following equations best represents marginal costing, where F = fixed costs, S = sales, C = contribution, V = variable costs, and P = profit?
   a $S - F = C, C - V = P$
   b $S - V = C, C - P = F$
   c $S - V = C, C - F = P$
   d $S - C = V, V - F = P$

5 If total sales revenue for 1,000 units is £5,000 and total variable costs are £3,000, the contribution per unit is:
   a £3,000
   b £2,000
   c £5
   d £2

6 If the variable costs per unit are £6, and 500 units have been sold for £5,000, the total contribution is:
   a £4,000
   b £2,000
   c £3,000
   d £8,000

7 If total fixed costs are £12,000, the selling price per unit is £12 and the variable costs per unit are £8, the break-even point is:
   a 12,000 units
   b 3,000 units
   c 1,500 units
   d 4,500 units

8 If the break-even point is 6,000 units and the contribution per unit is £6, total fixed costs must be:
   a £2,000
   b £18,000
   c £12,000
   d £36,000

9 If fixed costs are £32,000, maximum sales are £100,000 and variable costs are £60,000 at this level, the turnover required to break even is:
   a £80,000
   b £53,334
   c £19,200
   d £32,000

10 If fixed costs are £160,000 and the contribution per unit is £2, the number of units to be sold to achieve a profit of £60,000 is:
   a 80,000
   b 50,000
   c 110,000
   d 440,000

Further questions can be found on the accompanying website (www.booksites. net/black).

Question 11.1

Complete the shaded areas in the following table. Assume that A – E are separate businesses.

	A	B	C	D	E
Sales in units			4,000	6,000	15,000
Sales (£)	40,000	60,000	48,000	90,000	
Variable costs (£)	10,000		32,000	54,000	30,000
Contribution (£)	30,000	10,000	16,000		75,000
Contribution per unit (£)	6	0.5		6	
Fixed costs (£)	14,400		7,000		50,000
Profit/(loss) (£)		(5,000)		12,000	
Break-even point (units)	2,400	30,000		4,000	
Profit/(loss) if 3,000 units sold					

Question 11.2

Rumpole Ltd is proposing an expansion of their product range by manufacturing a new product. It is proposed that the new product will sell for £15 per item and will have a market between 10,000 and 15,000 items per year. An analysis of the costs at these levels of production is:

Units	10,000	15,000
	£	£
Materials	40,000	60,000
Labour	70,000	95,000
Overheads	50,000	55,000

a   Calculate the variable cost per unit and the total fixed cost.
b   Calculate how many units of the product must be manufactured to:
  ➤   break even
  ➤   earn a profit of £13,000.
c   Calculate how much profit or loss would be made if only 7,000 units were manufactured and sold.

Question 11.3

Indicate the following information on the proforma break-even chart in Figure 11.3. (Copy out the chart if this book is not your property).

➤   The break-even point
➤   The 'loss' area
➤   The margin of safety
➤   Fixed costs
➤   Variable costs
➤   Sales
➤   The 'profit' area

figure 11.3
**Break-even chart
proforma for
question 11.3**

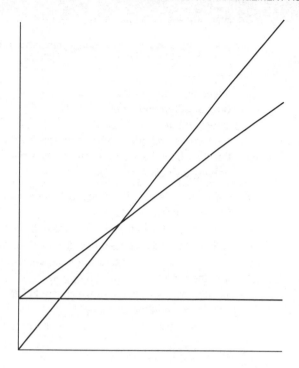

Question 11.4

From the following information produce a break-even chart for Basil Limited:

Maximum sales and production (units)	10,000
Fixed costs (£)	18,000
Sales price per unit (£)	6
Variable cost per unit (£)	1.50

From the chart, answer the following questions:

- What is the break-even point in units?
- How much profit or loss is made if 6,000 units are sold?
- What is the margin of safety in units?
- How many units must be sold for Basil Ltd to make a profit of £4,500?

Further questions can be found on the accompanying website (www.booksites.net/black).

Who is Mrs Eadale?

The directors of Machiq Limited (see previous case studies) decided to reject Esmeralda's take-over bid and instead devoted their talents to developing new products. Trixie, the managing director, had been sent an e-mail containing a recipe for a vanishing potion and decided to investigate the possibility of setting up a separate division to produce and promote it. The creator of the recipe, who had signed herself 'Mrs Eadale', said that the potion was totally harmless and caused only temporary invisibility. She also insisted that, as an absolute condition of her allowing Machiq Limited to use the recipe free of charge, the directors must test the potion on themselves before selling it to the general public.

Chiquita, the finance director, produced the following information:

Maximum production and sales per annum (bottles)	15,000
	£
Selling price per bottle	14
Ingredients per bottle	3
Cost of bottle and label	1
Direct labour cost per bottle	2
Rent, rates and other fixed costs relating to bottling division	20,000
Portion of company's other fixed costs to be absorbed by bottling division	130,000

a Using the *absorption costing* technique, would the new division be viable? Show your calculations.

b What recommendation might have been made if *marginal costing* had been used to evaluate the proposed new division? Show your calculations.

c Using marginal costing techniques, calculate:
- ➤ the break-even point (in bottles),
- ➤ the number of bottles which would have to be sold to earn £16,000 profit for the bottling division,
- ➤ how much profit or loss would be made if only 4,000 bottles were sold.

(Answers in Appendix 3)

A footnote:

Marvin, Chiquita and Trixie set up the bottling division. They sent an invitation to Esmeralda to join them at a celebration champagne 'test the potion' party to show there were no hard feelings after her failed take-over bid. Esmeralda replied saying that she would be *very* pleased to watch the three directors vanish and looked forward to toasting their health in champagne beforehand. Unfortunately, a waiter hired for the occasion inadvertently poured the potion into the champagne glasses, and the guests, after raising their glasses to the toast of 'Mrs Eadale', drank the 'champagne' and promptly disappeared without trace.

Reference
....

A companion volume devoted to management accounting:
Wright, D. (1996) *Management Accounting*, Longman Modular Texts in Business and Economics, Harlow: Longman

CHAPTER **12**
....

Revision chapter (2)

Objectives
....

When you have completed this chapter you will be able to:

➤ Relax, knowing that you have worked hard enough to get a very good pass mark in your accountancy course!

12.1 Introduction
....

This chapter consolidates the knowledge gained throughout the book, and is structured as follows:

Practice Examination Paper 1: a one-hour examination paper consisting of 40 multiple-choice questions, covering all chapters of the book.

Practice Examination Paper 2: a two-hour examination paper consisting of five questions. Solutions are provided in Appendix 4.

12.2 Practice Examination Paper 1
....

Time allowed ONE hour

This question paper contains FORTY multiple-choice questions. Read each question carefully and select ONE answer that you think is correct.

1 If a company is described as a 'going concern', it is:
    a   About to close down
    b   Not about to close down
    c   A company people are concerned about
    d   A rapidly expanding company

2 A company sells £150,000 of goods during the year, having been owed £12,000 by debtors at the start of the year and £18,000 at the end of the year. What sales figure will be shown in the profit and loss account for the year?
    a   £150,000
    b   £144,000
    c   £156,000
    d   £180,000

3 Which accounting concept overrides other concepts?
   a   Prudence concept
   b   Consistency concept
   c   True and fair view concept
   d   Accruals concept

4 An owner of a business had a capital balance of £85,000 at the end of the financial year. During the year, drawings of £14,000 had been made, and the business had made a net profit of £17,000. The owner paid in an inheritance of £40,000 into the business during the year. What was the opening capital balance?
   a   £14,000
   b   £156,000
   c   £42,000
   d   £122,000

5 In the accounting equation, assets plus expenses equals:
   a   Liabilities + Capital + Income
   b   Liabilities + Capital – Income
   c   Liabilities – Capital + Income
   d   Liabilities – Capital – Income

6 Why, if a business has money in the bank, does it appear as a debit balance in the business's ledger?
   a   It's a mistake – it should be a credit balance
   b   It is showing that the bank is a debtor of the business
   c   As all the debits equal all the credits, there is no difference between a debit and credit balance
   d   It shows that the business is in debt

7 A business pays a cheque for £4,100 for a van, of which £150 is for road tax. What would be the correct bookkeeping entries?
   a   Dr Van £4,100,   Cr Bank £4,100
   b   Dr Bank £4,100, Cr Van £3,950 and Cr Motor expenses £150
   c   Dr Motor expenses £4,100, Cr Bank £4,100
   d   Dr Van £3,950 and Dr Motor expenses £150, Cr Bank £4,100

8 A cash float is:
   a   A predetermined amount of petty cash which is paid out at regular intervals
   b   Cash used only for buying fixed assets
   c   A predetermined amount needed to meet petty cash expenditure, which is topped up at intervals
   d   The amount of petty cash after all the petty cash expenditure has been deducted

9 A bank reconciliation statement is used for:
   a   Ensuring that the business's own records of the bank account agree with the bank's records
   b   Ensuring that the bank manager knows what cheques the business has been paying
   c   Ensuring that the business does not exceed an agreed overdraft limit
   d   Summarising all the business's banking transactions for the financial period

10 A financial period:
    a   Is the same as a financial year
    b   Is the same as the balance sheet date
    c   Always ends on 31 December
    d   Can be as long or as short as the business needs for a specific purpose

11 Stock is usually valued in a balance sheet at:
    a   Selling price
    b   Lower of cost and net realisable value
    c   Lower of cost and gross realisable value
    d   Lower of selling price and net realisable value

12 A business has a combined rent and rates account. During the year ended 31 December 2001, the business had an opening rent prepayment of £200 and an opening rates accrual of £300. During the year it paid £11,000 for rent and rates. At the end of the year, £900 had been prepaid for rates and there was an accrual of £600 for rent. What figure for rent and rates would appear in the profit and loss account?
    a   £10,800
    b   £10,600
    c   £11,200
    d   £11,400

13 A fixed asset which cost £60,000 has been owned for three years. It is depreciated at 40% p.a. on the reducing balance method. What value would be shown as its net book value at the end of the third year of ownership?
    a   £21,600
    b   £8,640
    c   £12,960
    d   nil

14 Which of the following would be prime (direct) costs of a furniture manufacturer?
    a   Depreciation of wood-working machinery
    b   Wood used to make furniture
    c   Electricity used to heat the factory
    d   The rent of the factory

15 In a manufacturing business, what is 'work-in-progress'?
    a   Partly completed goods
    b   Goods in transit to a customer
    c   Raw materials
    d   Work about to start on manufacturing goods

16 Which one of the following statements is an integral part of the double-entry bookkeeping system?
    a   Cash flow statement
    b   Balance sheet
    c   Trial balance
    d   Profit and loss account

17 A car which cost £14,000 is part-exchanged for a new car exactly three years after its purchase. Cars are depreciated on the straight line basis over 5 years, assuming a residual value of 10% of the purchase price. If the part

exchange value of the car was £4,000, what profit or loss would be recorded in the profit and loss account in the year of disposal?

a £2,440 loss

b £1,600 loss

c £440 profit

d £2,600 profit

18 Theoretical stock valuation methods such as FIFO would be used where:

a Stock can be priced by looking at invoices

b Stock is always sold in a set order, e.g. oldest stock is sold first

c It is difficult or impossible to match stock with an invoiced price

d Stock has not been counted at the end of the financial period

19 The debtors' balances included within the total of current assets on a balance sheet should be:

a All the sales ledger balances

b Only the good debts of the business

c The sales ledger balances less any increase in a provision for doubtful debts

d All the sales ledger balances except the bad debts

20 Which of the following is the 'odd one out'?

a Provision for bad and doubtful debts

b Provision for good debts

c Provision for bad debts

d Provision for doubtful debts

21 Why might a partnership charge interest on partners' drawings?

a Because they want to increase the money taken out by partners

b To deter partners from taking excessive amounts from the business

c To ensure that all partners take an equal amount from the business

d The Partnership Act 1890 states that they have to charge interest

22 A convertible loan stock is:

a A loan issued by a company which can be converted into shares at a later date

b Money borrowed to buy the managing director a convertible car

c Raw materials lent to the business which are to be converted into a finished product

d A loan issued by a company which can be converted into a different currency at a later date

23 Two liabilities found in both a limited company and sole trader's balance sheet are:

a Corporation tax and dividends

b Creditors and overdraft

c Accruals and dividends

d Corporation tax and accruals

24 A holder of a preference share has the following advantages over an ordinary shareholder:

a A dividend which will increase if profits increase

b A greater number of votes for each share held

    c   Preferential prices if buying the company's products

    d   Priority over ordinary shareholders for payment of dividends and also capital repayment if the company fails

25 A bonus issue by a company has the following effect:

    a   Existing shareholders are given more shares

    b   Existing shareholders are given the right to buy more shares

    c   Non-shareholders are invited to buy shares in the company

    d   Directors receive a salary bonus

26 A share premium is:

    a   The amount shareholders pay for a share

    b   The increase in value in a share after it is sold

    c   The difference between the stock market price of a share and the nominal value of that share

    d   The difference between the price at which a company sells a share and the nominal value of that share

27 A 'statement of affairs' is broadly comparable to a:

    a   Cash flow statement

    b   Trial balance

    c   Balance sheet

    d   Profit and loss account

28 A business does not keep full accounting records, but you find that its opening debtors were £2,500 and its closing debtors were £6,000. Cash and cheques received from customers in the period totalled £49,300, bad debts suffered totalled £120, and £400 discount was allowed to customers for prompt payment. What is the total sales for the period?

    a   £53,320

    b   £52,720

    c   £46,320

    d   £52,800

29 Which of the following pairs *both* result in a positive cash flow?

    a   Decrease in stock and decrease in creditors

    b   Increase in stock and increase in creditors

    c   Increase in creditors and increase in debtors

    d   Decrease in stock and decrease in debtors

30 If a company shows Sales £60,000 and Gross Profit £12,000, which of the following calculations are correct?

    a   Mark-up 20%, Gross Margin 25%

    b   Mark-up 400%, Gross Margin 5%

    c   Mark-up 33%, Gross Margin 50%

    d   Mark-up 25%, Gross Margin 20%

31 Which one of the following statements is always true?

    a   The directors of a company own the company

    b   The auditors of a company produce the financial statements

    c   The company's reserves are represented by bank balances

    d   The shareholders of a company own the company

32 If a company has much more borrowed capital than equity capital, which of the following statements is always true?
    a   If interest rates rise, the company will have to close
    b   The company will expand faster than a company with no borrowings
    c   The company is said to be highly geared
    d   The company is said to be low geared

33 If the directors of a plc need to raise money for the company, which of the following would not achieve that effect?
    a   A bonus issue of shares
    b   A rights issue of shares
    c   A new issue of shares to the general public
    d   Issuing a debenture

34 A company has net current assets of £20,000, including stock valued at £22,000. The total of current assets is £60,000 and the current ratio is 1.5:1. What is the acid test ratio?
    a   2:1
    b   0.95:1
    c   0.5:1
    d   2.7:1

35 In a factory producing carpets, wool used in the production process would be classified as a:
    a   Fixed cost
    b   Indirect cost
    c   Direct cost
    d   Semi-variable cost

36 The technique of absorption costing is useful where:
    a   Pricing of products or services is on a 'cost-plus' basis
    b   Divisions need to be closed down
    c   It is impossible to allocate costs to different products
    d   The contribution of each product is to be calculated

37 A 'contribution' calculated under marginal costing is:
    a   The amount which each product unit contributes to the business's sales total
    b   The amount which each product unit contributes to the variable costs of the business
    c   The same as the fixed costs allocated to a product unit
    d   The amount which each product unit contributes to meeting the fixed costs of the business

38 A retail company sells cameras, all of which are sold at £40 each and bought from a manufacturer for £25 each. The retailer's fixed costs are £90,000, and all cameras bought in are sold. How many cameras must the retailer sell to break even?
    a   2,250
    b   3,600
    c   6,000
    d   1,385

39 From the details in question 38, how many cameras must the retailer sell to earn a profit of £15,000?

a   2,625

b   3,750

c   1,000

d   7,000

40 From the details in question 38, how much profit or loss would be made if 5,000 cameras were sold?

a   £75,000 profit

b   £15,000 loss

c   £200,000 profit

d   £90,000 loss

Further questions can be found on the accompanying website (www.booksites. net/black).

12.3 Practice Examination Paper 2

Time allowed TWO hours

Answer one of the two questions in Section A and all three questions in Section B. All questions carry equal marks.

Section A. Answer either question 1 or question 2.

Question 1

The trial balance of Aubrey Locke, a sole trader, at 31 May 2001 is as follows:

	Dr £	Cr £
Bank	3,840	
Cash	120	
Forklift truck: cost	20,000	
Forklift truck: depreciation to 31 May 2000		4,500
Motor cars: cost	18,000	
Motor cars: depreciation to 31 May 2000		6,000
Sales		375,000
Purchases	195,000	
Opening stock at 1 June 2000	62,000	
Rent	20,000	
Sales returns	420	
Electricity	8,000	
Debtors	16,200	
Creditors		14,600
Discount received		180
Wages and salaries	37,000	
Provision for doubtful debts at 1 June 2000		2,640
Bad debts written off	520	
General office expenses	18,000	
Owner's drawings	18,500	
Capital at 1 June 2000		14,680
	417,600	417,600

Notes:

1   Closing stock is £50,000.
2   Electricity of £2,000 is to be accrued at the year-end.
3   Rent of £4,000 has been prepaid at the year-end.
4   Depreciation on the forklift is calculated over 4 years on the straight line method, assuming a residual value of £2,000.
5   Depreciation on the cars is calculated at 40% on the reducing balance method.
6   The provision for doubtful debts is to be decreased by £400.

a   Prepare a profit and loss account for the year ended 31 May 2001 and a balance sheet as at that date.
b   If Aubrey Locke had been operating his business as a limited company, there are likely to be additional items of information you would expect to see when compared to the financial statements of a sole trader.
   (i)   List three additional items you would expect to find in a company's profit and loss account; and
   (ii) List three additional items you would expect to find in a company's balance sheet.

Question 2

Wilma Tonbridge started a business on 1 January 2000, with her own capital of £10,000 and an interest-free long-term loan of £20,000 from a friend. Her business retails Tonies, which are luxury fluffy toys sold at £80 each. Wilma, who has little knowledge of accounting, produced the following statement of her business's financial situation at the end of her first year's trading:

Balance account

	£	£
Cash received from selling 2,000 Tonies		160,000
Less Cash paid:		
Wages	56,000	
Purchases	127,200	
Rent and rates	16,000	
Office expenses	9,600	
Loan repayment	4,000	
		(212,800)
Loss		(52,800)

Wilma sent the statement to her bank manager, who immediately told Wilma to find an accountant to produce a set of financial statements drawn up according to generally accepted accounting principles. Wilma instructs you to prepare these statements.

You confirm that the amounts shown in Wilma's statements agree with details shown in the business's bank statements, but you find the following additional information:

1   A further 600 Tonies were sold in 2000, but not paid for during the year.
2   Wilma estimates that 5% of debtors are doubtful.
3   £7,000 is owed for purchases received in the year.

4 Wilma's starting capital and the loan were used to buy computers and office furniture and fittings with an estimated life of 5 years and an anticipated residual value of £5,000.

5 Wages of £1,600 and office expenses of £800 were accrued at the end of the year.

6 Stock at the end of the year was valued at £9,200.

7 The rent and rates covered the period from 1 January 2000 to 31 March 2001.

8 The wages figure included £32,000 taken by Wilma for her own personal use.

a Prepare a profit and loss account for the year ended 31 December 2000 and a balance sheet as at that date.

b Show, in as much detail as possible from the above information, the ledger accounts for Wages and also for Rent and Rates. Close off the two accounts and bring down balances at 1 January 2001.

Section B. Answer all three questions in this section.

Question 3

A company has just appointed a non-accountant as its new chairman. He makes the following comment to the managing director, who is a qualified accountant:

'I am under constant pressure from the shareholders, who always demand increased dividends from ever greater profits. You follow the prudence concept, which to my mind results in the lowest possible profits!'

a Explain the meaning of the prudence concept.

b Name and briefly explain three fundamental accounting concepts, other than the prudence concept.

c Analyse three relevant factors which either support or contradict the chairman's comments.

Question 4

The management of Eastbourne Ltd has calculated the following statistics from its results for the year ended 31 December 2001. Equivalent average figures from a relevant trade association are also given.

	Eastbourne Ltd	Trade average
(i) Gross profit margin	50%	40%
(ii) Net profit margin	10%	8%
(iii) Return on capital employed	16%	12%
(iv) Acid test	1:1	1.5:1
(v) Gearing percentage	80%	30%

a Explain the significance of, and the basis of calculation for, each of the five statistics listed above.

b Explain why, if you were informed that Eastbourne Limited's current ratio was 6:1, compared with a trade average of 2:1, this might not indicate a satisfactory situation.

Question 5

Solomon Limited manufactures coats. The company's management is preparing a budget for the next financial year and has prepared the following information:

	£
Selling price per coat	100
Materials per coat	25
Direct labour per coat	30
Overheads: variable per coat	5
Fixed overheads (total) £240,000 p.a.	

The company is planning to manufacture 16,000 coats in the next year.

a   Calculate:
  ➤ the break-even point (number of coats),
  ➤ the margin of safety (number of coats),
  ➤ the profit or loss if 11,000 coats are manufactured and sold.

b   A supermarket chain has approached Solomon Limited with a view to placing a special order for 5,000 coats bearing a prominent advertisement, but is prepared to pay only £70 per coat. The additional cost of embroidering the advertisement would be £6 per coat. This order would be within the capacity of the company and fixed costs would remain unchanged. Advise the company whether the special order should be accepted.

Further questions can be found on the accompanying website (www.booksites. net/black).

References
• • • • • • • • • • • • • •

Now that you have completed this book, you might be thinking of a career in accountancy. These are the website addresses of the main accountancy bodies in the UK:

Institute of Chartered Accountants in England and Wales: http://www.icaew.co.uk/

The Association of Chartered Certified Accountants: http://www.acca.org.uk/

Institute of Chartered Accountants in Scotland: http://www.icas.org.uk/

Chartered Institute of Management Accountants: http://www.cima.org.uk/

Association of Accounting Technicians: http://www.accountingtechnician.co.uk/

APPENDIX 1

Answers to self-check questions

					Chapter						
	1	2	3	4	5	6	7	8	9	10	11
Question											
1	d	c	b	c	c	a	c	c	d	a	c
2	a	d	b	b	a	c	d	a	d	d	a
3	c	a	c	a	d	b	d	a	a	b	a
4	b	c	c	d	b	d	a	c	d	c	c
5	a	b	c	a	a	a	b	d	b	a	d
6	b	c	d	c	d	a	b	a	c	a	b
7	c	d	a	b	b	c	a	c	c	c	b
8	c	a	a	c	c	b	c	d	a	b	d
9	d	c	c	d	a	d	c	b	c	d	a
10	a	b	d	a	c	b	d	b	a	c	c
11						a					
12						b					
13						d					
14						a					
15						c					
16						b					
17						b					
18						c					
19						a					
20						a					
21						c					
22						c					
23						d					
24						a					
25						b					
26						b					
27						c					
28						c					
29						a					
30						b					
31						c					
32						a					
33						a					
34						d					
35						b					

Answers to self-study questions

Chapter 1

Question 1.1

	Assets £	Liabilities £	Capital £
1	25,630	14,256	11,374
2	39,156	23,658	15,498
3	619,557	352,491	267,066
4	69,810	54,947	14,863
5	57,058	21,596	35,462
6	36,520	12,010	24,510
7	151,632	65,342	86,290
8	114,785	17,853	96,932
9	212,589	65,769	146,820
10	265,108	63,527	201,581
Totals:	1,591,845	691,449	900,396

Note that Assets less Liabilities = Capital.

Question 1.2

a   'Going concern' is a fundamental accounting concept, which assumes that the business can continue to trade for the foreseeable future. If it did not apply then that would indicate that the business had a very uncertain future, with a real possibility of failure.

b   *Accruals concept*: When calculating the profit or loss of an organisation, all income and related expenditure for a specified period should be included, not simply money paid or received.

Consistency concept: Accounting procedures used should be the same as those applied previously for similar items. This allows comparability of financial summaries over time.

Prudence concept: Accountants should be cautious in the valuation of assets or the measurement of profit. The *lowest* reasonable estimate of an asset's value should be taken, whilst a forecast loss would be included but not a forecast profit.

c   The overriding concept is that of 'true and fair view', which refers to the need for the financial statements to show truth and fairness, even if it means abandoning one or more of the fundamental accounting concepts.

Question 1.3

The most recent figures at the time of this publication are given below. The balance sheet information is from the 'group' figures, not 'company' figures. You may have been able to access more recent figures.

	Tesco (£m)		J.Sainsbury (£m)	
	Latest year	Previous year	Latest year	Previous year
(from the balance sheets)				
Total net assets (i.e. fixed and current assets, less liabilities)	4,377	3,903	4,689	4,165
(from the profit and loss account)				
Total sales for the year	18,546	17,779	17,587	15,496
Operating profit	934	849	836	762

Notes:

1   Overall value shows that Sainsbury has a greater balance sheet value than Tesco (6.7% higher).

2   Tesco's sales were higher than Sainsbury's by 5.5%.

3   Tesco's profit was higher than Sainsbury's, by 11.7%, and when profit is compared with the value of each company, Tesco's profit was 21.34% whereas Sainsbury recorded only 17.83%. This is known as the 'return on capital employed' – see Chapter 10.

4   The total net assets of Tesco have grown by 12.1% and those of Sainsbury by 12.6% between the two years, so both companies have been expanding. Tesco's sales increased by 4.3% in the year, whilst Sainsbury's sales increased by 13.5%, showing that Sainsbury were fighting hard to maintain their share of the market. Tesco's profit increased by 10%, slightly higher than Sainsbury's increase of 9.7%. A more detailed analysis of both companies is given in Chapter 10.

Chapter 2

Question 2.1

Sales account

	£		£
12 Dec Cash repaid to customer	65	17 Dec Cash received	84,000
31 Dec Balance c/d	209,535	22 Dec Sales day book	125,600
	209,600		209,600
		1 Jan Balance b/d	209,535

Bank charges account

	£		£
12 Oct Charges	112	13 Dec Refund due to bank error	26
12 Nov Charges	145	31 Dec Balance c/d	231
	257		257
1 Jan Balance b/d	231		

Question 2.2

	Assets	Expenses	Liabilities	Capital	Income
	£	£	£	£	£
1 The business pays a cheque of £100 for phone charges	− £100 (Bank)	+ £100 (Phone charges)			
2 The business pays a creditor £250	− £250 (Bank)		− £250 (Creditor)		
3 The owner takes out £100 in cash from the business	− £100 (Cash)			− £100 (Drawings)	
4 Goods are sold to a debtor for £900	+ £900 (Debtors)				+ £900 (Sales)
5 Petrol is bought on credit for £60		+ £60 (Petrol)	+ £60 (Creditor)		
Summary (overall change)	+ £450	+ £160	− £190	− £100	+ £900

Note that Assets + Expenses = Liabilities + Capital + Income.

Question 2.3

	Assets	Expenses	Liabilities	Capital	Income
	£	£	£	£	£
1 The owner pays in £6,000 to start the business's bank account	+ £6,000 (Bank)			+ £6,000 (Capital)	
2 The business pays wages of £200 by cheque	– £200 (Bank)	+ £200 (Wages)			
3 Goods are bought for £400 on credit from Goff Limited		+ £400 (Purchases)	+ £400 (Creditor)		
4 Goods are sold on credit to Plod plc for £510	+ £510 (Debtor)				+ £510 (Sales)
5 A computer is bought for £600 with a cheque	+ £600 (Fixed Asset) – £600 (Bank)				
6 Stationery is bought for £50 with a cheque	– £50 (Bank)	+ £50 (Stationery)			
Summary (overall change)	+ £6,260	+ £650	+ £400	+ £6,000	+ £510

Note that Assets + Expenses = Liabilities + Capital + Income.

Question 2.4

Rachel Roberts' business

Bank

		£			£
Oct 1	Capital	9,000	Oct 1	Purchases	4,000
2	Sales	600	3	Advertising	30
5	Sales	700		Printing	45
			4	Rent	100
			6	Drawings	400
			7	Sales returns	40
					4,615
			7	Balance c/d	5,685
		10,300			10,300
Oct 8	Balance b/d	5,685			

Cash

		£			£
Oct 1	Capital	100	Oct 1	Stationery	60
2	Sales	280	6	Wages	260
5	Sales	130			320
			7	Balance c/d	190
		510			510
Oct 8	Balance b/d	190			

Capital

		£			£
			Oct 1	Bank	9,000
				Cash	100
					9,100

Purchases

		£		£
Oct 1	Bank	4,000		

Stationery

		£		£
Oct 1	Cash	60		

Sales

		£			£
			Oct 2	Bank	600
				Cash	280
			5	Bank	700
				Cash	130
					1,710

Advertising

		£		£
Oct 3	Bank	30		

Printing

		£		£
Oct 3	Bank	45		

Rent

		£		£
Oct 4	Bank	100		

Wages

		£		£
Oct 6	Cash	260		

Drawings

		£		£
Oct 6	Bank	400		

Sales returns

		£		£
Oct 7	Bank	40		

Rachel Roberts
Trial balance as at 7 October

	Dr £	Cr £
Bank	5,685	
Cash	190	
Capital		9,100
Purchases	4,000	
Stationery	60	
Sales		1,710
Advertising	30	
Printing	45	
Rent	100	
Wages	260	
Drawings	400	
Sales returns	40	
	10,810	10,810

Question 2.5

Casper Peabody's business
Purchases Day Book

			£
May 1	C. Moss		630
	J. Carter		419
	A. McKeane		330
3	A. Iqbal		560
	A. McKeane		210
			2,149

Sales Day Book

			£
May 2	K. Palfreyman		199
	L. Patel		870
			1,069

Purchase Returns Day Book

			£
May 4	J. Carter		80
7	A. Iqbal		40
			120

Sales Returns Day Book

		£
May 5	L. Patel	62

Purchase Ledger

C. Moss

	£			£
		May 1	Invoice	630

J. Carter

		£			£
May 4	Returns	80	May 1	Invoice	419
6	Bank	339			
		419			419

A. McKeane

	£			£
		May 1	Invoice	330
		May 3	Invoice	210

A. Iqbal

		£			£
May 7	Returns	40	May 3	Invoice	560

Sales Ledger

K. Palfreyman

		£		£
May 2	Invoice	199		

L. Patel

		£			£
May 2	Invoice	870	May 5	Returns	62
			6	Bank	808
		870			870

General Ledger

Bank

		£			£
May 6	L. Patel	808	May 6	J. Carter	339

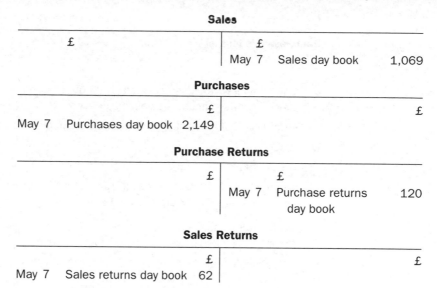

Sales

£				£
		May 7	Sales day book	1,069

Purchases

		£		£
May 7	Purchases day book	2,149		

Purchase Returns

	£			£
		May 7	Purchase returns day book	120

Sales Returns

		£		£
May 7	Sales returns day book	62		

Question 2.6

Lara Kelly: Petty Cash Book

£/p				£/p
200.00	Oct 14	Transfer from Cash Book		
		Travel expenses		25.56
	Oct 15	Window cleaning		14.29
	Oct 16	Train fares		18.45
	Oct 17	Dog kennel		40.00
		Dog food		19.00
	Oct 18	Postage		2.65
	Oct 19	Loan to Hiram Decker		10.00
	Oct 20	Window cleaning		23.85
		Total expenditure for the week		153.80
		Balance c/d		46.20
200.00				200.00
46.20	Oct 21	Balance b/d		
153.80		Transfer from Cash Book		
200.00				

Question 2.7

Paul Pascoe's journal

			Dr £	Cr £
a	Debit	Andrew Young's sales ledger account	400	
	Credit	Andrew Cheung's sales ledger account		400
		– Correction of misposting to A. Young's account		
b	Debit	Stationery	80	
	Credit	Bank		80
		– Correction of reversed entries (£40 to cancel incorrect entry, plus £40 for correct entry = £80)		
c	Debit	Purchases	200	
	Credit	Dingle Dynamics' purchase ledger account		200
		– Correction of omitted entry		

Chapter 3

Question 3.1

a   Controls are needed not only to ensure the accuracy and completeness of the data recorded within the bookkeeping system and financial summaries, but also to safeguard the business assets. Controls can help to minimise fraud by means of adequate supervision of tasks and a suitable allocation of duties. No one member of staff should have total responsibility for a financial function without the need for the work to be supervised or checked by others. Examples of controls include:

➤ Bank reconciliation statements
➤ Sales and purchase ledger control accounts
➤ The imprest system of petty cash
➤ The trial balance

b

Sales Ledger Control Account

	£		£
Opening debtors	86,250	Opening credit balances	370
Total sales invoices	610,200	Sales returns	3,200
		Cheques received	577,800
		Closing debtors	
		(balancing figure)	115,080
	696,450		696,450

Purchases Ledger Control Account

	£		£
Purchases returns	770	Opening creditors	92,100
Cheques paid	472,450	Total purchase invoices	463,750
Closing creditors	82,630		
(balancing figure)			
	555,850		555,850

Question 3.2

a The accruals concept ensures that all relevant income and expenditure appears in the profit and loss account, not just the cash paid and received. Adjustments for accruals and prepayments, opening and closing stock and provisions for depreciation are all examples of how the income for a period has to be matched with the relevant expenditure for the same period.

b

Polly Harris's books

General ledger

Stock

	£		£
1/5/00 Opening stock b/f	50,000	30/4/01 P & L account	50,000
30/4/01 P & L account	60,000	30/4/01 Closing stock c/d	60,000
	110,000		110,000
1/5/01 Opening stock b/d	60,000		

Telephone

	£		£
30/4/01 Bank	4,000	30/4/01 P & L account	4,900
Accrual c/d	900		
	4,900		4,900
		1/5/01 Accrual b/d	900

Rent

	£		£
1/5/00 Bank	15,000	30/4/01 P & L account	30,000
1/11/00 Bank	22,500	30/4/01 Prepaid c/d	7,500
	37,500		37,500
1/5/01 Prepaid b/d	7,500		

Question 3.3

a The official definition of depreciation contained within Financial Reporting Standard (FRS) 15, *Tangible Fixed Assets*, is:

'The measure of the cost or revalued amount of the economic benefits of the tangible fixed asset that have been consumed during the period. Consumption includes the wearing out, using up or other reduction in the useful economic life of a tangible fixed asset whether arising from use, effluxion of time or obsolescence through either changes in technology or demand for the goods and services produced by the asset'.

Depreciation is relevant to the fundamental accounting concepts in the following ways:

➤ *Accruals concept*: Depreciation ensures that a reasonable estimate of the loss in value of the fixed asset is matched to the accounting periods in which the loss is incurred.

➤ *Prudence concept*: It would be unrealistic to ignore the decline in value of fixed assets over time, and depreciation is the means by which such loss is recognised within the financial statements.

➤ *Consistency concept*: Once the accounting policy for depreciation is adopted, it should be applied consistently to all similar assets, unless the application of this concept results in a breach of the overriding 'true and fair view' concept.

➤ *Going concern concept*: It is always assumed that the business is a going concern unless it is stated otherwise, so it is reasonable to assume that fixed assets will be depreciated over their useful economic life based on the estimates made at the time of acquisition. If a business is not considered as a going concern, assets should be written down to a realistic value, possibly based on a 'forced sale' (i.e. the value which would be realised if the business was forced to sell them by creditors).

b

Machinery

		£			£
1/1/00	Cost	65,000	31/12/00	Balance c/d	65,000
1/1/01	Balance b/d	65,000	31/12/01	Balance c/d	65,000
1/1/02	Balance b/d	65,000	31/12/02	Balance c/d	65,000
1/1/03	Balance b/d	65,000			

Computers

		£			£
1/1/00	Cost	20,000	31/12/00	Balance c/d	20,000
1/1/01	Balance b/d	20,000	31/12/01	Balance c/d	20,000
1/1/02	Balance b/d	20,000	31/12/02	Balance c/d	20,000
1/1/03	Balance b/d	20,000			

Motor cars

£			£		
1/1/01	Cost	45,000	31/12/01	Balance c/d	45,000
1/1/02	Balance b/d	45,000	31/12/02	Balance c/d	45,000
1/1/03	Balance b/d	45,000			

Provision for depreciation on machinery

		£			£
31/12/00	Balance c/d	12,000	31/12/00	P & L account	12,000
31/12/01	Balance c/d	24,000	1/1/01	Balance b/d	12,000
			31/12/01	P & L account	12,000
		24,000			24,000
			1/1/02	Balance b/d	24,000
31/12/02	Balance c/d	36,000	31/12/02	P & L account	12,000
		36,000			36,000
			1/1/03	Balance b/d	36,000

Provision for doprociation on computers

	£		£
31/12/00 Balance c/d	5,000	31/12/00 P & L account	5,000
31/12/01 Balance c/d	10,000	1/1/01 Balance b/d	5,000
		31/12/01 P & L account	5,000
	10,000		10,000
		1/1/02 Balance b/d	10,000
31/12/02 Balance c/d	15,000	31/12/02 P & L account	5,000
	15,000		15,000
		1/1/03 Balance b/d	15,000

Provision for depreciation on motor cars

	£		£
31/12/01 Balance c/d	18,000	31/12/01 P & L account	18,000
		1/1/02 Balance b/d	18,000
31/12/02 Balance c/d	28,800	31/12/02 P & L account	10,800
	28,800		28,800
		1/1/03 Balance b/d	28,800

c

Profit and loss account for the year ended 31 December 2002 (extract)

Expenses include:

	£
Depreciation on machinery	12,000
Depreciation on computers	5,000
Depreciation on motor cars	10,800

Balance sheet as at 31 December 2002 (extract)

	Cost	Accumulated depreciation	Net book value
	£	£	£
Fixed assets			
Machinery	65,000	36,000	29,000
Computers	20,000	15,000	5,000
Motor cars	45,000	28,800	16,200
	130,000	79,800	50,200

Question 3.4

Louise Jones
Profit and loss account for the year ended 30 November 2001

	£	£
Sales		75,972
Less **Cost of goods sold**		
Opening stock at 1 December 2000	7,224	
Add Purchases	49,600	
	56,824	
Less Closing stock at 30 November 2001	(12,400)	
		(44,424)
Gross profit	c/f	31,548

	b/f	31,548

Less Expenses

Wages	11,590
Accountancy	350
Advertising	285
Bank charges	74
Depreciation: fixtures and fittings	800
Depreciation: motor van	1,600
Light and heat	1,030
Motor expenses	518
Postage and printing	390
Rent and rates	2,900
Repairs	810
Telephone and insurance	619

		(20,966)
Net profit		10,582

Louise Jones
Balance sheet as at 30 November 2001

	Cost	Accumulated depreciation	Net book value
Fixed assets	£	£	£
Fixtures and fittings	11,400	4,200	7,200
Motor van	8,900	4,800	4,100
	20,300	9,000	11,300

Current assets

Stock	12,400
Debtors	7,384
Prepayments	200
Bank	3,600
Cash	120
	23,704

Less Current liabilities

Creditors	8,140	
Accruals	130	
		(8,270)
Net current assets		15,434
Total net assets		26,734

Capital

Opening balance, 1 December 2000	23,652
Add Net profit	10,582
	34,234
Less Drawings	(7,500)
Closing balance at 30 November 2001	26,734

Chapter 4

Question 4.1

Amber: Profit and loss account for the year ended 30 April 2001

	£	£
Raw materials		
Opening stock at 1 May 2000	8,320	
Add Purchases of raw materials	52,450	
	60,770	
Less Closing stock at 30 April 2001	(9,641)	
Cost of raw materials		51,129
Other direct costs:		
Production labour		47,653
Prime cost of production		98,782
Indirect factory costs:		
Factory expenses	89,322	
Depreciation of factory	6,000	
		95,322
		194,104
Add Opening work-in-progress	35,620	
Less Closing work-in-progress	(32,040)	
		3,580
Total factory production cost c/d		197,684
Sales		253,620
Less **Cost of goods sold**		
Opening stock at 1 May 2000	12,634	
Add Total factory production cost b/d	197,684	
	210,318	
Less Closing stock at 30 April 2001	(13,671)	
		(196,647)
Gross profit		56,973
Add Discount received		114
		57,087
Less Expenses		
Office expenses	34,000	
Discount allowed	840	
Depreciation	3,600	
		(39,040)
Net profit		10,047

Blue: Profit and loss account for the year ended 31 May 2002

	£	£	£
Sales		184,162	
Less Sales returns		(580)	
			183,582
Less **Cost of goods sold**			
Opening stock at 1 June 2001		12,700	
Add Purchases	65,210		
Carriage inwards	360		
	65,570		
Less Purchases returns	(2,600)		
		62,970	
		75,670	
Less Closing stock at 31 May 2002		(10,700)	
			(64,970)
Gross profit			118,612
Add Discount received			120
			118,732
Less **Expenses**			
General office expenses		54,923	
Carriage outwards		240	
Depreciation (office)		2,300	
Discount allowed		320	
			(57,783)
Net profit			60,949

Cerise: Profit and loss account for the year ended 30 June 2003

	£	£
Fees from clients		85,400
Less **Expenses**		
General office expenses	21,500	
Discount allowed	160	
Depreciation (office)	1,600	
		(23,260)
Net profit		62,140

Question 4.2

Wesley Timpson
Profit and loss account for the year ended 30 November 2002

	£	£	£
Sales		245,610	
Less Sales returns		(2,350)	
			243,260
Less **Cost of goods sold**			
Opening stock at 1 December 2001		15,684	
Add Purchases	124,100		
Carriage inwards	6,200		
	130,300		
Less Purchases returns	(2,910)		
		127,390	
		143,074	
Less Closing stock at 30 November 2002		(16,822)	
			(126,252)
Gross profit			117,008
Add Discount received		640	
Bank interest received		140	
			780
			117,788
Less **Expenses**			
Wages and salaries		47,231	
Carriage outwards		900	
Depreciation (office furniture)		2,500	
Depreciation (computers)		900	
Depreciation (motor cars)		4,500	
Postage and stationery		2,710	
Sundry office expenses		3,571	
Telephone		1,499	
Light and heat		5,230	
Discount allowed		533	
			(69,574)
Net profit			48,214

Question 4.3

Betta Buys
Profit and loss account for the year ended 28 February 2002

	£	£	£
Sales			425,000
Less **Cost of goods sold**			
Opening stock at 1 March 2001		90,000	
Add Purchases		204,000	
		294,000	
Less Closing stock at 28 February 2002		(70,000)	
			224,000
Gross profit		c/f	201,000

Gross profit	b/f	201,000
Less **Expenses**		
Wages and salaries	62,000	
Rent	12,000	
Electricity	5,000	
Depreciation: shop fittings	5,200	
Depreciation: car	2,880	
		(87,080)
Net profit		113,920

Betta Buys
Balance sheet as at 28 February 2002

	Cost	Accumulated depreciation	Net book value
Fixed assets	£	£	£
Shop fittings	30,000	15,600	14,400
Motor car	12,000	7,680	4,320
	42,000	23,280	18,720
Current assets			
Stock		70,000	
Debtors		35,200	
Prepayments		3,000	
Bank		960	
Cash		250	
		109,410	
Less **Current liabilities**			
Creditors	27,600		
Accruals	1,000		
		(28,600)	
Net current assets			80,810
Total net assets			99,530
Capital			
Opening balance, 1 March 2001		10,610	
Add Net profit		113,920	
		124,530	
Less Drawings		(25,000)	
Closing balance at 28 February 2002			99,530

Question 4.4

Helen Thorne
Profit and loss account for the year ended 31 May 2001

	£	£
Sales	324,650	
Less Sales returns	(1,250)	
		323,400
Less **Cost of goods sold**		
Opening stock at 1 June 2000	34,500	
Add Purchases	168,220	
	202,720	
Less Closing stock at 1 May 2001	(27,880)	
		(174,840)
Gross profit		148,560
Add Discount received		690
		149,250
Less **expenses**		
Assistants' wages	33,100	
Insurance	5,900	
Telephone and e-mail	5,400	
Light and heat	6,230	
Security guards' wages	12,800	
Repairs to premises	3,970	
Amortisation of leasehold premises	3,000	
Depreciation of safe	2,880	
Depreciation of shop fittings	3,400	
Rent and rates	17,000	
Discount allowed	1,520	
Website charges	905	
Publicity and advertising	9,740	
Sundry expenses	3,940	
		(109,785)
Net profit		39,465

Helen Thorne
Balance sheet as at 31 May 2001

	Cost	Accumulated depreciation	Net book value
Fixed assets	£	£	£
Leasehold premises	60,000	21,000	39,000
Safe	12,000	7,680	4,320
Shop fittings	34,000	13,600	20,400
c/f	106,000	42,280	63,720

	£	£	£
b/f			63,720
Current assets			
Stock		27,880	
Debtors		3,400	
Prepayments		525	
Cash		520	
		32,325	
Less **Current liabilities**			
Creditors	19,670		
Accruals	600		
Bank overdraft	2,380		
		(22,650)	
Net current assets			9,675
Total net assets			73,395
Capital			
Opening balance, 1 June 2000		58,630	
Add Net profit		39,465	
		98,095	
Less Drawings		(24,700)	
Closing balance at 31 May 2001			73,395

Chapter 5

Question 5.1

Profit and loss account for the year ended 31 December 2005 (extract)

Expenses include:

	£
Provision for depreciation on vessels	240,000
Loss on disposal of vessels	152,500

Balance sheet as at 31 December 2005 (extract)

	Cost £	Accumulated depreciation £	Net book value £
Vessels	1,600,000	645,000	955,000

Note:

Vessels	£
Cost at 1 January 2005	1,950,000
Add additions in year	700,000
	2,650,000
Less disposals at cost	(1,050,000)
Cost at 31 December 2005	1,600,000

Depreciation at 1 January 2005	1,102,500
Add provision for the year	240,000
	1,342,500
Less depreciation on disposals	(697,500)
Depreciation as at 31 December 2005	645,000
Net book value as at 31 December 2005	955,000
Net book value as at 1 January 2005	847,500

Workings (figures in £000):

	Vessel				
	Invisible	*Submersible*	*Outrageous*	*Implausible*	*Total*
Depreciation p.a.	$\frac{£450 \times 75\%}{5}$ $= 67.5$	$\frac{£600 \times 75\%}{5}$ $= 90$	$\frac{£900 \times 75\%}{5}$ $= 135$	$\frac{£700 \times 75\%}{5}$ $= 105$	
Depreciation to 1/1/05	67.5×5 $= 337.5$	90×4 $= 360$	135×3 $= 405$	(none)	1,102.5
Depreciation for 2005	(none)	(none)	135	105	240
Net book value at disposal	$450 - 337.5$ $= 112.5$	$600 - 360$ $= 240$	n/a	n/a	
'Proceeds' of disposal	nil	200	n/a	n/a	
Loss on disposal	112.5	40	n/a	n/a	152.5

Question 5.2

a   FIFO method

	Purchase price			
	70p	90p	£1.10	1.30
Years ended 30 September:				
2001 Purchases	120,000			
Sales (FIFO)	(100,000)			
Sub-total	20,000			
2002 Purchases		120,000		
Sales (FIFO)	(20,000)	(80,000)		
Sub-total	—	40,000		
2003 Purchases			120,000	
Sales (FIFO)		(40,000)	(100,000)	
Sub-total		—	20,000	
2004 Purchases				120,000
Sales (FIFO)			(20,000)	(80,000)
Sub-total			—	40,000

Value of stock under the FIFO method = 40,000 × £1.30 = **£52,000.**

LIFO method

	Purchase price			
	70p	90p	£1.10	£1.30
Years ended 30 September:				
2001 Purchases	120,000			
Sales (LIFO)	(100,000)			
Sub-total	20,000			
2002 Purchases		120,000		
Sales (LIFO)	–	(100,000)		
Sub-total	20,000	20,000		
2003 Purchases			120,000	
Sales (LIFO)	–	(20,000)	(120,000)	
Sub-total	20,000	–	–	
2004 Purchases				120,000
Sales (LIFO)	–	–	–	(100,000)
Sub-total	20,000	–	–	20,000

Value of stock under the LIFO method = (20,000 × 70p) + (20,000 × £1.30) = **£40,000.**

AVCO method

	Mats in stock	Price	Value (£)	Average
Purchases, year ended 30/9/01	120,000	70p	84,000	
Sales, year ended 30/9/01	(100,000)	70p	(70,000)	
Sub-total at 30/9/01	20,000		14,000	
Purchases, year ended 30/9/02	120,000	90p	108,000	
Sub-total	140,000		122,000	
Average (£122,000/140,000)				87.14p
Sales, year ended 30/9/02	(100,000)	87.14p	(87,140)	
Sub-total at 30/9/02	40,000		34,860	
Purchases, year ended 30/9/03	120,000	£1.10	132,000	
Sub-total	160,000		166,860	
Average (£166,860/160,000)				£1.043
Sales, year ended 30/9/03	(140,000)	£1.043	(146,020)	
Sub-total at 30/9/03	20,000		20,840	
Purchases, year ended 30/9/04	120,000	£1.30	156,000	
Sub-total	140,000		176,840	
Average (£176,840/140,000)				£1.263
Sales, year ended 30/9/04	(100,000)	£1.263	(126,300)	
Closing stock	**40,000**	**£1.263**	**50,540**	

Value of stock (allowing for rounding adjustments) under the AVCO method = **£50,540.**

b   In the UK, FIFO is preferred to LIFO because:

➤   The Inland Revenue does not accept profit figures based on LIFO stock valuations.

➤ SSAP 9, the accounting standard relating to stock valuations, does not consider the method acceptable, as LIFO results in unrealistically high cost of sales figures.

➤ The stock valuation tends to be outdated (as in the above example, where stock at 30 September 2004 is partly based on values current at 30 September 2001).

Question 5.3

a This is the application of the prudence concept to stock valuation, to ensure that asset values are not overstated. Cost represents all those costs incurred in the normal course of business in bringing the product to its present location and condition. Net realisable value is the estimated proceeds from the sale of items of stock less all further costs to completion and less all costs to be incurred in marketing, selling and distributing directly related to the items in question.

b

Orange Lace
Cost £9,000
Net realisable value £2,000 – £500 = £1,500
Therefore valued at the lower figure, £1,500

Injured Turtles
Cost £16,000
Net realisable value £4,000 – (2,750 + 2,650) = £1,400 loss
Therefore it would be omitted from the stock calculation (stock written down to zero) as the stock would be thrown away rather than be exported at a loss.

Question 5.4

a Bad debts occur when a customer has bought goods or services and does not pay for them. The company selling the goods or services has given up trying to recover the debt, and accepts that it has lost money on the transaction.

Doubtful debts occur when there is an element of doubt as to whether a customer will pay for goods or services, but it has not reached the stage where the company is prepared to write off the debt as bad.

b

Bickley Brothers
Profit and loss account for the year ended 31 May 2002

	£	£
Expenses include:		
Bad debts written off		2,400
Increase in provision for doubtful debts		500

Balance sheet as at 31 May 2002

	£	£
Current assets include:		
Debtors	11,125	
Less Provision for doubtful debts	(3,500)	
		7,625

Bickley Brothers
Profit and loss account for the year ended 31 May 2003

	£	£
Added to gross profit:		
Decrease in provision for doubtful debts		300
Expenses include:		
Bad debts written off		600

Balance sheet as at 31 May 2003

	£	£
Current assets include:		
Debtors	17,030	
Less Provision for doubtful debts	(3,200)	
		13,830

Chapter 6

Question 6.1

Felicity Frankton
Profit and loss account for the year ended 30 September 2003

	£	£	£
Sales			105,800
Less **Cost of goods sold**			
Opening stock at 1 October 2002		16,520	
Add Purchases	32,410		
Add Carriage in	320		
		32,730	
		49,250	
Less Closing stock at 30 September 2003		(14,560)	
			(34,690)
Gross profit			71,110
Less **Expenses**			
Wages and salaries		18,500	
Bad debts		500	
Carriage outwards		430	
Discount allowed		340	
Light and heat		2,200	
Provision for doubtful debts (1,210 – 800)		410	
Rent and rates (3,200 + 600)		3,800	
Sundry office expenses (10,200 – 200)		10,000	
Loss on sale of car[1]		400	
Depreciation on car[2]		4,200	
Depreciation on computer[3]		722	
			(41,502)
Net profit			29,608

Notes:

1 (7,900 – 6,000) – 1,500.

2 60% × [(16,500 – 7,900) – (7,600 – 6,000)].

3 3,610/5.

Felicity Frankton
Balance sheet as at 30 September 2003

Fixed assets	Cost	Accumulated depreciation	Net book value
	£	£	£
Computers	3,610	2,572	1,038
Motor cars	8,600	5,800	2,800
	12,210	8,372	3,838

Current assets			
Stock		14,560	
Debtors	24,200		
Less provision for doubtful debts	(1,210)		
		22,990	
Prepayments		200	
Bank		1,260	
		39,010	
Less Current liabilities			
Creditors	13,600		
Accruals	600		
		(14,200)	
Net current assets			24,810
Total net assets			28,648

Capital			
Opening balance, 1 October 2002		15,940	
Add Net profit		29,608	
		45,548	
Less Drawings		(16,900)	
Closing balance at 30 September 2003			28,648

Question 6.2

Patrick Cooper
Profit and loss account for the year ended 31 December 2003

	£	£	£
Sales (289,512 – 100)			289,412
Less Cost of goods sold			
Opening stock at 1 January 2003		5,620	
Add Purchases		132,950	
		138,570	
Less Closing stock at 31 December 2003		(4,900)	
			(133,670)
Gross profit		c/f	155,742

Gross profit		b/f	155,742
Less expenses			
Wages and salaries	39,540		
Bad debts written off	250		
Discount allowed	200		
Bank interest	950		
Administration expenses (55,500 – 150)	55,350		
Increase in provision for doubtful debts	250		
Selling expenses (37,790 + 300)	38,090		
Depreciation on equipment[1]	2,680		
Loss on sale of equipment[2]	140		
			(137,450)
Net profit			18,292

Notes

1 20% × (14,000 – 600).

2 Cost – Depreciation to date of sale = 600 – (60% × 600) = 240.
Loss = 240 – 100 proceeds = 140.

Patrick Cooper
Balance sheet as at 31 December 2003

	Cost	Accumulated depreciation	Net book value
Fixed assets	£	£	£
Equipment	13,400	4,670	8,730
Current assets			
Stock		4,900	
Debtors	6,300		
Less provision for doubtful debts	(550)		
		5,750	
Prepayments		150	
Cash		140	
		10,940	
Less Current liabilities			
Creditors	5,210		
Accruals	300		
Bank overdraft	1,600		
		(7,110)	
Net current assets			3,830
Total net assets			12,560
Capital			
Opening balance, 1 January 2003		16,268	
Add Net profit		18,292	
		34,560	
Less Drawings		(22,000)	
Closing balance at 31 December 2003			12,560

Chapter 7

Question 7.1

A partnership is not a collection of sole traders, as the partners run the business in the knowledge that they will be sharing the risks and rewards. Although sole trading suits many people, it can be helpful to be able to draw on the expertise of others. Sharing of problems and the ability to discuss business possibilities is also a very positive aspect of a partnership. It is very difficult to expand a business with only one owner, and bringing in partners can draw in finance which is otherwise unavailable.

Question 7.2

Disraeli and Gladstone
Profit and loss account (appropriation section)
for the year ended 31 December 2000

	£	£
Net profit for the year		40,000
Less Salary to Disraeli		(9,000)
		31,000
Less Interest on capital		
Disraeli (5% × £20,000)	1,000	
Gladstone (5% × £15,000)	750	
		(1,750)
		29,250
Disraeli: share of profit ($\frac{2}{3}$ × £29,250)	19,500	
Gladstone: share of profit ($\frac{1}{3}$ × £29,250)	9,750	
		29,250

Disraeli and Gladstone
Balance sheet as at 31 December 2000

	£	£
(Assets less liabilities)		43,000
Disraeli's Capital Account		
Opening balance, 1 January 2000	20,000	
Add: Salary	9,000	
Interest on capital	1,000	
Share of profit	19,500	
	49,500	
Less: Drawings	(18,000)	
Closing balance, 31 December 2000		31,500
Gladstone's Capital Account		
Opening balance, 1 January 2000	15,000	
Add: Interest on capital	750	
Share of profit	9,750	
	25,500	
Less: Drawings	(14,000)	
Closing balance, 31 December 2000		11,500
		43,000

Question 7.3

a   Problems:

- ➤ Partners may be incompetent, and there may be personality clashes.
- ➤ Partners have unlimited liability for the debts of the partnership.

b   There is a grain of truth in the quotation, but it must be recognised that trading as a limited company requires compliance with a much stronger regulatory framework than applies to a partnership. This is to protect the interest of creditors who, though warned of the limited liability of the owners by the inclusion of 'Ltd' or 'plc' in the business's name, are still entitled to the assurance that the business is run properly and in accordance with the law by the directors.

c   See Chapter 7 (pp. 125–26) for the advantages and disadvantages of limited liability status.

Question 7.4

Although there have been many well-publicised cases of unscrupulous directors defrauding shareholders and creditors, the vast majority of limited liability companies are run on perfectly legal lines, providing returns to shareholders, salaries to employees and trade with suppliers nationally and internationally. Limited liability status has obvious attractions to entrepreneurs as they can take business risks without the burden of placing their personal assets in jeopardy. However, their own investments in the company have no special safeguard, and will be lost if the business fails. Company law and financial reporting standards exist to try to protect shareholders and creditors from crooked business people, but it could be argued that there have been swindlers and confidence tricksters in existence for thousands of years, before limited liability status was ever thought of.

Question 7.5

Morse Ltd
Profit and loss account for the year ended 31 December 2000

	£	£
Sales		462,600
Less **Cost of goods sold**		
Opening stock at 1 January 2000	14,900	
Add Purchases	140,800	
	155,700	
Less Closing stock at 31 December 2000	(17,650)	
		(138,050)
Gross profit		324,550
Add Decrease in provision for doubtful debts		600
c/f		325,150

		c/f	325,150
Less Expenses			
Directors' remuneration		59,200	
Salesforce wages		65,230	
Office salaries		34,900	
Advertising and website charges (15,300 – 160)		15,140	
Interest		2,502	
Carriage out		632	
Bad debts		750	
Depreciation on delivery vehicles			
(30% × (143,600 – 27,800))		34,740	
Office expenses (33,897 + 800)		34,697	
			(247,791)
Net profit for the year, before taxation			77,359
Less Provision for taxation			(24,000)
Net profit for the year, after taxation			53,359
Less Dividends:			
Final (proposed)			(5,000)
Retained profit for the year			48,359

Morse Ltd
Balance sheet as at 31 December 2000

	Cost	Accumulated depreciation	Net book value
Fixed assets	£	£	£
Delivery vehicles	143,600	62,540	81,060
Current assets			
Stock		17,650	
Trade debtors	64,100		
Less Provision for doubtful debts	(1,000)		
		63,100	
Prepayments		160	
Bank		11,500	
		92,410	
Less Creditors due for payment within			
one year			
Trade creditors	32,711		
Accruals	800		
Taxation	24,000		
Proposed dividend	5,000		
		(62,511)	
Net current assets			29,899
			110,959
Less Creditors due for payment after			
more than one year			
Debenture (repayable 2012)			(10,000)
Total net assets		c/f	100,959

		£	£
Total net assets	b/f		100,959
Capital and reserves			
Called-up share capital (50p shares)			25,000
Share premium account			15,000
Profit and loss account:			
Balance at 1 January 2000		12,600	
Retained profit for the year		48,359	
			60,959
			100,959

Question 7.6

a   Reserves do not equal cash. The total of reserves, when added to the nominal value of the share capital, equal the *total net assets* (i.e. all the assets less all the liabilities) of the company.

b   A revenue reserve (the profit and loss account) has been built up from profits accumulated as a result of the trading operations of the business reflected in the profit and loss account. Such reserves are referred to as being *distributable* – they are available for dividend payments.

A capital reserve (share premium account, asset revaluation reserve) represents share capital (nominal value plus any premium) paid into the company by shareholders, plus any *unrealised gains* recorded as a result of revaluing assets. Capital reserves are *undistributable* – they are not available for the payment of dividends.

c   A share premium is the difference between the price paid to a company for shares and the nominal value of those shares. In the example, the company must have sold its shares at £1.75 each (called-up share capital = £100,000, plus share premium account £75,000 = £175,000, divided by 100,000 shares).

d   An asset revaluation reserve is created to record an increase in the valuation of a fixed asset (usually land). If several years have elapsed since the purchase of the land (or its last revaluation), the value as recorded in the balance sheet may be unrealistically low, and distort the overall net asset values shown. The other balance sheet item affected is the fixed asset being revalued.

e   A bonus issue could be made, which effectively returns reserves (capital or revenue) without cash payments being made. The bonus issue is a free issue of shares to shareholders, pro rata to their existing shareholdings.

f   The rights issue would be for 150,000 shares (100,000 × 3/2). 150,000 shares at £2.40 each = £360,000 of which £150,000 is the nominal value (added to 'called-up share capital') and £210,000 is share premium (added to 'share premium account').

Chapter 8

Question 8.1

a

Delia Trelawney – 'Soul Trading'
Profit and loss account for the year ended 31 May 2003

	£	£
Sales (see Working 1)		39,220
Less Cost of goods sold		
Opening stock (balancing figure)	5,625	
Purchases (see Working 2)	15,069	
	20,694	
Less Closing stock	(3,045)	
		(17,649)
Gross profit (55% × £39,220)		21,571
Less **Expenses**		
Wages	6,000	
Advertising	520	
Rent and rates	1,500	
Telephone and electricity (203 + 871 – 140)	934	
Sundry expenses	603	
Loss on sale of van	480	
Depreciation of shop fittings (see Working 3)	3,082	
		(13,119)
Net profit		8,452

Delia Trelawney – 'Soul Trading'
Balance sheet as at 31 May 2003

Fixed assets	£	£	£
Shop fittings at cost brought forward		7,900	
Additions in the year		6,402	
		14,302	
Depreciation to 1 June 2002 (see Working 3)	4,029		
Depreciation for the year (see Working 3)	3,082		
		(7,111)	
			7,191
Current assets			
Stock		3,045	
Bank		6,340	
		9,385	
Less **Current liabilities**			
Trade creditors	6,320		
Accruals	203		
		(6,523)	
Net current assets			2,862
Total net assets		c/f	10,053

Total net assets		b/f	10,053

Capital

Opening balance (see Working 4)		8,991	
Add Net profit		8,452	
		17,443	
Less Drawings (6,670 + 720)		7,390	
			10,053

Working 1:

Cash banked	35,500
Less Sale of van	3,000
	32,500
Add Used for holiday and wages	6,720
	39,220

Working 2:

Purchases Control a/c

	£		£
Cheques paid	10,854	Creditors b/f	2,105
Creditors c/f	6,320	Purchases (=)	15,069
	17,174		17,174

Working 3:

Depreciation of shop fittings

	Owned at 31 May 2002	Bought in year to 31 May 2003	Total
	£	£	£
Cost	7,900	6,402	14,302
2000/1 Depreciation	(2,370)	—	(2,370)
	5,530		
2001/2 Depreciation	(1,659)	—	(1,659)
	3,871		
2002/3 Depreciation	(1,161)	(1,921)	(3,082)
	2,710	4,481	7,191

Depreciation to 1 June 2002 = 2,370 + 1,659 = 4,029.

Working 4:

Opening balance sheet at 1 June 2002

	£	£	£
Fixed assets: Van			3,480
Shop fittings (see Working 3)			3,871
		c/f	7,351

		b/f	7,351
Current assets			
Stock		5,625	
Less Current liabilities			
Creditors	2,105		
Accrual	140		
Bank overdraft	1,740	(3,985)	
			1,640
			8,991
Capital			8,991

b Ways of keeping better control over creditors' invoices include:

- ➤ Maintain a creditors' ledger.
- ➤ File invoices systematically and have a set period for payment.
- ➤ Check invoices against statements received.
- ➤ Keep a purchases day book.
- ➤ Stamp invoices paid when cheques are sent.
- ➤ Don't pay individual invoices; pay only monthly statements from creditor.

Question 8.2

Tilly Snowdon
Profit and loss account for the year ended 31 December 2002

	£	£
Sales (see Working 1)		97,650
Less Cost of goods sold		
Opening stock	16,800	
Purchases (see Working 2)	67,100	
	83,900	
Less Closing stock	(23,700)	
		(60,200)
Gross profit		37,450
Less **Expenses**		
Wages	9,070	
Rent and rates	4,600	
Light and heat	3,900	
Van running expenses	1,400	
Adverts (840 − 140 + 120)	820	
Insurance (560 + 80 − 120)	520	
Bad debts	100	
Depreciation − van (see Working 3)	1,500	
Depreciation − fittings (see Working 4)	1,215	
Loss on sale of van (see Working 3)	400	
Sundries	2,800	
		(26,325)
Net profit		11,125

Tilly Snowdon
Balance sheet as at 31 December 2002

	£	£	£
Fixed assets			
Van – at cost		6,000	
Less Depreciation		(1,500)	
			4,500
Fittings – cost b/f		1,500	
Additions in year		3,000	
		4,500	
Depreciation b/f	450		
Provision for year	1,215		
		(1,665)	
			2,835
			7,335
Current assets			
Stock at cost		23,700	
Debtors		750	
Prepayments		120	
		24,570	
Less **Current liabilities**			
Creditors	3,300		
Accruals	120		
Bank overdraft	6,670		
		(10,090)	
Net current assets			14,480
Total net assets			21,815
Capital			
Opening balance (see Working 5)		21,190	
Net profit		11,125	
		32,315	
Less Drawings		(10,500)	
			21,815

Working 1:
Sales

	£		£
Debtors b/f	600	Cash*	97,400
Sales =	97,650	Written off	100
		Debtors c/f	750
	98,250		98,250

* cash banked 86,900, plus drawings 10,500 = 97,400.

Working 2:
Purchases

	£		£
Cheques	66,200	Creditors b/f	2,400
Creditors c/f	3,300	Purchases =	67,100
	69,500		69,500

Working 3:

Van Account (at net book value)

	£		£
b/f	2,400	Proceeds (contra)	2,000
Cost	4,000	P & L depreciation (on new van)	1,500
Trade-in (contra)	2,000	P & L loss on sale	400
		c/f	4,500
	8,400		8,400

Note: 'contra' means that both debit and credit entries cancel each other within the same ledger account.

Working 4:
Depreciation on fittings = [(1,500 + 3,000) − 450] × 30% = 1,215.

Working 5:
Opening capital

	£	£
Van (2,400 less depreciation 450)		1,950
Fittings		1,500
Stocks		16,800
Debtors		600
Prepayments		80
Bank		2,800
		23,730
Less:		
Creditors	2,400	
Accruals	140	
		(2,540)
		21,190

Question 8.3

Razmatazz Sports and Social Club
Income and Expenditure Account for the year ended 31 December 2003

	£	£
Income		
Subscriptions (see Working 1)		14,160
***Less* Expenditure**		
Wages	8,450	
Loss on Dances (2,060 − 1,778)	282	
Competitions ([850 + 2,200 − 450] − 2,590)	10	
Depreciation on van (25% × £6,300)	1,575	
Depreciation on computer	200	
Depreciation on sports equipment	800	
Loss on sale of van (see Working 2)	1,250	
Printing and advertising	2,070	
Repairs	800	
Motor expenses	1,200	
Sundry expenses	1,180	
		(17,817)
Surplus of Expenditure over Income		(3,657)

Razmatazz Sports and Social Club
Balance sheet as at 31 December 2003

	Cost	Accumulated depreciation	Net book value
Fixed assets	£	£	£
Van	6,300	1,575	4,725
Computer	2,000	600	1,400
Sports equipment	8,000	2,600	5,400
	16,300	4,775	11,525
Current assets			
Stock of prizes		450	
Debtors: subscriptions		1,620	
		2,070	
Less **Current liabilities**			
Creditors: prepaid subscriptions	720		
Bank overdraft	2,722		
		(3,442)	
Net current liabilities			(1,372)
Total net assets			10,153
Accumulated fund			
Opening balance (see Working 3)		13,810	
Less Surplus of expenditure over income		(3,657)	
			10,153

Working 1:

Subscriptions

	£		£
Owing b/f	1,440	Cash re 2002	620
Income and Expenditure a/c	14,160	Cash re 2003	14,080
Prepaid c/f	720	Owing c/f	1,620
	16,320		16,320

Working 2:

Sale of van

	£		£
Cost	4,000	Depreciation*	1,750
		Bank	1,000
		Loss on sale (I & E a/c)	1,250
	4,000		4,000

* 1st year: 25% × £4000 = £1,000, plus (2nd year) 25% × (£4,000 − £1,000) = £750.

Working 3:

Opening accumulated fund balance

	£
Van (cost £4,000 less depreciation £1,750)	2,250
Computer	1,600
Sports equipment	6,200
Prizes	850
Debtors: subscriptions owing	1,440
Bank	1,470
	13,810

Question 8.4

a

Vim and Vigour Sports and Social Club
Income and Expenditure Account for the year ended 31 December 2001

	£	£
Income		
Subscriptions (see Working 1)		27,540
Competitions: fees	3,150	
prizes	(2,250)	
		900
Dance: ticket sales	2,460	
expenses	(1,350)	
		1,110
		29,550
Less **Expenditure**		
Wages	29,700	
Depreciation on photocopier	600	
Depreciation on sports equipment	1,800	
Loss on sale of equipment	2,000	
Printing and advertising	2,250	
Repairs	1,500	
Sundry expenses	2,460	
		(42,210)
Surplus of Expenditure over Income		(12,660)

Vim and Vigour Sports and Social Club
Balance sheet as at 31 December 2001

	Cost	Accumulated depreciation	Net book value
Fixed assets	£	£	£
Photocopier	6,000	2,400	3,600
Sports equipment	25,800	10,800	15,000
	31,800	13,200	18,600
Current assets			
Stock of prizes		600	
Debtors: subscriptions		1,560	
c/f		2,160	18,600

		£	£
b/f		2,160	18,600
Less **Current liabilities**			
Bank overdraft		(12,810)	
Net current liabilities			(10,650)
Total net assets			7,950
Accumulated fund			
Opening balance (see Working 2)		20,610	
Less Surplus of Expenditure over Income		(12,660)	
			7,950

Working 1:

Subscriptions

	£		£
Owing b/f	1,800	Prepaid b/f	840
Refund	60	Cash re 2000	1,800
Income and Expenditure a/c	27,540	Cash re 2001	25,200
		Owing c/f	1,560
	29,400		29,400

Working 2:

	£
Accumulated fund as at 1 January 2001	
Photocopier	4,200
Sports equipment	12,000
Prizes	1,050
Debtors: subscriptions owing	1,800
Bank	2,400
	21,450
Less: Subscriptions in advance	(840)
	20,610

b

	Members	£
No. of members in 2001 (£27,600*/£80)	345	
Less members resigning (20% × 345)	(69)	
	276	
New members	40	
	316	
Cash due in 2002:		
316 members × £120		37,920
Add cash due in 2002 re 2001		1,560
Total cash due		39,480

* (840 + 25,200 + 1,560)

Chapter 9

Question 9.1

A: £10,080
B: £22,570
C: £(7,930)
D: £(6,270)

Question 9.2

(£)	A	B	C	D
Net profit before interest	36,620	29,937		20,060
Net loss before interest			(22,660)	
Depreciation	12,000	16,000	24,000	15,000
Increase in stock	(9,650)			(14,850)
Decrease in stock		5,840	5,622	
Increase in debtors			(2,240)	(12,795)
Decrease in debtors	7,980	6,722		
Increase in creditors	3,380		9,713	
Decrease in creditors		(6,840)		(11,629)
Cash flow from operating activities	50,330	51,659	14,435	(4,214)

Question 9.3

Dombey plc
Cash Flow Statement for the year ended 31 May 2001

	£000
Net cash inflow from operating activities (see Note 1)	28,800
Interest paid	(1,200)
Tax	(4,000)
Net capital expenditure (22,000 – 1,800)	(20,200)
Changes in financing	(8,900)
Dividends	(2,000)
Business acquisitions/disposals	–
Decrease in cash for the year (see Note 2)	(7,500)

Note 1:
Reconciliation of operating profit to net cash inflow from operating activities

	£000
Operating profit before interest (24,700 + 1,200)	25,900
Depreciation charges (see Working)	6,000
Loss on sale of tangible fixed assets	3,200
Increase in stock	(1,000)
Increase in debtors	(1,500)
Decrease in creditors	(3,800)
	28,800

Note 2:

Analysis of changes in cash during the year	£000
Balance at 1 June 2000	4,800
Decrease in cash for the year	(7,500)
Balance at 31 May 2001	(2,700)

Working:

Disposals Account

	£000		£000
Cost	8,000	Proceeds	1,800
		Depreciation*	3,000
		P & L	3,200
	8,000		8,000

Depreciation Account

	£000		£000
Disposals (see Depreciation a/c)	3,000	Balance b/f (76,000 – 32,000)	44,000
Balance c/f (90,000 – 43,000)	47,000	P & L*	6,000
	50,000		50,000

* Balancing figures

Question 9.4

The forecast (see Figure A2.1) appears to show a healthy business, with the closing bank balance reaching £17,700 by the end of the year. However, payments in January 2003 are forecast to reach £19,400 (rent, general overheads and the 60% of December's sales due to artists). No overdraft limit has been agreed, so Clara would have to convince the bank that her business can survive into the following year. She would need a temporary overdraft for September (£750) and at least £1,700 in January (£19,400 – £17,700). The worrying aspect of the business is that it may be seasonal, so the overdraft might have to rise sharply in the first quarter of 2003.

Chapter 10

Question 10.1

There is no set answer to this question.

Question 10.2

a Roden Limited is likely to be the food retailer, for the following reasons.
- ➤ Food retailing produces a small gross profit margin, but the fast turnover ensures that profit is earned much faster than in a manufacturing business.
- ➤ Very few retail food sales are made on credit terms, so the year-end debtors' figure will be very low. Due to the fast stock turnover, creditors' totals might be twice as much as stock, giving rise to the negative current (working capital) ratio for Roden Limited of 0.4:1.

figure A2.1
Clara Pilbeam: The Marshes Gallery cash flow forecast from 1 July 2002 to 31 December 2002

Clara Pilbeam: The Marshes Gallery cash flow forecast from 1 July 2002 to 31 December 2002

Period – Monthly (£s)	July	August	September	October	November	December
Receipts						
Sales – cash	8,000	4,000	7,000	12,000	18,000	24,000
Capital injected	4,000	–	–	–	–	–
Other receipts: grant	–	5,000	–	–	–	–
A: Total Receipts	12,000	9,000	7,000	12,000	18,000	24,000
Payments						
Due to artists	–	4,800	2,400	4,200	7,200	10,800
Wages	750	750	750	750	750	750
Deposit to landlord	3,000	–	–	–	–	–
Rent	–	–	–	3,000	–	–
Redecorating premises	–	4,000	3,000	–	–	–
General overheads	–	2,000	2,000	2,000	2,000	2,000
Clara's drawings	600	600	600	600	600	900
Equipment	–	–	3,000	–	–	–
Advertising	–	500	–	–	–	–
B: Total Payments	4,350	12,650	11,750	10,550	10,550	14,450
C: Net Cashflow (A – B)	7,650	(3,650)	(4,750)	1,450	7,450	9,550
D: Opening Bank Balance	–	7,650	4,000	(750)	700	8,150
E: Closing Bank Balance (D +/– C)	7,650	4,000	(750)	700	8,150	17,700
Note: Agreed Overdraft Facility	(none)	(none)	(none)	(none)	(none)	(none)

Note: depreciation does not appear in the forecast, as it is a 'non-cash' expense.

b Debtors:

Ercall Limited's sales can be calculated as £200,000 × 100/40 (because the gross margin of 60% means that cost of sales must be 40% of the sales figure). If the debtors' collection period is 30 days, then the debtors' total is 30/365 of the sales figure: (30/365) × £500,000 = £41,096.

Creditors:

The current ratio (current assets: current liabilities) is 2:1. Current assets for Ercall Limited are:

	£
Stock	40,000
Debtors (as calculated above)	41,096
Bank and cash	11,004
	92,100

Therefore current liabilities are $1/2 \times £92,100 = £46,050$.

c Roden Limited is high-geared, which indicates that the company has significant borrowings. As an ordinary shareholder, you would need to be satisfied that the company can repay the interest due on such loans and that the return generated by the borrowed capital is greater than the cost of financing it. High-geared companies carry more risk than low-geared companies, but can produce higher returns if the company and its profits expand as a result of the borrowings.

Question 10.3

a

	Rodington	Rowton	Comments
(i) Gearing	Nil	$\dfrac{100}{100+113} = 47\%$	Gearing for Rowton is a high 47%, whereas Rodington has no fixed-return borrowings
(ii) Current ratio	123:135 = 0.9:1	177:168 = 1.05:1	Both companies have low working capital ratios, Rodington worse than Rowton
(iii) Acid test ratio	38:135 = 0.28:1	57:168 = 0.34:1	Both companies are exposed to liquidity problems if creditors start demanding payment
(iv) ROCE	$\dfrac{40,000}{113,000} = 35.4\%$	$\dfrac{40,000}{113,000 + 100,000} = 18.8\%$	Rodington has almost twice the ROCE compared to Rowton. Are they in comparable business sectors?

b Rowton is more vulnerable due to high gearing and lower ROCE. Both companies show poor working capital/acid test ratios, but this may be a feature of their type of trade (e.g. supermarkets).

If Rodington would be prepared to issue a debenture secured on its assets, then the investor might be better off with Rodington, though again the lack of liquidity would be worrying. Neither seems suitable for a cautious investor!

c If the going concern concept was not applicable, then Rodington would be heading for receivership, with asset values (almost certainly) being downgraded, and provisions being made for the likely costs of liquidation.

The advice to the potential investor in that situation would be to steer well clear of the company.

Question 10.4

a Any eight of the following ratios:

From P & L Account:

Mark-up	190/480 × 100	39.6%
Gross profit margin	190/670 × 100	28.4%
Net profit margin	51,050/670,000 × 100	7.6%
ROCE	51,050/265,000 × 100	19.3%
Earnings per share	40,000/100,000	40p
Interest cover	51,050/5,600	9.1 times
Dividend cover	40,000/15,000	2.7 times

From Balance Sheet:

Asset turnover	670,000/185,800 × 100	360.6%
Current ratio	158,450/79,250	2:1
Acid test	68,450/79,250	0.86:1
Gearing	80,000/185,000 + 80,000 × 100	30.2%
Stock turnover	90,000/480,000 × 365	68.4 days
Debtors' collection	43,650/670,000 × 365	23.8 days
Creditors' payment	48,000/570,000 × 365	30.7 days

Comment: One year's figures should never be taken by themselves as a measure of a company's performance, as other figures are needed for comparison, e.g. those of previous years or competitors. With this major proviso, we can see that the company had a 'textbook' current ratio, a seemingly strong ROCE (when compared with what we know of prevailing interest rates), a good safety level for interest payments (profit available being 9.1 times the interest) and realistic debtors and creditors ratios. Gearing is on the high side, but as we have seen, the interest is covered strongly.

b £6m is a significant amount for a company which only made £40,000 profit after taxation. However, possibilities for raising capital include:

➤ A rights issue (but it is a new company, so would shareholders put in so much more capital so quickly?)

➤ Loans (but existing debentures could be secured on assets – so it is unlikely that there would be enough security available for more loans)

Note that as a private limited company it could not sell its shares to the general public.

Chapter 11

Question 11.1

	A	B	C	D	E
Sales in units	5,000	20,000	4,000	6,000	15,000
Sales (£)	40,000	60,000	48,000	90,000	105,000
Variable costs (£)	10,000	50,000	32,000	54,000	30,000
Contribution (£)	30,000	10,000	16,000	36,000	75,000
Contribution per unit (£)	6	0.5	4	6	5
Fixed costs (£)	14,400	15,000	7,000	24,000	50,000
Profit/(loss) (£)	15,600	(5,000)	9,000	12,000	25,000
Break-even point (units)	2,400	30,000	1,750	4,000	10,000
Profit/(loss) if 3,000 units sold	3,600	(13,500)	5,000	(6,000)	(35,000)

Question 11.2

a

	@10,000 units	@15,000 units	Change + 5,000 units
	£	£	£
Total costs	160,000	210,000	+ 50,000

Therefore variable costs =

$$£50,000/5,000 \text{ units} = £10 \text{ per unit}$$

Variable costs @ £10 per unit	100,000	150,000
Therefore fixed costs =	60,000	60,000

Answer: fixed costs = £60,000

b   Break-even = Fixed costs/contribution per unit
Contribution per unit = Selling price (£15) – Variable cost (see **a** above) (£10) = £5
Therefore the break-even point = £60,000/£5 = 12,000 units

To earn a profit of £13,000, total contribution must be
Fixed costs £60,000 + Profit £13,000 = £73,000
As contribution per unit is £5, they must sell 73,000/5 = **14,600 units**

c   If only 7,000 units were manufactured and sold, the total contribution would be 7,000 × £5 = £35,000, which is £25,000 less than the fixed costs of £60,000. Therefore a loss of **£25,000** is made.

Question 11.3

figure A2.2
**Break-even chart for
question 11.3**

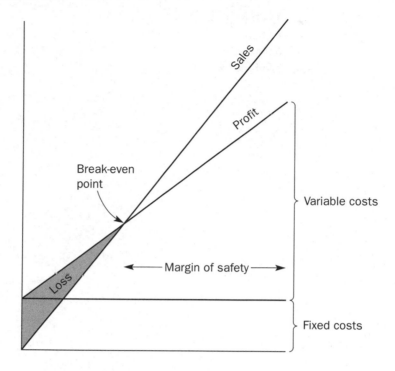

Question 11.4

figure A2.3
**Break-even chart for
Basil Limited,
question 11.4**

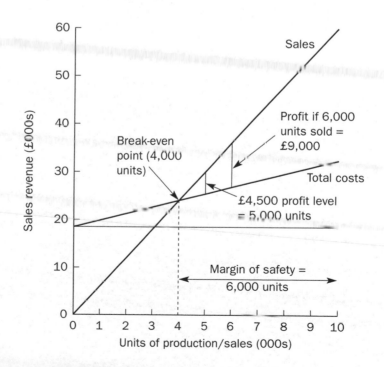

The answers to the four questions are as follows:

- ➤ 4,000 units
- ➤ £9,000
- ➤ 6,000 units
- ➤ 5,000 units

Answers to case study questions

Chapter 1 – Marvin makes a career choice

1

	£
Income in week ending 7 July:	
Fee for Flower Show appearance	750
Less Travel expenses	(20)
Profit	730

2

Fixed assets	£	£
Costume		3,000
Magic Book		2,000
Cards		400
		5,400
Current assets		
Bank account	750	
Less **Current liability**		
Creditor (Kazam Limited)	(400)	
		350
		5,750

Because of the accounting equation ($A – L = C$), Marvin's capital at 7 July was £5,750.

Proof:

Marvin paid for the costume, the book and the travel expenses out of his own private resources (£3,000 + £2,000 + £20 = £5,020), and the business made a profit during the week of £730 which increased the value of his capital to £5,750.

Chapter 2 – Marvin buys rabbits!

Cash Book

	Cash £	Bank £		Cash £	Bank £
Jul 7 Fee		750	Jul 10 Travel	15	
Jul 10 Fee	100		Jul 11 Cleaning		18
Jul 12 Fee		120	Jul 12 Travel	9	
	100	870	Jul 14 Utd Rabbit		240
			Jul 14 Kazam Ltd		400
				24	658
			Jul 14 Bal c/d	76	212
	100	870		100	870
Jul 15 Bal b/d	76	212			

General Ledger

Capital

	£		£
Jul 14 Balance c/d	5,020	Jul 1 Costume	3,000
		Jul 2 Magic Book	2,000
		Jul 7 Travel	20
	5,020		5,020
		Jul 15 Balance b/d	5,020

Costume

	£		£
Jul 1 Capital	3,000	Jul 14 Balance c/d	3,000
Jul 15 Balance b/d	3,000		

Magic Book

	£		£
Jul 2 Capital	2,000	Jul 14 Balance c/d	2,000
Jul 15 Balance b/d	2,000		

Playing Cards

	£		£
Jul 3 Kazam Limited	400	Jul 14 Balance c/d	400
Jul 15 Balance b/d	400		

Fees

	£		£
Jul 14 Balance c/d	1,220	Jul 7 Bank	750
		Jul 10 Cash	100
		Jul 12 Bank	120
		Jul 13 Mr & Mrs Peter	250
	1,220		1,220
		Jul 15 Balance b/d	1,220

Travel Expenses

	£		£
Jul 7 Capital	20	Jul 14 Balance c/d	44
Jul 10 Cash	15		
Jul 12 Cash	9		
	44		44
Jul 15 Balance b/d	44		

Rabbits (an expense)

	£		£
Jul 8 United Rabbit Corp'n	240	Jul 14 Balance c/d	240
Jul 15 Balance b/d	240		

Rabbit Food

	£		£
Jul 8 Amalgamated Carrots	250	Jul 14 Balance c/d	250
Jul 15 Balance b/d	250		

Cleaning

	£		£
Jul 11 Bank	18	Jul 14 Balance c/d	18
Jul 15 Balance b/d	18		

Purchase Returns

	£		£
Jul 14 Balance c/d	60	Jul 14 Amalgamated Carrots	60
		Jul 15 Balance b/d	60

Purchase Ledger

Kazam Limited

	£		£
Jul 14 Bank	400	Jul 3 Playing cards	400

United Rabbit Corporation

	£		£
Jul 14 Bank	240	Jul 8 Rabbits	240

Amalgamated Carrots plc

	£		£
Jul 14 Purchase returns	00	Jul 8 Rabbit food	250
Jul 14 Balance c/d	190		
	250		250
		Jul 15 Balance b/d	250

Sales Ledger

Mr & Mrs Peter

	£		£
Jul 13 Fees	250	Jul 14 Balance c/d	250
Jul 15 Balance b/d	250		

Marvin the Magician
Trial balance as at 14 July

	Dr £	Cr £
Cash	76	
Bank	212	
Capital		5,020
Costume	3,000	
Magic book	2,000	
Playing cards	400	
Fees		1,220
Travel expenses	44	
Rabbits (an expense)	240	
Rabbit food	250	
Cleaning	18	
Purchase returns		60
Amalgamated Carrots plc (creditor)		190
Mr & Mrs Peter (debtor)	250	
	6,490	6,490

Chapter 3 – Esmeralda appears, then disappears

Marvin the Magician
Profit and Loss Account for the six months ended 31 December 2000

	£	£
Sales of novelties (2500 + 350)		2,850
Less Cost of sales		
Opening stock at 1 July 2000	—	
Add Purchases	1,700	
	1,700	
Less Closing stock at 31 December 2000	(80)	
		(1,620)
Gross profit on sales of novelties		1,230
Add Appearance fees as entertainer		18,320
		19,550
Less Expenses		
Wages (1200 + 100)	1,300	
Travel (2600 – 50)	2,550	
Rabbit expenses	430	
Cleaning	140	
Depreciation – magician's equipment	540	
Depreciation – disappearing lady apparatus	400	
		(5,360)
Net profit		14,190

Balance sheet as at 31 December 2000

	£	£	£
Fixed assets			
Magician's equipment, at cost (3,000 + 2,000 + 400)		5,400	
Less Depreciation (20% for half year)		(540)	
			4,860
Disappearing lady apparatus		2,000	
Less Depreciation (40% for half year)		(400)	
			1,600
			6,460
Current assets			
Stock		80	
Debtors		350	
Prepayment – travel		50	
Bank		120	
Cash		560	
		1,160	
Less **Current liabilities**			
Creditors (Kaboosh Ltd, 1,700 – 1,500)	200		
Accrual – wages	100		
		(300)	
Net current assets			860
Total net assets			7,320
Capital			
Opening balance (as per Case Study 2)		5,020	
Add Net profit		14,190	
		19,210	
Less Drawings		(11,890)	
Closing balance at 31 December 2000			7,320

Chapter 4 – Marvin makes magic

**Manufacturing, trading and profit and loss account
for the year ended 30 June 2001**

	£	£
Raw materials		
Purchases of raw materials		
(note: no opening stock)	15,621	
Less Closing stock at 30 June 2001	(6,320)	
Cost of raw materials		9,301
Other direct costs:		
Production labour		5,820
Prime cost of production		15,121
Indirect costs:		
Rent and rates	3,600	
Light and heat	2,500	
Other workshop expenses	4,100	
Depreciation of workshop machinery	500	
		10,700
Total production cost c/d		25,821

Sales		45,821
Less Cost of goods sold		
Purchases (*note*: no opening stock)	3,400	
Total production cost b/d	25,821	
	29,221	
Less Closing stock at 30 June 2001	(2,400)	
		(26,821)
Gross profit		19,000
Add Appearance fees as entertainer		34,500
		53,500
Less Expenses		
Assistant's wages	12,400	
Travel	5,510	
Rabbit expenses	430	
Cleaning	280	
Depreciation – magician's equipment	1,080	
Depreciation – disappearing lady apparatus	800	
		(20,500)
Net profit		33,000

Balance sheet as at 30 June 2001

	£	£	£
Fixed assets			
Magician's equipment, at cost		5,400	
Less Depreciation		(1,080)	
			4,320
Disappearing lady apparatus		2,000	
Less Depreciation (40%)		(800)	
			1,200
Workshop machinery		3,600	
Less Depreciation		(500)	
			3,100
			8,620
Current assets			
Stock (6,320 + 2,400)		8,720	
Debtors (Mrs Featherskew)		200	
Prepayment – rent and rates		600	
Bank		660	
Cash		40	
		10,220	
Less Current liabilities			
Creditors (Kaboosh Ltd)	240		
Accruals (£200 + £100)	300		
		(540)	
Net current assets			9,680
Total net assets		c/f	18,300

Total net assets		h/f	18,300

Capital

Opening balance (as per Case Study 2)	5,020	
Add Net profit	33,000	
	38,020	
Less Drawings	(19,720)	
Closing balance at 30 June 2001		18,300

Chapter 5 – Esmeralda doesn't disappear, so Chiquita appears

a

	£
Cost of the equipment	2,000
Depreciation to 30 June 2001	800
One month's depreciation to disposal date:	
$\frac{1}{12} \times (40\% \, [2,000 - 800])$	40
Total depreciation to date of disposal	(840)
Net book value at date of disposal (2,000 – 840)	1,160
Proceeds	1,000
Loss on disposal	160

b   The £200 bad debt will be written off to profit and loss account, thus reducing net profit. Debtors (current assets) also decrease by this amount.

Doubtful debts do not affect the sales ledger as the account is kept alive as long as there is a glimmer of hope of payment. However, to abide by the prudence concept, profits are set aside from the profit and loss account to ensure that all the doubtful debts are covered by the provision. The total provision is then deducted from the total debtors (after any bad debts have been deleted). The effect on profits depends on whether the provision is being created, increased or decreased:

➤   Created: the full amount of the provision comes out of profit.
➤   Increased: only the extra amount needed comes out of profit.
➤   Decreased: the surplus provision is added back to increase the profit.

Chapter 6 – Marvin's second birthday

Profit and loss account for the year ended 30 June 2002

	£	£
Sales		35,900
Less **Cost of goods sold**		
Opening stock at 1 July 2001	2,400	
Add Purchases	15,600	
	18,000	
Less Closing stock at 30 June 2002	(2,500)	
		(15,500)
Gross profit		20,400
Add Appearance fees as entertainer		45,200
	c/f	65,600

		b/f	65,600

Less Expenses

	£
Assistant's wages	24,600
Travel (£6,220 – prepaid £450)	5,770
Bad debt	200
Increase in provision for doubtful debts (5% × £2,600)	130
Cleaning	1,570
Depreciation – magician's equipment	1,300
Depreciation – 'saw the lady in half' prop ((3000 – 600)/4)	600
Loss on disposal of disappearing lady apparatus	160

	(34,330)
Net profit	31,270

Balance sheet as at 30 June 2002

	£	£	£
Fixed assets			
Magician's equipment, at cost		7,700	
Less Depreciation (1,080 + 1,300)		(2,380)	
			5,320
'Saw the lady in half' prop		3,000	
Less Depreciation		(600)	
			2,400
			7,720
Current assets			
Stock		2,500	
Debtors	2,600		
Less Provision for doubtful debts	(130)		
		2,470	
Prepayment – travel		450	
Bank		5,160	
		10,580	
Less Current liabilities			
Creditors	480		
Accruals	250		
		(730)	
Net current assets			9,850
Total net assets			17,570
Capital			
Opening balance, 1 July 2001		18,300	
Add Net profit		31,270	
		49,570	
Less Drawings		(32,000)	
Closing balance at 30 June 2002			17,570

Chapter 7 – Marvin and Chiquita make Machiq, but Esmeralda makes trouble

a

Machiq & Co
Profit and loss account (appropriation section) for the year ended 30 June 2003

	£	£
Net profit for the year		58,800
Appropriated as follows:		
Marvin: share of profit (60% × £58,800)	35,280	
Chiquita: share of profit (40% × £58,800)	23,520	
		58,800

Machiq & Co
Balance sheet as at 30 June 2003 (extract)

	£	£
(Total net assets)		35,000
Marvin's Capital Account		
Opening balance, 1 July 2002	17,570	
Add Share of profit	35,280	
	52,850	
Less: Drawings	(32,850)	
Closing balance, 30 June 2003		20,000
Chiquita's Capital Account		
Opening balance, 1 July 2002	10,000	
Add: Share of profit	23,520	
	33,520	
Less: Drawings	(18,520)	
Closing balance, 30 June 2003		15,000
		35,000

b

Machiq Limited
Profit and loss account for the year ended 30 June 2004 (extract)

	£
Net profit for the year, before taxation	92,000
Less Provision for taxation (20% × £92,000)	(18,400)
Net profit for the year, after taxation	73,600
Less Dividends (£2.25 × 14,000 shares)	(31,500)
Retained profit for the year	42,100

Machiq Limited
Balance sheet as at 30 June 2004 (extract)

	£
Capital and reserves	
Called-up share capital (£1 shares)[1]	14,000
Share Premium Account[2]	21,000
Profit and Loss Account:	
Retained profit for the year	42,100
	77,100

Notes.

1   The balances transferred from Machiq & Co (see above) were Marvin £20,000, Chiquita £15,000 (ratio 4:3), so the share capital of £14,000 is allocated as follows: Marvin (4/7) = 8,000 shares, Chiquita (3/7) = 6,000 shares.
2   The partners' balances totalled £35,000, so the share premium must be £35,000 less the nominal value of £14,000 = £21,000.

Chapter 8 – The treasurer of the Abracadabra Club does a vanishing trick

a   Workings to establish 100 Club receipts:

Subscriptions Account (number of members in brackets)

		£			£
1/1/03	Opening debtors (4)	360	31/12/03 Bank: subs re 2002 (3)		270
31/12/03	Income and Expenditure Account (100)	9,000	Bad debt written off to I&E Account (1)		90
			Bank: subs re 2003 (95)		8,550
			Closing debtors (5)		450
		9,360			9,360

Bank summary:

	£	£
Opening balances (2,099 + 711)		2,810
Add Subscriptions (see workings above) (270 + 8,550)	8,820	
Other receipts as listed	2,352	
		11,172
		13,982
Less Payments as listed		(6,118)
Closing balance at bank should have been		7,864

Therefore, as the bank balances were nil, **£7,864** is the amount missing.

b

The Abracadabra Club
Income and Expenditure Account for the year ended 31 December 2003

	£	£
Income		
Membership subscriptions (see workings)	9,000	
Profit on sale of drinks[1]	47	
Profit on dances[2]	401	
Bank interest	120	
	c/f	9,568

	b/f	9,568

Less Expenditure

100 Club prizes	2,000
Bad debt written off	90
Loss on sale of computer (1,000 − 700)	300
Depreciation on computer (20% × £1000)	200
Sundries	87
Exceptional expenditure: theft of cash	7,864

	(10,541)
Surplus of expenditure over income	(973)

Notes:

1 Profit on sale of drinks:

Sales		265
Less Cost of sales		
Opening stock	200	
Purchases (165 + 28)	193	
	393	
Less Closing stock	(175)	
		(218)
Profit		47

2 Profit on dances

Ticket sales	1,267
Less Band fees	(866)
Profit	401

ç

The Abracadabra Club
Balance sheet as at 31 December 2003

	£	£	£
Fixed assets			
Computer		1,000	
Less Depreciation		(200)	
			800
Current assets			
Bar stock		175	
Subscriptions owing		450	
Bank		–	
		625	
Less Current liabilities			
Creditors – drinks		(28)	
Net current assets			597
Total net assets			1,397
Accumulated fund			
Opening balance, 1 January 2003		2,370	
Less Surplus of expenditure over income		(973)	
Closing balance, 31 December 2003			1,397

d One advantage and one disadvantage of presenting a simple Receipts and Payments Account, rather than an Income and Expenditure Account and Balance Sheet, are as follows.

> ➤ *Advantage*: Requires no knowledge of accounting principles, just the ability to summarise cash and bank information.
> ➤ *Disadvantage*: Does not disclose the club's surplus or deficit for the financial period, nor its assets and liabilities at the end of that period.

e Clubs could minimise the risk of a treasurer misappropriating funds by the following means:

> ➤ ensuring that more than one person must sign cheques
> ➤ requiring an external audit of the club's finances
> ➤ seeking references before appointing the treasurer
> ➤ always ensuring that more than one person is present when cash receipts are being counted
> ➤ requiring regular reports of the financial position from the treasurer
> ➤ asking the bank to send duplicate bank statements to another club official at regular intervals.

Chapter 9 – There's the profit, but where's the cash?

a

Machiq Limited
Cash Flow Statement for the year ended 30 June 2005

	£
Net cash inflow from operating activities[1]	120,060
Interest paid	(1,800)
Tax	(18,400)
Capital expenditure	(97,000)
Changes in financing	20,000
Dividends	(31,500)
Decrease in cash for the period	(8,640)
Reconciliation of cash balances at start and end of the period:	
Opening bank balance, 1 July 2004	6,240
Closing bank overdraft, 30 June 2005	(2,400)
Decrease in cash for the period	(8,640)

Note:	£
1 Operating profit (116,000 + 1,800)	117,800
Depreciation (see Working 1)	5,060
Increase in stock (32,650 – 17,370)	(15,280)
Decrease in debtors (39,560 – 30,950)	8,610
Increase in creditors (14,080 – 10,210)	3,870
Net cash inflow from operating activities	120,060

Working 1:

Fixed Assets (at net book value)

	£		£
Balance b/f	74,040	P & L account (depreciation for the year)*	5,060
Additions (2 cars)	97,000	Balance c/f	165,980
	171,040		171,040

* There were no disposals during the year, so the balance on this account must be the depreciation charged for the year.

b The Cash Flow Statement clearly shows the main cause of the decrease in cash for the year: the purchase of the two luxury cars for Marvin and Chiquita. If more modest vehicles costing, say, £15,000 each had been purchased, there would have been a positive cash flow of nearly £60,000. If Trixie can curb the extravagance of her fellow shareholders then the company can both be profitable and have strong liquidity.

c

Cash flow forecast from 1 July 2005 to 31 December 2005
Period – Monthly

(£)	Jul	Aug	Sept	Oct	Nov	Dec
Receipts						
Sales – cash	15,000	15,000	15,000	15,000	20,000	15,000
Sales – debtors	30,950	15,000	15,000	15,000	15,000	20,000
A: Total receipts	45,950	30,000	30,000	30,000	35,000	35,000
Payments						
Purchases and office expenses – creditors	14,080	35,000	35,000	35,000	35,000	35,000
Wages and salaries	6,000	6,000	6,000	6,000	6,000	14,000
B: Total payments	20,080	41,000	41,000	41,000	41,000	49,000
C: Net cash flow (A – B)	25,870	(11,000)	(11,000)	(11,000)	(6,000)	(14,000)
D: Opening bank balance	(2,400)	23,470	12,470	1,470	(9,530)	(15,530)
E: Closing bank balance (D +/– C)	23,470	12,470	1,470	(9,530)	(15,530)	(29,530)
Note: Agreed overdraft facility	6,000	6,000	6,000	6,000	6,000	6,000

The company will have to renegotiate its bank overdraft facility during October, or alternatively will have to either increase its forecast sales income or reduce its expenditure.

Chapter 10 – Esmeralda springs a surprise

a   Ratio analysis:

Group	Name of ratio	Machiq Limited	Kaboosh Limited
Profitability	ROCE (Return on Capital Employed)	76.4%	22.7%
	Gross Margin (or Gross Profit Margin)	25%	40%
	Mark-up	33.3%	66.7%
	Net Margin (or Net Profit Margin)	16.7%	24.1%
Efficiency	Fixed assets turnover	4.25 times	1.16 times
	Stock turn	22.5 days	138.7 days
	Debtors' collection period	16 days	47.2 days
	Creditors' payment period	9.7 days	59.6 days
Short-term solvency and liquidity	Current ratio (or 'working capital' ratio)	0.84:1	2.05:1
	Acid test (or 'quick assets' test)	0.41:1	0.85:1
Long-term solvency and liquidity	Gearing	nil	17.1%
	Interest cover	65 times	22 times
Investment ratios	eps (earnings per share	18.6p	10.35p
	p/e (price/earnings)	(assume) 15	(assume) 15
	Dividend cover	2.78 times	3.76 times
	Dividend yield	2.4%	1.77%

Commentary:

1   Profitability

We are comparing just one year's results for each company, so we must be cautious in drawing conclusions, as trends may show an improvement or decline when compared with previous years. With this proviso, Machiq Limited's ROCE is impressively high compared with Kaboosh's, indicating that Machiq is operating profitably from a relatively low capital base. It could also mean that Kaboosh has been investing in new fixed assets, and expects profitability to increase significantly as a result.

Kaboosh's margins are higher than Machiq's. If we assume that they are selling the same type of goods, then Machiq could seemingly raise its prices without affecting sales. Another interpretation is that Kaboosh is controlling its costs and buying prices much more efficiently than Machiq.

2 Efficiency

In terms of efficiency, in all respects Machiq is performing better than Kaboosh. Fixed assets are producing over three times as much sales, stock is sold every 22.5 days (compared to a lengthy 138.7 days) and debts are being collected three times as quickly. The only surprise is that creditors are paid so quickly – it would be more efficient to take advantage of interest-free credit and pay creditors after approximately 30 days. Kaboosh's stock turn is very worrying – why have they let stock build up to such an extent? Is part of the stock unsaleable and perhaps overvalued?

3 Short-term solvency and liquidity

Kaboosh has a 'textbook' current ratio, though the acid test could be slightly stronger. Machiq's ratios are very low, and the acid test shows only 41p of quickly realisable assets for every £1 of current liabilities. Machiq's management should reassess the dividend levels to improve the current and acid test ratios.

4 Long-term solvency and liquidity

Machiq has no long-term borrowings (it is assumed that the interest shown in the profit and loss account is overdraft interest), so the gearing is zero. Kaboosh is low-geared at 17.1%. Neither company has any problems over safety of interest payments, with cover of 65 and 22 times respectively.

5 Investment ratios

Neither company would have a stock market price (not being 'listed' plc's), so the p/e ratio may not be a realistic comparison. However, the dividend yield has been calculated on the basis of a share price 15 times the eps. Both companies have reasonable safety of dividend, though Machiq's generous dividend policy results in a higher yield than that of Kaboosh.

b Purely on the basis of the ratio comparison with Machiq Limited, the key concerns within Kaboosh Limited's financial statements are:

➤ Low return on capital employed
➤ Poor working capital control, especially stock.

Within Machiq Limited's statements, the key concerns are:

➤ Lower profit margins
➤ Poor liquidity.

The poor liquidity, if uncorrected, could prove fatal to Machiq Limited, so they need to address this problem urgently. Once they can overcome this, they may feel that they do need to sell out to Kaboosh Limited, especially in view of Machiq's massively higher return on capital employed. Before a decision can be taken, the following further information is needed:

➤ How much is Kaboosh Limited offering for the shares in Machiq Limited?
➤ What steps are Kaboosh Limited taking to overcome its poor working capital control?

➤ What plans does Kaboosh Limited have for improving its return on capital employed?

➤ What roles will the three directors of Machiq Limited have in the new company, and are they acceptable? What salaries would they be paid?

Chapter 11 – Who is Mrs Eadale?

a   Using absorption costing principles, the bottling division would 'absorb' all the relevant costs, as follows:

	£	£
Forecast sales revenue (15,000 × £14)		210,000
Direct costs (15,000 × £6)	90,000	
Fixed costs of bottling division	20,000	
		(110,000)
Gross profit		100,000
Company costs absorbed by division		(130,000)
Net loss		(30,000)

b   Using marginal costing techniques, the information would be redrawn as follows:

	£
Forecast sales revenue (15,000 × £14)	210,000
Less Variable costs (15,000 × £6)	(90,000)
Contribution	120,000
Less Fixed costs of division	(20,000)
Profit of division	100,000

On this basis it can be seen that the bottling division would make a positive contribution of £120,000 to meeting the fixed costs (which would increase by only £20,000) of the business as a whole.

c   The answers to the questions are as follows:

➤ The contribution per bottle is £14 – £6 = £8, so to meet the fixed costs of £20,000 (i.e. the break-even point), **2,500 bottles** must be sold (£20,000/£8).

➤ To earn £16,000 profit for the division, total contribution would need to be £32,000 (P + F = C). At a contribution of £8 per bottle, **4,000 bottles** would need to be sold.

➤ If 4,000 bottles were sold, total contribution would be £32,000. After deducting fixed costs of £20,000, profit would be **£12,000**.

Postscript:

Scotland Yard detectives, after months of painstaking research, identified 'Mrs Eadale' as none other than an anagram of the name 'Esmeralda'!

Answers to practice examination papers 1 and 2

Paper 1 (multiple choice)

Question	
1	b
2	a
3	c
4	c
5	a
6	b
7	d
8	c
9	a
10	d

Question	
11	b
12	b
13	c
14	b
15	a
16	d
17	a
18	c
19	b
20	b

Question	
21	b
22	a
23	b
24	d
25	a
26	d
27	c
28	a
29	d
30	d

Question	
31	d
32	c
33	a
34	b
35	c
36	a
37	d
38	c
39	d
40	b

Paper 2

Question 1

a

Aubrey Locke

Profit and loss account for the year ended 31 May 2001

	£	£
Sales	375,000	
Less Sales returns	(420)	
		374,580
***Less* Cost of goods sold**		
Opening stock at 1 June 2000	62,000	
Add Purchases	195,000	
	257,000	
Less Closing stock at 31 May 2001	(50,000)	
		(207,000)
Gross profit	c/f	167,580

		b/f	167,580
Gross profit			
Add Decrease in provision for doubtful debts		400	
Discount received		180	
			580
			168,160
Less **Expenses**			
Wages and salaries		37,000	
Rent		16,000	
Electricity		10,000	
Bad debts written off		520	
General office expenses		18,000	
Depreciation on forklift truck (20,000 – 2,000)/4		4,500	
Depreciation on cars 40% × (18,000 – 6,000)		4,800	
			(90,820)
Net profit			77,340

Aubrey Locke
Balance sheet as at 31 May 2001

	Cost	Accumulated depreciation	Net book value
Fixed assets	£	£	£
Forklift truck	20,000	9,000	11,000
Motor cars	18,000	10,800	7,200
	38,000	19,800	18,200
Current assets			
Stock		50,000	
Debtors	16,200		
Less Provision for doubtful debts	(2,240)		
		13,960	
Prepayments		4,000	
Bank		3,840	
Cash		120	
		71,920	
Less **Current liabilities**			
Creditors	14,600		
Accruals	2,000		
		(16,600)	
Net current assets			55,320
Total net assets			73,520
Capital			
Opening balance at 1 June 2000		14,680	
Add Net profit		77,340	
		92,020	
Less Drawings		(18,500)	
			73,520

b A limited company's profit and loss account contains:

> ➤ Directors' salaries
> ➤ Corporation tax
> ➤ Dividends

A limited company's balance sheet contains:

> ➤ Additional creditors (taxation and dividends owing)
> ➤ Share capital
> ➤ Reserves

Question 2

a

Wilma Tonbridge
Profit and loss account for the year ended 31 December 2000

	£	£
Sales		208,000
Less **Cost of goods sold**		
Add Purchases	134,200	
Less Closing stock at 31 December 2000	(9,200)	
		(125,000)
Gross profit		83,000
Less **Expenses**		
Wages and salaries	25,600	
Rent and rates	12,800	
Provision for doubtful debts	2,400	
Office expenses	10,400	
Depreciation on computers, etc.	5,000	
		(56,200)
Net profit		26,800

Wilma Tonbridge
Balance sheet as at 31 December 2000

	Cost	Accumulated depreciation	Net book value
Fixed assets	£	£	£
Computers, etc.	30,000	5,000	25,000
Current assets			
Stock		9,200	
Debtors	48,000		
Less Provision for doubtful debts	(2,400)		
		45,600	
Prepayments		3,200	
	c/f	58,000	25,000

		b/f	58,000	25,000

Less Current liabilities

Creditors	7,000
Accruals	2,400
Bank overdraft	52,800

	(62,200)	
Net current liabilities		(4,200)
		20,800
Less Long-term loan		(16,000)
Total net assets		4,800

Capital

Opening balance at 1 January 2000	10,000	
Add Net profit	26,800	
	36,800	
Less Drawings	(32,000)	
		4,800

b

Wages Account

	£		£
31/12/00 Bank	56,000	31/12/00 Transfer to Drawings	32,000
31/12/00 Accrual c/d	1,600	31/12/00 Profit and loss account	25,600
	57,600		57,600
		1/1/01 Accrual b/d	1,600

Rent and Rates Account

	£		£
31/12/00 Bank	16,000	31/12/00 Profit and loss account	12,800
		31/12/00 Prepaid c/d	3,200
	16,000		16,000
1/1/01 Prepaid b/d	3,200		

Question 3

a   Prudence, also known as 'conservatism', is the concept whereby revenue and profits are not anticipated but are recognised by inclusion in the profit and loss account only when realised in the form of either cash or other assets, the ultimate cash realisation of which can be assessed with reasonable certainty. Provision is made for all known liabilities (expenses and losses), whether the amount of these is known with certainty or is a best estimate in the light of the information available.

b

➤   Going concern concept
➤   Accruals concept
➤   Consistency concept

(see Chapter 1 for descriptions)

c   Factors include (any three)

- ➤ The need not to overstate profits or assets
- ➤ The need not to understate losses or liabilities
- ➤ It is up to the management to resist shareholders' demands if they are against the interests of the company
- ➤ The need for accountants to follow existing statute and accounting standards in producing published information.

Question 4

a

Gross profit margin	(GP/Sales) × 100	Eastbourne Ltd's margin is higher than average. Possible reasons include lack of competition, better buying policies, errors in stock counts
Net profit margin	(NP/Sales) × 100	Eastbourne Ltd's margin is higher than average. Possible reasons include greater control of expenses, more automation (lower wage costs)
ROCE	PBIT/Capital employed (total net assets + loans) × 100	Eastbourne Ltd's margin is higher than average. Possible reasons include greater efficiency overall, less competition.
Acid test	Ratio of (Current assets – Stock): Current liabilities	Eastbourne Ltd's margin is lower than average. Possible reasons include better use of interest-free credit from trade creditors, fewer credit sales than average
Gearing	Fixed % borrowing/ capital employed or Fixed % borrowing/ capital employed plus fixed % borrowing	Eastbourne Ltd's margin is much higher than average. Possible reasons include past expansion financed by borrowings, or borrowing in anticipation of future expansion

b   A current ratio of 6:1 might indicate too much stock being carried, poor control of debtors, or surplus bank balances not being reinvested into fixed assets.

Question 5

a   Contribution per coat = £100 – (25 + 30 + 5) = £40
Break-even point = Fixed costs/Contribution per coat = £240,000/10
= 6,000 coats.

Margin of safety = Maximum production less sales at break-even point
= 16,000 – 6,000 = 10,000 coats.

If 11,000 coats are manufactured and sold, total contribution will be £40 × 11,000 = £440,000. Fixed costs are £240,000, so profit will be (£440,000 – 240,000) = £200,000.

b   The contribution from the special order will be £70 – (25 + 30 + 5 + 6) = £4.
Total additional contribution = 5,000 × £4 = £20,000 with no additional
fixed costs, so the order should be accepted.

Index